Between Humanist Philosophy and Apocalyptic Theology

Between Humanist Philosophy and Apocalyptic Theology

The Twentieth Century Sojourn of Samuel Štefan Osuský

Paul R. Hinlicky

Bloomsbury T&T Clark
An imprint of Bloomsbury Publishing Plc

B L O O M S B U R Y
LONDON • OXFORD • NEW YORK • NEW DELHI • SYDNEY

Bloomsbury T&T Clark
An imprint of Bloomsbury Publishing Plc

50 Bedford Square
London
WC1B 3DP
UK

1385 Broadway
New York
NY 10018
USA

www.bloomsbury.com

Bloomsbury is a registered trade mark of Bloomsbury Publishing Plc

First published 2016

British Library Cataloguing-in-Publication Data
A catalogue record for this book is available from the British Library.

ISBN: HB: 978-0-56766-018-3
ePDF: 978-0-56766-019-0
ePUB: 978-0-56766-020-6

Library of Congress Cataloging-in-Publication Data
A catalog record for this book is available from the Library of Congress.

Typeset by Fakenham Prepress Solutions, Fakenham, Norfolk NR21 8NN
Printed and bound in Great Britain

To the Protestant Theological Faculty of Comenius University in Bratislava, where I was blessed to serve 1993–6.

Contents

A Very Personal Preface

The Marxist-Leninist regime in Czechoslovakia (1948–89) tried to erase the theologian Samuel Štefan Osuský (1888–1976) and his life's work from living memory – as it did with many others whose intellectual legacy would present rival accounts of reality.[1] Students who discovered his considerable literary legacy during the brief Prague Spring in 1968, when Alexander Dubček attempted democratic reform within Marxism-Leninism, had heard little if anything of the man. What they did hear always highlighted his reputation as a Slovak nationalist and philosopher and included a coded warning about the 'outdated' elements in his thought. But he had been bishop of the Western District of the Slovak Church of the Augsburg Confession for sixteen tumultuous years, and a leading intellectual at its theological faculty in Bratislava, from 1920 to 1950 when he was purged. Like the contemporaneous efforts of Karl Barth in the *Epistle to the Romans*,[2] or of Dietrich Bonhoeffer in *Creation and Fall*,[3] Osuský, at the pinnacle of his writing career, strove to articulate a new, 'post-liberal', way of theological exegesis of the Bible. Pastor, bishop and theologian of the minority Lutheran Church in Slovakia, in a dramatic lifetime that saw the passage from imperialism to democracy to fascism to Stalinism, Osuský died in obscurity. This book is an endeavour in small part to right that wrong of history.

Slovakia is often confused with Slovenia, the northern and westernmost land bordering Italy, emerging from the breakup of the Balkan Yugoslavia, which, like Czechoslovakia, was a hybrid multicultural nation state carved from the corpse of the Austro-Hungarian Empire after the First World War. Since 1992, Slovakia is a new country but an old culture and territory, north of Hungary and east of today's Czech Republic, which emerged at the same time, after the end

1 The experience of the churches in the Soviet bloc during the Cold War was diverse and varied in intensity through the period of some 40 years. See *Christian World Community and the Cold War: International Research Conference in Bratislava on 5–8 September 2011* ed. Július Filo (Bratislava: Evangelical Theological Faculty of the Comenius University, 2012). An instructive English language study of a country neighbouring Slovakia is H. David Baer, *The Struggle of Hungarian Lutherans under Communism* (College Station: Texas A & M University Press, 2006).

2 Karl Barth, *Epistle to the Romans*, trans. E.C. Hoskyns (London: Oxford University Press, 1972).

3 Dietrich Bonhoeffer, *Creation and Fall*, Dietrich Bonhoeffer Works, Vol. 3 trans. D. S. Bax (Minneapolis: Fortress, 1997).

of the Cold War, from the former Czechoslovakia. It is a relatively small nation with under six million citizens. Its language is closest to Czech, but distinct from the other Slavic languages like those spoken in the Balkans, such as Serbian and Croatian, or to the north in Poland, or to the east in Ukraine. Slovakia had been yoked with the Czech lands of Moravia and Bohemia by the post-First World War settlement in a new democratic republic, Czechoslovakia. But the cultures of the Czechs and Slovaks were significantly different in geo-political orientation and cultural development, which led to tensions between the two groups that ended finally in the so-called Velvet Divorce in 1992.

The Czech lands are surrounded on three sides by German-speaking peoples, and previously belonged to the Austrian Habsburg crown. The Slovak land was called Upper Hungary, as it belonged to the Hungarian crown, and, to complicate matters further, as mentioned in passing above, the Austrians and Hungarians belonged to a united empire, the Austro-Hungarian Empire. But the Slovak territory was surrounded on three sides by Slavic-speaking lands, and to the south by the imperial overlord, Hungary. While the earliest manifestation of Slovak nationalism, led in significant part by Lutheran pastors in the first half of the nineteenth century,[4] envisaged regional autonomy within this multicultural empire, a repressive policy of Hungarianisation, which outlawed the Slovak language in education and government,[5] caused profound enmity to emerge, especially from the Slovak side.

All this is mentioned by way of table-setting for the complex meal in four courses about to be served. For Osuský, as mentioned, passed from Austro-Hungarian imperialism to Czechoslovak democracy to Slovak fascism to Czecho-Slovak[6] Stalinism, in a twentieth century journey between the humanist philosophy of Christian Platonism that he inherited and the apocalyptic theology of the New Testament that he rediscovered in his lifetime of eighty-eight years.

Yet another painful wrinkle to his story has to be lifted up already here by way of preface, concerning relations with the majority Roman Catholic tradition in Slovakia. Osuský was pastor and bishop and theologian of the largest minority Protestant tradition (in his lifetime perhaps as high as 20 per cent of the Slovak population), although it had once been religiously

4 *Slovakia in History*, ed. Mikuláš Teich, Dušan Kováč, and Martin D. Brown (Cambridge: Cambridge University Press, 2013), 87–119.

5 Ibid., 120–36.

6 The new spelling of the name for the reunited nation, with the hyphen, following the Second World War, was intended to honour the demands of the Slovaks for regional autonomy.

predominant in Upper Hungary. More about this history will emerge in the pages that follow, but for here it suffices to note that, to this day, the relationship between Lutherans and Catholics remains strained and, from the Lutheran side, often bitter. The first time I visited Slovakia, in 1989, I was taken on a tour of the old city of Bratislava by a young pastor. We were speaking in German, as my Slovak was at that time the 'kitchen' language of my peasant grandparents, who had immigrated to the United States before the First World War. As we passed every old church on every other corner, he would tell me how this had once been one of *their* churches. Not knowing the history, I didn't grasp what he was talking about. Finally, thinking to myself of the Marxist-Leninist suppression of religion, I asked when and how the Lutherans had lost all these churches. Indignantly, he replied to me: *In der Gegenreformation!* Subsequently, I learned that in a terrible decade between 1670 and 1680 the 880 parishes of Upper Hungary were forcibly re-Catholicized. The Lutheran remnant lived an underground existence for the next century, until the Enlightenment brought about a legal toleration.[7] This legal tolerance in fact made possible the leadership role of the Lutheran intelligentsia in the nineteenth century national awakening,[8] although the repressive policy of Hungarianisation with which it was met quickly smothered that blossoming.

The present author learned of Osuský as a visiting professor in Bratislava in the 1990s. I was told about him for the first time by one of the 'prison pastors'. This term refers to the circle of defiant Lutheran clergy and theological students formed after the February 1948 seizure of power in Czechoslovakia by the Marxist-Leninists backed by the occupying force of the Red Army. Many of these, who were, otherwise, inclined like Osuský to moderate forms of democratic socialism, resisted the communist party's assertion of total domination over culture, hence, also, if not especially, over religion. About one-third of the church's leadership suffered some form of legal persecution.[9]

Daniel Veselý was a theological student at the time of Osuský's deposition. He was arrested and held without trial for a number of months before being sentenced to prison for counter-revolutionary activity in opposition to the

7 For a current and objective account, see the contribution of Viliam Čičaj, 'The Period of Religious Disturbances in Slovakia', in *Slovakia in History*, 71–86.

8 *Slovenské Národné Zhromaždenie v Turčianskom Sv. Martine 1861: Teologické aspekty memorandových udalostí a ich odkaz pre dnešok* [The Slovak National Assembly in St. Martin 1861: Theological Aspects of the Events surrounding the Memorandum on Slovak Nationality and their Message for Today]. Edited by Michal Valčo and Andrej-Braxatoris-Sládkovič (Žilina: University Press, 2011).

9 For a memoir translated into English, see Pavel Uhorskai, *Uncompromising Faith: One Man's Notes from Prison* trans. Jaroslav Vajda (St. Louis: Concordia, 1992).

still-young regime,[10] although he did not discover until many years later what specifically had been his alleged crime. After several years in prison, he was released to work on a collective farm. There he repeatedly appealed to be readmitted to the theological faculty, so that he could finish his studies and become a pastor. When, in 1963, this permission finally came, he learned that a fellow student had under secret police intimidation denounced him, reporting that Veselý had commented on current events: 'Fascism and Bolshevism are alike plagues.' Veselý, who told me this story, did not deny making that statement. In the course of my discussing this history with him, Veselý then told me about Osuský's 1937 lecture at a pastors' theological conference, where he had predicted the coming disasters of fascism/Nazism and communism. When I read this 1937 lecture (to be discussed in detail below in Chapters 2 and 4), I was overwhelmed by Osuský's prescience, a veritable voice crying in the wilderness. I translated it years later and published it in English in several places.[11] From that moment, I had to make this lost testimony known and better understood. This book is the fulfilment of that promise I made to myself.

But my drama of discovery only began with the 1937 lecture. What I went on to discover at first struck me as very curious. Osuský, insofar as he has been remembered at all by the Slovak Lutheran intelligentsia, was remembered as a philosopher, or historian of philosophy, or a philosophical theologian. But his most significant works, as it seemed to me as I worked through the materials, were major war-time commentaries on the biblical books of Revelation and Job. This was followed by the covert production of a major work of biblical theology, *A Gallery of New Testament Figures*, which was published posthumously in 2009. This great and final work will be the focus of attention in the culminating Chapter 4 of this book.

In his Foreword to the 2009 edition, editor Igor Kišš, later post-communist dean of the Protestant Theological Faculty in Bratislava where Osuský had taught, tells how, during 1958, Osuský began dictating from his 1000-page handwritten manuscript for Igor Kišš to type. They made four copies, but, so far as is known, only the one Kišš kept survived. 'I want to express thanks to the good Lord for helping me to preserve this work for more than fifty years in my personal archives and who has now has given me strength to prepare it

[10] Veselý's testimony to his arrest is recorded in Jan Pešek, *Odvrátena tvár totality: Politické perzekúcie na Slovensku v rokoch 1948–1953* [Totalitarian Shunning: Political Persecution in Slovakia 1948–1953] (Bratislava: Nádádci Milana Šimečku, 1998), 145. His testimony will be further considered below, in Chapter 4.

[11] I will refer to the version printed in Paul R. Hinlicky, *Before Auschwitz: What Christian Theology Must Learn from the Rise of Nazism* (Eugene, OR: Cascade, 2014), 193–220.

for publication. Without God's help I could not have mastered the situation in 1962 when the State Security Police searched my house'– Osuský's manuscript would surely have been confiscated and destroyed. Kišš called it 'an honour to the Slovak nation that one of us succeeded in writing such a magnificent book'.[12]

With this brief survey, the reader can see already that there is considerable prima facie evidence for this book's interpretative thesis that what is fascinating about Osuský and salient about his work for us today was his twentieth century sojourn between humanist philosophy and apocalyptic theology that ended in his (re-)turn to the Bible. What follows cannot pretend to be a comprehensive account of Osuský's life and work; it is, rather, a theological and historical interpretation of this dramatic new turn to the Bible for the 'post-modern' world that emerges for us today after fascism, after communism (and perhaps also after liberalism).

Since Osuský's work is written in a language that is inaccessible for so many, this book must be largely concerned to present sufficient drafts of Osuský's thinking to make it known and intelligible to the English language world. All translations from Slovak are my own, unless explicitly noted, or referenced to another author. Since none of Osuský's corpus has ever been translated into English (apart from my several exceptions as noted in the Works Cited), I will frequently provide exact translations of direct quotations of the most significant passages. More often than not, however, I will employ a method of synopsis and paraphrase to present the argumentative or interpretative lines that Osuský pursues. In the latter case, I will embed page notations to the Slovak original in parenthesis at the turning of a page in the original Slovak text. I will employ footnotes only for references to literature other than the Osuský text under consideration, as indicated by the subheadings. Distinguishing voices when I expand on or comment on Osuský's thought as may be needed in the course of paraphrase is a necessary, and, I hope, not overly burdensome requirement placed on the reader. I also draw frequently on the Slovak Lutheran Church's journal, *Cirkevné Listy* (hereafter *CL*).

Osuský's material so presented will in either case be explicated in close connection with the historical circumstances which engaged him. Needless to say, this description and selection is guided by the author's interpretative thesis that what is of interest to us is Osuský's turn to the Bible as *representative for the current plight of Christian theology in post-Christendom*. The claim is *this* author's

12 Samuel Štefan Osuský, *Galéria Postáv Novej Zmluvy: Historicko-psychologická trilógia* [Gallery of New Testament Figures] Mikuláš: Tranoscius, 2009), 7–8. All citations in the author's translation are printed here with the permission of the publisher, Tranoscius, in Mikulaš, Slovakia.

theological thesis, of course, for which *he* is responsible, not Osuský! What I aim for is thus a hermeneutical engagement with Osuský in a shared deliberation over the problems and possibilities of post-modern theology that thinks in the matrix of the Scriptures to speak to the maelstrom of new messianisms that fill the spiritual vacuum of post-Christendom in the West.[13] Admittedly, this endeavour may be as quixotic as was Osuský's own project in writing his final work under the shadow of an internal exile that lasted to his dying day.

I am grateful to readers of my manuscript. Long-time friend and colleague Bob Benne offered encouraging feedback in the course of the drafting, dissenting only on how I chose to lay the emphasis in my 'equally personal conclusion'. I am thankful for his critical engagement and perspective, close enough to my own to make our disagreements interesting. Sarah Hinlicky Wilson returned to commenting on this book as it was being written, offering valuable stylistic as well as substantive comments. The latter I have absorbed with gratitude, but concerning the former I fear I continue to fall short of the standards of this more excellent stylist. John Palka, who has written an extraordinary book in *My Slovakia, My Family*, agreed to risk venturing from his disciplinary specialisation in the natural sciences to offer the critical commentary of a knowledgeable lay person. His counsel has been invaluable and he has saved me from numerous mistakes. We share a love for Slovakia and its people and for making known its unknown story to the English-speaking world. I express my gratitude to him here in hope for our blossoming friendship. Michael DeJonge is among the best and brightest young American scholars of religion and the history of ideas in modern Germany. He generously took time to not only read and comment but to engage substantively with my text. His Bonhoeffer scholarship together with his own insights and queries have made this book better than it would have been otherwise. Finally I would like to acknowledge and thank my long-time friend and colleague, the Rev Paul Brndjar. Health problems prevented his engaging as thoroughly as he would have liked to, but his support and encouragement for many, many years have been one of the many blessings of my life.

Among Slovak colleagues, I must first of all thank Dr Peter Gažik, who provided invaluable access to scholarly sources discovered in his own research

[13] The claim of the 'end of Christendom' is, however, not this author's alone. See *Christian Churches in Post-Communist Slovakia: Current Challenges and Opportunities*, ed. Michal Valčo and Daniel Slivka (Salem, VA: Center for Religion and Society, Roanoke College, 2012). 'For a Slovakia troubled by post-communist changes and post-Christian culture, the authors individually and collectively make a case for a solid, relevant, faithful public theology' (17). A constructive effort to respond to the situation of post-Christendom may be seen in Michal Valčo and Katarína Valčová, *Teologické posolstvo Lutherovej reformácie a výzvy sučasnej doby* [The Theological Message of the Lutheran Reformation and the Challenges of the Contemporary Period] (Žilina: EDIS, 2012).

on Osuský, and in a series of consultations also lent to me important perspectives on Osuský's legacy, as will be shown in the frequent referencing I make to his work in the course of this book. Librarian Vlastislav Svoboda of the theological faculty in Bratislava generously gave time, and invested labour, in response to my research requests. Retired professor and former Dean Igor Kišš likewise shared with me valuable reminiscences of Osuský. His dramatic role in preserving Osuský's magnum opus during the period of communist persecution has already been mentioned. Finally, the current Dean, Ĺubomir Batka, made himself available in response to numerous questions, as I engaged in the translation into English of Slovak language materials. I am a blessed man for having so many friends and colleagues, here and abroad, as acknowledged in these paragraphs.

I am greatful to the The Mednick Foundation for a grant in 2012–3 that supported my research. All the works of Osuský discussed in this book are long out of print and in the public domain, with the exception of his posthumous *Gallery of New Testament Figures*. Permission to quote from this book in the author's translations has been generously granted from the publisher, Tranoscius, in Mikulaš, Slovakia. This book is dedicated to the Evanjelická Bohoslecká Fakulta, Univerzita Komenského v Bratislave, where I first learned of Osuský and his dramatic twentieth century theological journey.

Paul R. Hinlicky
October, 2015

Introduction

Problems in Remembering Osuský

Osuský's obscured, if not distorted, reputation stands in the way of the retrieval of his theological witness that this book seeks. The previously mentioned Daniel Veselý, for example, stood in the line of so-called 'Gnesio-Lutheran', that is, 'authentic' Lutheran theologians, who flirt with philosophical obscurantism, biblical fundamentalism and un-nuanced dogmatism in a black-and-white world where the children of light and the children of darkness belong to clearly delineated camps. For such theologians, 'God's Word and Luther's Doctrine Endure Forever', and theology becomes the endless repetition of the same slogans. Ironically, the name Veselý means 'happy, joyful', but Daniel was one of the angriest people I have ever known – an anger exacerbated, no doubt, by his brutal treatment by the Stalinist regime. Such people, as we shall see, had in fact opposed Osuský already in the 1920s; they did consider him too rational, too philosophical, too 'liberal'.

Within the smaller world of Slovak Lutheranism, then, it is not wholly wrong to remember Osuský as a theologically 'liberal', philosophically aware, theologian. But, as I shall show, Osuský is better understood as standing in the Melanchthonian line of Lutheran tradition, which is more responsive to culture and philosophy,[1] more self-critical and ecumenically inclined, but, in the end, no less biblically oriented than the Gnesio-Lutherans. One can put the difference summarily in this way: Luther expected the imminent end of

[1] Gažik underscores the Melanchthonian background to Osuský's more 'open' relation to philosophy, *Samuel Štefan Osuský: Moderný filozof náboženstva* [Modern philosopher of religion], (Žilinská univerzita, 2012) 90.

the world and prophesied.[2] Melanchthon expected the renewal of Christendom by reformation and philosophized accordingly.[3] Indeed, for his interest in the problem of theodicy and his doctrine of God as the harmony of power, wisdom and love, the 'philosopher' to whom I find Osuský closest is that last prince in Melanchthon's line, Gottfried Leibniz, as much a theologian as a philosopher.[4]

Insofar as Osuský was remembered during communist times, it was *as a philosopher* and 'progressive' in his own day (but no longer). On the centennial of Osuský's birthday in 1988, the man who later occupied the chair in philosophy and religious studies at the Protestant Theological Faculty in Bratislava from which Osuský had been deposed in 1950 commemorated him. The circumstances of this 1988 commemoration should be recalled. There are stirrings of *perestroika* and *glasnost* in the Soviet Union. The Solidarity Movement in neighbouring Poland is sending waves of light across the dark border to the beleaguered Charter 77 movement of intellectuals and artists of Czechoslovakia, 'normalized' since 1968, when the Warsaw Pact invasion ended Alexander Dubček's brief Prague Spring. But in 1988 no one in Czechoslovakia yet imagined the fall of the walls to come in 1989. The Soviet empire seems impregnable and its post-1968 satellite regime in Czechoslovakia has now become one of its stalwarts. The minority Lutheran Church in Slovakia in the interim has accommodated itself to this 'new normal'.

Osuský, accordingly, could not be remembered in 1988 as the theological foe that he had in fact been of fascism, Hitlerism and Bolshevism alike, nor recognized as a new champion of theologizing from the Scriptures under post-modern conditions. In memorializing Osuský, Professor Dušan Ondrejovič[5] made a politically acceptable mention of Osuský's imprisonment by the Gestapo, during the Nazi occupation of Slovakia in 1944, for lending the moral support of the Lutheran church leadership to the Slovak National Uprising against Hitler's

[2] Heiko Oberman, *Luther: Man between God and the Devil* trans. E. Walliser-Schwarzbart (Yale University Press, 1989).

[3] *Philip Melanchthon: Orations on Philosophy and Education* ed. Sachicko Kusukawa, trans. C. F. Salazar (Cambridge, UK: Cambridge University Press, 1999). See further the studies of Günther Frank: 'Gott und Natur: Zur Transformation der Naturphilosophie in Melanchthons humanistischer Philosophie' in *Melanchthon und die Naturwissenschaften seiner Zeit*, ed. G. Frank & S. Rhein (Sigmaringen: Jan Thorbecke Verlag, 1998); *Die Vernunft des Gottesgedankens: Religionsphilosophische Studien zur fruehen Neuzeit* (Frommann-Holzboog, 2003); *Die Theologische Philosophie Philipp Melanchthons (1497–1560)* Erfurter Theologische Studien Band 67 (Benno).

[4] On Melanchthonian Lutheranism, including its final flowering in Leibniz, see Paul R. Hinlicky, *Paths Not Taken: Fates of Theology from Luther through Leibniz* (Grand Rapids, MI: Eerdmans, 2009).

[5] Dušan Ondrejovič, 'PhDr. ThDr. h.c. Samuel Štefan Osuský 7.6.1888–14.11.1975', photocopy from the archives of the library of the Protestant Theological Faculty, Comenius University, Bratislava, accessed in 2014 with the aid of librarian Vlastislav Svoboda and Dr Peter Gažik.

puppet regime. But Ondrejovič made no mention of Osuský's being purged in 1950 from the theological faculty and forced into premature 'retirement', forbidden to preach, lecture or publish. In this connection, Ondrejovič only alluded vaguely to now 'outdated' views of Osuský, as we shall see.

Ondrejovič made two chief points in his memorial lecture. First, he claimed, Osuský laboured in 'service to the nation': 'a new state [Czechoslovakia] was being built [after the First World War] and so professors had to fill in the gaps, since there were not enough educated people. Also here Osuský was known for his industriousness'. Such a patriotic 'nation-builder' was Osuský, Ondrejovič reports, that he even wrote a five-act drama, 'The Fall of the Great Moravian Empire',[6] on the tenth anniversary of the founding of the new Czechoslovak state. It was a clumsy morality play, drawing lessons for the new state from a millennium before; Ondrejovič conceded that this amateurish effort lacked 'greater artistic merit'.

Second, according to Ondrejovič, Osuský's labour was that of a religious philosopher or, perhaps, a philosophical theologian. Osuský's 'most significant work' was his 1939 *The First Slovak History of Philosophy*, which argued the cases simultaneously for Slovak culture in spite of centuries of Hungarian domination, and for the role of Lutheranism as educator of the nation through this long national ordeal. Osuský's exploration of the thought of patriotic predecessors thus undergirded his own contemporary task of nation-building in the new Czechoslovakia. But, ironically, this cultural and pedagogical task compromised Osuský's theological posture in the eyes of conservative churchmen. Thus, in conclusion, Ondrejovič wrote:

> Much of what the bishop and professor Osuský wrote proceeded from the needs of the time and later became untimely. But he was already conscious of this then. He did not claim permanence for his work, because he did not give principles in them. His principle was deep in his heart and conscience and it is possible to call it "the principle of Slovak Lutheran Protestantism." He was a great personality, even though many in his age did not understand him. Those who would have been glad to see a theologian in him recognized a philosopher in him and conversely those who wanted to see in him only a philosopher saw in him a theologian. From this many suspicions arose. Whoever wants to understand him must look upon him as a philosophizing theologian, who wanted always by his opinions to address also those who are in the church but influenced by secularization.

6 Samuel Štefan Osuský, *Pad ríše Veľkomoravskej* (Myjava, 1928).

Thus Ondrejovič depicted Osuský as engaged in a time-bound but systematic apologetics, concerned to keep the religious flock intact under the pressure of modern secularization. We will return to this characterization of Osuský shortly.

Thinkers like Ondrejovič, who could not have taught on the Protestant faculty in 1988 without the approval of the post-1968 Czechoslovak regime committed to the 'normalcy' of Brezhnev's 'real, existing socialism,' profiled themselves as intellectual opponents of reactionary obscurantism, fundamentalism and dogmatism. They asserted both the right and the need for mediating the theological tradition to modern thought and culture. Paul Tillich, accordingly, became their 'Lutheran' hero and alternative to 'fundamentalism,' old and new ('new,' to wit, the Czech Brethren theologian Josef Hromádka, a champion of Karl Barth's 'new' orthodoxy).[7] In his centennial memorialisation, then, Ondrejovič produced an Osuský portrait suitable to his own times in 1988: one who was progressive in his day, battling fundamentalism and open to socialism, a practitioner of the 'method of correlation,' according to which theology responds to the questions posed by contemporary culture. Such would be a theology 'facing life,' as Ondrejovič's bishop, Ján Michalko (1912–90), a systematic theologian and then dean of the theological faculty, would put it.

Peter Gažik, who now occupies the seat once held by Osuský and Ondrejovič, has followed Ondrejovič's line of interpretation,[8] albeit with important post-1989 modifications. Gažik sees Osuský as a theological philosopher, where this classification stands for opposition to narrow-mindedness and irrationalism in theology. Yet Gažik also sees Osuský *after* Marxism; that is, he sees that narrow-mindedness and irrationalism are not the exclusive properties of religion but can equally attend the self-identified forces of enlightenment and progress, especially in the form of the twentieth century 'political religions'[9] of fascism and communism. The Marxist-Leninist regime, in other words, tried to erase Osuský from living memory, not least because he represented something other than the Marxist caricature of the narrow-minded, irrational and reactionary theologian hawking pie in the sky in the sweet bye and bye. While Osuský

[7] Peter Gažik distances Osuský from Barth and identifies him with Brunner with respect to the controversy over the 'point of contact' provided by religion. Gažik 26–8.

[8] Gažik, 94. As we shall see, this interpretation is justified to the degree that it vindicates Osuský from the criticisms made of him after he was deposed. Gažik, who came of age during the Prague Spring, told me that when he learned of Osuský late in his theological education he had never before heard of one who only twenty short years earlier had been the church's leading intellectual. Gažik has dedicated his own scholarship, in part, to remedying that erasure of memory. I will accordingly gratefully draw on Gažik's scholarship throughout this book.

[9] Emilio Gentile, 'Fascism as Political Religion,' *Journal of Contemporary History*, 25/2–3 (May–June, 1990), 229–51.

never wholly shed the vocabulary and thought-forms of nineteenth century liberalism's faith in progress, and continued to engage in corresponding forms of conservative apologetics regarding the historical credibility of the Bible, he in fact took steps beyond modern epistemological foundationalism and swam anew in the bracing waters of the apocalyptic and narrative theology of the Bible. Gažik's monograph on Osusky as 'modern philosopher of religion' concludes with the statement that 'treatment of Osuský as a theologian would be an independent theme. Osuský was not only a religious philosopher but also a Protestant theologian, who wrote several theological books. He did not avoid the basic Reformation problem of the grace of God in relation to the justification and salvation of humanity'.[10] We may take this as a mandate for the present work, coming from the best study to date of Osuský's legacy.

Gažik's view of Osuský is shared by contemporary Slovak philosophers. Ján Letz, for example, describes Osuský as one who came from nationally self-conscious surroundings; he reports that already, in 1906, as a student at the Lyceum in Bratislava, Osuský signed a petition in which students demanded that lectures be given in their native Slovak language, not the imperial language of Hungary. Dedicating his life to the improvement of Slovak Protestant theological education, Letz continues, Osuský educated several generations of the Protestant clergy intelligentsia. After the Second World War, but before the communist seizure of power, Osuský received considerable public recognition, not only for his wartime witness but academically in his areas of expertise. Letz summarizes the contribution as follows:

> The gravamen of his production is philosophy, especially its history in Slovakia. A second gravamen is his religious and theological work, which was presented especially in his books, *The End of the World* (1941) and *The Mystery of the Cross* (1943) [expositions of the biblical books of Revelation and Job respectively, to be discussed below in Chapter 3]. Osuský was not a religious philosopher but rather a philosophizing theologian. His positive relation to philosophy arose in the Protestant context of mistrust in philosophy. Just because of the philosophical accent in his thought, many of his fellow believers subjected him to criticism and received his reflections with mistrust. They rebuked him for dependence on liberal theology and too much theological speculation. But Osuský did not blindly trust in philosophy...[11]

[10] Gažik, 97.

[11] Ján Letz, *Slovenská kresťanská filozofia 20. Storočia a jej perspektívy* [Slovak Christian Philosophy of the 20th Century and its Perspectives] (Spolok Slovákov v Polsku & Filozofická fakulta Trnavskej univerzity v Trnave, 2010), 248–9.

Such constructions of Osuský – as much a philosopher as a theologian – are not fabricated out of whole cloth, to be sure. As mentioned, in a single lifetime Osuský lived through the war-time collapse of Austro-Hungarian imperialism, the twenty-year experiment of multicultural Czechoslovak democracy betrayed by the West into Hitler's hands, then Slovak fascism allied with Hitler; and, as the latter's reward, the Stalinist nightmare. In this context, Ondrejovič, Gažik and Letz are not wrong to highlight Osuský's work in service to the nation as a philosophizing theologian as well as his opposition to fundamentalism and obscurantism. We shall carefully examine, in Chapter 1, this aspect of Osuský's work, including a significant episode of this conflict with fundamentalism.

But Osuský opposed *all* forms of fundamentalism; Nazism, then, but also the fascisms of the secular and self-identified 'progressive' left. Furthermore, as I shall show in this book, Osuský battled fundamentalism in the crucible of these dramatic times with the aid of the Bible and for the sake of the Bible and its liberating message concerning Christ, as understood in his Lutheran tradition, precisely for modern people vulnerable to new messianisms bringing about new bondages with recurring episodes of apocalyptic horrors. Osuský, also in accord with his Lutheran theological tradition, took that biblical message to entail service to one's native land and its people. There is a dialectic here that is palpable in his life's work. On the one hand, the principle of incarnation in Christian theology requires indigenization, enculturation; but the principle of the cross of the Incarnate One, on the other hand, demands prophetic critique of every indigenization. Where this dialectic is not recognized and received, the theologian who works in accord with it inevitably looks too conservative to those who protest the malice and injustice structured into the culture and too liberal to those who would merely conserve the cultural synthesis thus far achieved.

It is important, then, to shed a little more light at the outset on this dialectic Osuský embodied. The chair that Osuský occupied would today be called 'religious studies'. It is critical, however, to explicate the Slavic language etymology of the words translated by 'nation' and 'religion'. *Narod* derives from the verb *rodit*, to give birth, while the noun form, *rod*, literally means one's biological lineage through the generations. These words are kindred, then, to the word for family, *rodina*, so that *narod* has the connotation of something like the English 'motherland'. Nation, then, does not entail ethnically exclusive political sovereignty for Osuský, nor does patriotism associate with hatred of other peoples of other lineages. But love of one's own naturally reflects the organic unity of place with the development and tradition of human culture and language in any given, historically specific form of humanity.

Naboženstvo, translated by the English word 'religion', derives from *Boh*, God, and means literally the human state of being oriented to God, as in Augustine's famed remark from the beginning of his Confessions: 'Thou hast made us for Thyself, and our hearts are restless until they find their rest in Thee, O God.' Religion, then, does not have the primary sense of social ritual that binds a people together, as in secular and sociological theories of religion current in Western Europe and North American 'religious studies' today; rather it denotes, especially as we shall see, for Osuský, that Augustinian anthropological universal of desire, howsoever corrupted, for the one, true God. Thus, when Osuský describes himself and his work as 'religious' study, he is very far from imagining a non-theological inquiry, as we might imagine under contemporary epistemic conditions in the English-speaking world.

These understandings of nation and religion, moreover, deeply correlate with Osuský's *Melanchthonian* Lutheranism. Luther, too, had derived all social authority from the cultural activity of parenting, even as at the same time he regarded the coercive mechanism of the state as a super-added 'emergency order' after the human fall into sin and violence.[12] Luther also regarded 'religion' not as a theologically indifferent ritual for social bonding but as human desire, howsoever corrupted, for the 'one, true God'. 'There has never been a people so wicked', Luther wrote in his influential *Large Catechism*, 'that it has not erected some form of worship of God'. Note the association of 'people' – for Osuský, *narod*, 'nation' – with the cult, 'worship', that is, *naboženstvo*, orientation to God. For Melanchthon, *praeceptor Germaniae*, but also of Upper Hungary in the 16th and 17th centuries, these theological truisms mandated the construction of a new, Protestant reform of national culture in the framework of European Christendom. The gymnasium and the university, as reformed under Melanchthon's influence for this task of a reformed Christendom, deeply influenced Slovak cultural development, as Michal Valčo has shown.[13]

Under these presuppositions, Osuský, Slovak patriot *and* Czechoslovak multicultural social democrat *and* Melanchthonian Lutheran, was able to oppose the nativist forces of fascism that turned a decent love of homeland into xenophobic hatred. In historical fact, it was precisely a Slovak *national* uprising consisting for the most part of Lutherans and Marxists that opposed Nazi biological racism

[12] Oswald Bayer, *Martin Luther's Theology: A Contemporary Interpretation* trans. Thomas H. Trapp (Grand Rapids, MI: Eerdmans, 2007).

[13] See Michal Valčo and Daniel Škoviera, *Katechizmus Leonarda Stőckela a jeho theologicko-filozofický odkaz* (Martin: Slovenská národná knižnica, 2014).

and domestic 'political Catholicism'.[14] In parallel, Osuský embraced a kind of democratic socialism that made him the peculiar target of Marxist-Leninist antipathy for any and all rivals to allegedly 'scientific' socialism. He suffered at the hands of both forces, accordingly, as a confessor of the faith who at the end of his life became increasingly and explicitly biblical – another hallmark of his always tacit and at the end of his life increasingly explicit Lutheranism. Thus, he gravitated towards Luther's apocalypticism, yet, as we shall see, in deliteralised fashion.

Osuský's intellectual legacy should not be construed, then, as that of an accommodating modernist, giving the unbeliever less and less in which to disbelieve in order to stay 'relevant'. What is rather more striking about Osuský's trajectory through the twentieth century tragedies was his turn to the Bible from (but also on the basis of) the cultural, philosophical, sociological and psychological studies of his early career in nation-building, in order to speak to the collapse of Christendom. In his forays into biblical exposition, he strove to speak from the Scriptures to the crises of mid-century Europe. In these works, he pioneered a new (to use George Lindbeck's term) 'post-liberal' way of reading Scripture as the Spirit's formative narrative of a particular kind of person-cum-society, as we shall see, that no longer depends on or seeks political privilege.[15]

Life, Works and the Plan of This Book

Osuský was born in the western region of Slovakia approaching its border with Moravia from a working class family of leather-tanners. He studied at the gymnasium in Trnava before joining the historic Protestant Lyceum in Bratislava from 1903 to 1906; he then continued his studies at his church's Theological Academy in Bratislava from 1906 to 1910. Following that, Osuský enjoyed study abroad at the German theological faculties in Erlangen, Jena and Leipzig. He served as a war-time pastor in Dacov Lom, where, in 1916, he published his first book, *War and Religion*. In the years 1919 to 1922, he worked on his doctorate in philosophy at Charles University in Prague, culminating in a dissertation on the psychology of religion in 1922. He continued in legal studies at the Academy of Law in Prešov by distance learning, earning a doctorate in jurisprudence in 1941. In the interim he was employed by the Slovak Protestant

[14] On the Hlinka Slovak National Party, and 'political Catholicism', see below, Chapter 2.

[15] George A. Lindbeck, *The Nature of Doctrine: Religion and Theology in a Postliberal Age* (Philadelphia: Westminster, 1984).

Theological Faculty in Bratislava, first, in 1919, as an unpaid professor; from 1920 to 1933 as a paid professor; and from 1933 until 1950 as tenured. He lectured on topics in the history of philosophy, the psychology of religion, pedagogy and sociology. He chaired various learned societies, and was elected after the war to membership in the Philosophical Section of the prestigious cultural research institute and national museum, *Matica Slovenska*. He founded a short-lived academic journal, *Faith and Science,* which published from 1930 to 1933, dying a financial death during the Great Depression. He ably represented his church at international congresses in Fanő and Oxford in his years as a bishop of the Western District of his church from 1933, a post that he voluntarily gave up in 1946 in order to dedicate his remaining years to his life-long project of the Slovak Protestant Theological Faculty. After being deposed in 1950 by the regime and its collaborators, he retired to obscurity in his hometown.[16]

A survey of the prolific Osuský's literary legacy that tried to be comprehensive would take us far afield. In the following, enough of a sketch is provided to give the measure of the man and define the contours of the material to be traversed in the coming chapters. We have already mentioned Osuský's first book, to be discussed in the next chapter. Written while he was a pastor in Dacov Lom (1912–18), *War and Religion* (1916) bewailed the carnage of the First World War and queried the uncritical war theology of German Protestant boosters, setting off by contrast the deep reserve Osuský found in his Slovak peers, especially the Lutheran poet, essayist and politician Martin Rázus (1888–1937). *War and Religion* is more of an extended essay than an academic monograph, yet it is significant for displaying the critical spirit and social engagement that would attend Osuský's work throughout his career.

His next book, published in several editions, was *The History of Religion* (2nd edition, 1922). This was a textbook written for Protestant educational purposes (religious schools still predominated at this time). It exudes the teleological spirit of nineteenth century liberal Protestant accounts of the progress of religions towards Christianity, and, at the pinnacle of perfection, Protestantism. Despite dependence on the German scholarship of his pre-war education at Erlangen, Jena and Leipzig, Osuský took the opportunity in this little textbook to widen considerably the culturally narrow horizons of his readership, introducing them to the various worldviews represented by the religions. It is significant, also, as we shall see, for revealing the considerable extent to which the young Osuský was under the spell of the liberal theology in which he had been educated.

[16] I am drawing this biographical information from Letz, 248.

In this regard, the text book on the religions stands in some tension with the prophetic earlier effort, *War and Religion*.

The pedagogical task of educating a people for democratic citizenship in the post-war world community of nation-states provides proper orientation for understanding Osuský's studies and writings in the 1920s on to the 1930s: catch as catch can, he was 'filling the gaps', as Ondrejovič rightly put it, in writing to educate a small and backward nation just recently emerged from centuries of foreign domination and cultural infantilization. For example, in 1930 Osusky produced in two volumes the first Slovak language *Introduction to Sociology*.[17] In the process of this broad cultural and pedagogical work, as Letz remarked on Osuský's studies in *The First Slovak History of Philosophy* (1939),[18] Osuský was able to show his readership: 'Slovaks also in the distant past dedicated themselves to philosophy and committed themselves to research on philosophical problems… in close relation to their Christian religion and faith. He succeeded in this way to refute incorrect views of the philosophical inferiority of Slovaks and thus by the mediation of their intellectual legacy was able to contribute to the self-knowledge of the Slovak person and nation'.[19] More specifically, Osuský published a three volume monograph, *The Philosophy of Štur and His Followers* (1926–32),[20] which became part of the later, 1939, *First Slovak History of Philosophy*, investigating in detail the thought of nineteenth century Protestant pastors and intellectuals who led the national awakening of the Slovaks.

Ľudovit Štur (1815–56) is the chief figure here; he received his higher education in Germany, where he fell under the spell of Herder and Hegel. Returning to Slovakia, he inspired his generation to fight for Slovak cultural autonomy within the multicultural Austro-Hungarian Empire. In the process, he contributed greatly to the modern codification of the Slovak language. Štur ended in a kind of mystical Panslavism: that is, he thought that Russian Orthodox liturgical theology could mediate the Western conflict between Reformation Christianity and the Enlightenment and overcome the sterile reaction of Roman Catholicism against modernity.

Osuský's discerning judgment in these matters, as reported by Letz, is illustrative of his analytical prowess in interpreting intersections of philosophy and theology:

[17] Samuel Štefan Osuský, *Úvod do sociologie* (Pa, 1930).
[18] Samuel Štefan Osuský, *Prvé slovenské dejiny filozofie* (Myjava, 1939).
[19] Letz, 249.
[20] Samuel Štefan Osuský, *Filozofia Štúrovcov* 1–3 (Myjava, 1926–32).

> Štur is a true pupil of Hegel. He took over his philosophy of history with many of its virtues, but also its inadequacies... In metaphysics the difference is that while Hegel is unclear about his absolute, whether it is theistic or pantheistic, Štur is decisively theistic... In Hegel's philosophy of history there can only be talk about nations, which form states, but in Štur it is about nations which create events, deeds, that spring from their own spirit; in Hegel the state stands supreme, but with Štur, even in the acknowledgement of the greatness of the state, the nation in the sense of a human tribe stands in the forefront.[21]

These are significant differentiations for Osuský, which led him to the conclusion that, even though the nineteenth century Slovak patriots borrowed from Hegel's idealism, they also brought every element of it immediately to life. As Letz puts it, for Osuský the nineteenth century Protestant pastors who led the national awakening 'overcame objective idealism, and its philosophical worldview became both ideal *and real.* Osuský also worked towards this realism of the ideal, even if he did not expressively put it this way'.

As mentioned, these investigations came to final form in Osuský's *First Slovak History of Philosophy* (1939), published at the very moment when Hitler was dissecting the First Czechoslovak Republic, granting Slovak state autonomy under the leadership of 'political Catholicism' in exchange for a loyal satellite (further to be discussed in Chapter 2, below). Osuský's book was attacked at this tense moment from both the left and the right. The left attacked Osuský's non-pantheistic theological notion of divine providence as superstitious supernaturalism, while the right decried his multicultural tendencies towards the alliance with the Czech peoples in a democratic and multicultural state. For the left, Osuský represented 'bourgeois nationalism', and for the right, 'Czechoslovakism'.

It is from this critical juncture in the 1930s that Osuský's authorship began to take the surprising turn to the Bible.[22] In his 1937 lecture on the 'Philosophy of Fascism, Bolshevism and Hitlerism' (to be discussed below in Chapter 2) he was still confining himself to his academic specialization in philosophy and the social sciences, leaving it to colleagues on the Protestant Theological Faculty to sound biblical and theological warnings about the dire events on the horizon. But by 1941, with the twisted cross of the Nazi conquest now flying the swastika all across the continent, Osuský published his commentary on Revelation, *The*

[21] Cited by Letz, 250, from Osuský's *Philosophy of Štur and His Disciples.*

[22] Gažík describes the same turn more abstractly as a turn to 'revelation' (73, 80) and as a turn from 'idealism' (77).

End of the World.[23] It was followed two short years later by *The Mystery of the Cross,*[24] a commentary on Job, informed by his Lutheran tradition's 'theology of the cross'. We shall examine these important works carefully in Chapter 3 below.

During 1944, Osuský gave moral support to the participation of Lutherans among Slovak partisans, many of whom were Marxists, in preparation for an uprising against the fascist satellite state as the Red Army approached from the East. But already Osuský knew that this tactical alliance would not last. During 1944, he composed an apologetics, *Defence of the Truth,*[25] which appeared in 1946 in anticipation of the ascent of Marxism-Leninism. In this book, Osuský appears unmistakably as a Christian theologian speaking directly to Marxist criticisms of 'religion' (recall: *Na-Boh*, human desire for God), Christianity and Protestantism. Interestingly, as we shall see, these three categories, around which he organized his thinking, reflect the Christian Trinity of Father, Son and Holy Spirit respectively. During this period he also published occasional articles, and presented some unpublished public lectures which are also preserved; these we will have occasion to study in Chapters 2 and 3. Since *Defence of the Truth* is in several respects a culmination of Osuský's work as a philosophical theologian, I will treat its first part on religion in general (or, First Article theism) at the conclusion of Chapter 1, below, and its third part on Protestantism (or the Holy Spirit's work) at the end of Chapter 2. I will treat the second part of it on Christianity (or, concerning the incarnate Son, Jesus Christ) at the end of Chapter 3, where it will serve as a segue to the final chapter in Osuský's writing career. This concerns the most astounding fruit from Osuský's pen, already mentioned in the Preface, the book of New Testament theology which never appeared in his lifetime. An examination of this final and quite remarkable effort, amounting to a post-modern narrative theology of the Bible, will occupy us in Chapter 4.

[23] Samuel Štefan Osuský, *Koniec Sveta z Jánovho Zjavenia Vyložil* [The End of the World Exposited from the Revelation of John] (Mikulaš: Tranoscius, 1941).

[24] Samuel Štefan Osuský, *Tajomstvo Kríža z Joba vyklade* [The Mystery of the Cross exposited from the book of Job] (Mikuláš: Tranoscius, 1943).

[25] Samuel Štefan Osuský, *Braň Pravdy* [Defence of the Truth] (Mikuláš: Tranoscius, 1946).

1

From Dissent under Imperialism to Nation-building

The young Osuský adopted, but also modified, the religious socialism of the reformed Zurich theologian Leonhard Ragaz (1868–1945) to address the burning social questions of his poor and traditionally rural land undergoing rapid industrialization and painful social transformation in the time of his youth. He affiliated politically with the Czech leader, Tomaš Masaryk, joining forces after the war with the Czechoslovak movement for democracy and national self-determination within the framework of a multi-ethnic democratic republic in the European family of nations. The young Osuský matured to these positions from within the decay of the Austro-Hungarian Empire, when, as mentioned, in 1916 he cautiously but unmistakably questioned the war in his first book, a potentially prosecutable offence. Affiliation with the Czech intellectuals, among whom he studied for his doctorate in philosophy in Prague, brought him, however, under theological suspicion in the eyes of some very conservative Slovak Lutherans. Osuský successfully rebutted this attack, but in the process also revealed a definite ambivalence towards the modern world, optimistically championed by liberal theology.

One observer puts the matter well:

> Although as a Lutheran Osuský had a definite freedom of movement in philosophy, we do not meet in him an effort to work out an original philosophical standpoint, nor with any tendency to attach himself to a certain philosophical direction or personality. Almost all the problems, which he solved and in which he revealed his more liberal standpoint, were identical with the problems Catholics tried to solve. Although he saw many dark shadows in modernity, he did not condemn it, but revealed an understanding for its secularizing and laicizing tendencies; indeed, he himself sought to explain in a lay, historical-evolutionary way, what Catholics explained more in a

> theological-dogmatic way. Primarily it was about contemporary social, political and ideological problems, which disturbed him just as they disturbed Catholics. When however it came to the basic questions of worldview, to religion itself, he denied in himself the philosopher, but not the theologian and so he solved the problems the same way, and often by the same arguments, as did Catholics.[1]

Philosophically, in other words, Osuský turns out to be a standard Christian Platonist theist, trying like so many others in so many ways to accommodate the challenge of modernity.

In this chapter, in order to contextualize the somewhat misleading claim that his chief legacy is that of (such) a philosophizing theologian, we will trace Osuský's early intellectual movement from dissent under imperialism to nation building in the new Czechoslovak state. In fact, the philosophical positions he took were the conventional ones of the Christian Platonism, which he shared, as the preceding citation indicates, with the Catholic tradition.[2] This is particularly visible in his 1946 apologetics, *Defence of the Truth*, the first part of which concerning religion, taken as theism, I will interpret below as a final, indeed desperate, act in his early work as a nation-builder.

Imperialism, Nationalism and Western Christianity

Even though the last regime that could described with any empirical weight as 'imperial' passed from the stage of world history in 1989, one would never know that from some quarters of contemporary theology. By this terminology, given today's absence of any actual political empire (although Vladimir Putin seemingly wants to revive one), one intends something like Lenin's theory of a new formation of capital to trans-national, global formations, that is, *economic* imperialism. In this extended sense, 'imperialism' holds conceptual sway as the demythologized political bogey-man in certain interpretations of the theology

1 Teodor Münz, 'Náboženská filozofia na Slovensku v prvej polovici 20. Storočia,' *Filozofia* 49/7 (1994), 469.

2 Münz is undoubtedly right about this, despite the anti-Catholicism in which Osuský indulges, as we shall amply witness. But on the way up to his magnum opus, the *Gallery of New Testament Figures*, the Augustinian themes of the restless heart (433), the two societies driven by the two loves (693), the sharp critique of the religion business and the *libido dominandi* (607–8, 687–8), in short, Catholic Christianity's *Platonism* saturates Osuský's thought by way of the Augustinian doctrine of the hierarchy of value: 'If God is the highest value, then all other values must give way before Him … For [Jesus], spiritual values, bonds and connections are higher than the connections of blood, body and matter' (197). Osuský resolved problems of theodicy, like Jesus in the Sermon on the Mount, Augustine and Leibniz before him, with 'the consequent Christian relativization of all earthly values in relation to eternal values' (Gažík, 66).

of the Apostle Paul.[3] Lost from view in this demonizing of the ideal of empire is both the Apostle's cautious endorsement of the imperialism of his times, which he makes a matter of *conscience* for Christians on account of God's institution (Romans 13.6), but also the proper political antinomy of empire, which is *nationalism*. One would think that after the twentieth century of nationalist idolatries that soaked Europe in blood, something like the multicultural unity of the imperial ideal would rather attract theological interest as a form of human unity better approximating the eschatological kingdom of God composed of every nation, tribe and tongue. The fragile, still developing, European Union might be understood this way. Nationalism is, in any event, the idol which filled the modern European spiritual vacuum after the collapse of old dreams for a 'holy' Roman empire under Christendom stretching back to Charlemagne.

In his *The Rise of Western Christendom*, Peter Brown has shown how, in case after case, the tribes of Europe were Christianized in a complex symbiosis with the cultural task of nation-building and the corresponding work of political centralization. The centralization of power in political sovereignty with its new, Christian sacralisation, together with the codification of law and language and the cultivation of learning for the new tasks of diplomacy and policy – all this took place by way of a new covenant with Europe's new religion. The monastery became the reservoir of sacred power within the nation, taken in its turn under the protection of the crown. The crown likewise became the instrument of the Christianization of the masses by the monasteries. The resulting synthesis was *Christendom*, or, rather, a plethora of micro-Christendoms emerging from 750 AD onwards, in which church and nation were profoundly synthesized. Brown gives a crisp account of the Christian theological problem involved, in muted but unmistakable terms:

> A small body of clergymen (notably Alcuin…) were challenged by [Charlemagne's] brusqueness to restate, more forcibly than even before, a view of Christian missions which emphasized preaching and persuasion. But, in fact, when it came to Charlemagne's treatment of the Saxons, most later writers took no notice of Alcuin's reservations. They accepted the fact that, as befitted a strong king, Charlemagne was entitled to preach to the Saxons with "with a tongue of iron" – as a later Saxon writer put it without a hint of blame. Force was

3 Walter Wink, *Naming the Powers: Then Language of Power in the New Testament* (Philadelphia: Fortress, 1984), and *Engaging the Powers: Discernment and Resistance in a World of Domination* (Minneapolis: Fortress, 1992). N. T. Wright, 'Paul and Caesar: A New Reading of Romans, in *A Royal Priesthood: The Use of the Bible Ethically and Politically*, ed. C. Bartholemew (Carlisle: Paternoster, 2002) 173–93. John M. G. Barclay, *Pauline Churches and Diaspora Jews* (Mohr Siebeck), criticizes Wright's 'reading between the lines' to discover a 'hidden transcript', 379.

> what was needed on a dangerous frontier. Education began, rather, at home. In the reigns of Charlemagne and his successors, a substantially new Church was allied with a new political system, both of which were committed, to a quite unprecedented degree, to the "correction" and education of their subjects.[4]

Lutheranism, as a much later reform movement within this Christendom project, did not overcome this theological problem, but rather reiterated it in a new key. Osuský was heir to this more subtle entanglement.

John Witte has written perceptively about the dark side of this Christian fusion of state paternalism with its monopoly on the means of coercion. The ancient commonwealths were, in the view of Melanchthon and his disciples, 'incomplete. They can speak only to a "civil goodness", not to a "spiritual goodness"... For none of these classical civilizations had the full biblical revelation of the heavenly kingdom on which the earthly kingdom must be partly modelled'.[5] The 'law of the prince must coerce citizens to a "civil goodness", and also cultivate in them a "spiritual goodness"'.[6] Lutheranism in this way 'went beyond Luther... in articulating the divinely imposed task of Christian magistrates to promulgate... "rational positive laws" ("*rationes iuris positive*") for the governance of the earthly kingdom'.[7] The Christian magistrate was to be 'the "custodian" of both tables of the Decalogue, "a voice of the Ten Commandments" within the earthly kingdom... magistrates must pass laws against idolatry, blasphemy, and violations of the Sabbath – offence that the First Table prohibits on its face. Magistrates are also, however, to pass laws to "establish pure doctrine" and right liturgy, "to prohibit all wrong doctrine", "to punish the obstinate", and to root out the heathen and the heterodox'.[8] While this 'move toward the establishment of religion by positive law was a marked departure from Luther's original teaching ...',[9] the *cuius regio, eius religio*

[4] Peter Brown, *The Rise of Western Christendom: Triumph and Diversity A.D. 200–1000*, second edition (Oxford: Blackwell, 2003), 433. It is intriguing but also salient to note here Adolf Hitler's admiration for Charlemagne's empire-building, i.e. not for the Christianization but for the 'tongue of iron': 'Charlemagne gathered the Germans into a well-cemented community, and created an empire that continued to deserve the name long after his death...The fact that this German empire was named "the Holy Roman Empire" has no religious significance, i.e. no Christian significance'. Trevor-Roper, H. R. ed., *Hitler's Table Talk 1941–1944: His Private Conversations*, New Updated Version trans. N. Cameron and R.H. Stevens (NY: Enigma Books, 2008) 288. See the discussion of 'Napoleon's Mantle' in Paul R. Hinlicky, *Before Auschwitz: What Christian Theology Must Learn from the Rise of Nazism* (Eugene, OR: Cascade, 2014), 134–8.

[5] John Witte, Jr., *Law and Protestantism: The Legal Teachings of the Lutheran Reformation*, with a Foreword by Martin E. Marty (Cambridge University Press, 2002), 147.

[6] Ibid., 151

[7] Ibid., 129.

[8] Ibid., 131.

[9] Ibid.

principle at length of 'the Peace of Westphalia (1648), rested ultimately on the Lutheran Christendom theory that the magistrate's positive law was to use the First Table of the Decalogue to establish for his people proper Christian doctrine, liturgy, and spiritual morality'.[10]

Witte's conclusion here serves well to locate the Lutheran parameters within which the more liberal young Osuský is thinking as an exponent of the Melanchthonian theological tradition. On the positive side, Witte urges that 'a good deal of our modern Western law of marriage, education, and social welfare, for example, still bears the unmistakable marks of Lutheran Reformation theology'.[11] He emphasizes that '... the state has a role to play not only in fighting wars, punishing crime, and keeping peace, but also in providing education and welfare, fostering charity and morality, facilitating worship and piety... law has not only a basic use of coercing citizens to accept a morality of duty but also a higher use of inducing citizens to pursue a morality of aspiration'. But on the negative side, Witte notes that ever since the Reformation times 'Germany and other Protestant nations have been locked in a bitter legal struggle to eradicate state establishments of religion and to guarantee religious freedom for all ...'.[12] It is in this latter regard that Osuský's Lutheranism finally turned against him as nation-builder and returned him to the defenceless posture of the biblical witness/martyr in the complex evolutions that transpired in his life's course from imperialism to democracy to fascism to Stalinism.

As mentioned in the Preface, the territory of present day Slovakia in the centuries since the fall of the Great Moravian Empire in the ninth century had been under the hegemony of the Hungarian crown, just as the Moravians and Bohemians in the Czech lands to the immediate west had been under the hegemony of the Austrian Habsburgs. In these imperial configurations, these Slavic peoples experienced distinct if not in some ways antagonistic developments. The indigenous Czech reform stemming from Jan Hus had been crushed at the Battle of White Mountain in 1620 and the population re-Catholicized under the tutelage of the Jesuits, even though Czech nationalism continued to identify with Hus. And so a profound divergence between nation and religion came about (I have been told that the German term for a 'none', *Bekenntnislos*, 'without a confession', originated in the Czech language, *bezvyznany*). Today the Czech Republic ranks among the most atheist nations in Europe. By contrast, thanks to extensive German colonialization due to the

[10] Ibid., 132.
[11] Ibid., 295.
[12] Ibid., 296.

mining industry in mountainous Slovakia, the Reformation message of Luther quickly spread into the Slovak territory of Upper Hungary and thence into Hungarian-speaking lands. By the year 1670, some 880 parishes on this territory were served by preachers subscribed to the Augsburg Confession. Although this 'Lutheranizing' of Slovakia for 150 years was accompanied by magisterial acts of political power, and sacralised in the Melanchthonian way, as Witte described, it was not so violent and traumatic as the decade of forced re-Catholicizing of these parishes.[13] The imperial action that commenced in 1670, in coordination with the Jesuit order, was a bloody and traumatic event that ever after stamped the consciousness of surviving Slovak Lutherans as a persecuted (religious) minority within a (national) minority. To preserve an identity of victimization, however, is a decidedly mixed blessing.

The Lutheran pastors of these parishes were given the choice of converting to Catholicism, going into exile or being executed or sold into slavery to Muslim galley ships in the Adriatic Sea. For more than one hundred years afterwards, until the enlightened emperor, Joseph II, promulgated an Edict of Toleration, the surviving Slovak Lutherans led a barely tolerated, often underground, existence. Even with the Toleration, their churches were not permitted to compete in public spaces with Catholic buildings.[14] Only with the passing of the Hungarian empire in the rubble of the First World War and the new laws of religious liberty that came with the Czechoslovak republic did Slovak Lutherans emerge from second-class citizenship. This burden of history must always be borne in mind in understanding Osuský, who as a young man passionately threw himself into the patriotic project of religiously inspired nation-building afforded by the post-war regime. This motive is palpable in the concluding words of the Foreword to the first edition of his 1919 textbook, *The History of Religion*: 'May this book serve to the glory of God and to the uplift of the nation'. Now, at long last, thanks to the Reformation, thanks to the Enlightenment, and thanks to the Wilsonian principle of national self-determination, the Slovak Lutherans were free to take a leading role in the pursuit of the project of a reformed and renewed Christendom in their own place, among their own people.

Yet from the beginning, with a conscience sensitized by the experience of historical victimization, Osuský was suspicious of secularized nationalism. His commitment to Czechoslovakia was a commitment to a *reformed* imperialism, so to speak, in the sense that the new republic was itself a multicultural society

[13] *Slovakia in History*, 83–6.
[14] Ibid., 87–100.

containing Sudetenland and other Germans, Bohemians, Moravians, Slovaks, Ruthenians, Hungarians, Romani, as well as a significant Jewish population. In his 1916 *War and Religion*, Osuský had written:

> Bad exegesis leads to the attempt to nationalize Christianity. The nationalization of Christianity would transplant us from the soil of the New Testament back to the soil of the Old Testament and lead us into polytheism, where every nation would have its own God. Chauvinism would grow. Surely the task of Christianity is to teach us love of humanity and a better patriotism than one drawn from hatred of other nations. In place of pagan patriotism must come a Christian patriotism. Human beings have to respect and love human beings, both of one's own nation and of others, because each one has its own talents and mission. The internationalism of Christianity does not intend to erase national life, but rather to leaven it with the good, so that in relation to other nations and states it behaves in accord with divine commandments.[15]

One should note here, for further reference, both the nineteenth century theological trope about Jewish particularism as opposed to Christian universalism and the favoured metaphor of Christianity as 'leaven that leavens the whole lump of dough'. We will take up the deeply rooted problem of Osuský's habitual anti-Judaism in the Conclusion to this book. For the interim, however, it is necessary to underscore what an 'earthquake' the First World War was, as Osuský's younger colleague from a later time in life, Karol Gábriš (1919–98), once noted: 'Whoever wants to understand the formation of theological thought in the 20th century must take into consideration everything that the First World War brought with it. It was an earthquake, which was certainly long in preparation, but its extent and quality was by far greater than expected at the outbreak of the war'. Gažik, who records this comment of Gábriš that is so pertinent to understanding Osuský, comments: 'This situation meant the need to correct in a principled way the dependence of theology on modern idealistic philosophy, to overcome theological liberalism and to take a stance towards antichristian streams and increasingly powerful secularism'.[16] Bearing in mind, then, both this situation, and the dialectic of indigenization on the one side, and prophetic critique of nationalistic enculturation of the gospel on the other, we will now trace Osuský's path as a prophetic theologian, from the earthquake of the First World War to the religious philosopher of culture in the twenties and thirties

15 *War and Religion*, 50.
16 Gažik, 55.

of the last century. Following out the latter trajectory of a religious philosophy of culture, we will conclude this chapter with an account of the first part of his post-war apologetic, *Defence of the Truth*, on religion as the ineradicable human orientation to God.

Prophetic Protest: *War and Religion* (1916)

There is no more current question than war and religion, the 1916 essay begins. Christianity has never been in such a state of tension as in today's world war. Doubts, he continues, multiply: 'How can a good and just God allow such bloodshed? How can today's exceedingly celebrated culture and humanity inflict such horrors on the poor shoulders of humanity? How can the most Christian and equally the most enlightened nations ignite with such bloodthirsty anger against themselves that they forget everything that is Christian, honourable, and conscientious? How is it that the better ones fall into the flame instead of the worse? Why do the church and clergy do nothing? And so on …' (3). Publishing this little book, Pastor Osuský is trying to do something about the war. Already 180 young men from his parish have been drafted and sent to the front. But who can speak objectively in a state of war?

At 'one moment the Christian theologian prevails, but in the next moment the citizen, the patriot … Our most excellent Protestant theological minds both of Germany and of England are interested parties. In vain then do we await from them complete objectivity. And the neutrals? They too are not without interests' (3). But theology is eminently practical and it must intervene in this crisis despite all such obstacles. It must 'examine the war in the light of the Bible but also the Bible in the light of history, especially of such serious times, since someone once said that history is the illustration of Holy Scripture'. This must be the collective task of theologians of all nations. To be sure: 'our Slovak Protestantism is poorly prepared for this task. Why, our theological science is very poor, uncultivated, undeveloped, our language is not agile in theological expressions'. But anxiety for our sons and fathers and the fate of our people gives us no choice. It is our duty to join our theological voice to the solution of the problem of war and religion. 'We must shed light on this problem through the prism of our Slovak soul, which is more inclined to love and service than domination' (4).

There are several notable features in the foregoing opening of the little book. The question of *theodicy* emerges as one that will occupy Osuský theologically, culminating in his 1942 study of Job, but continuing on even to his final work.[17] His early-on understanding of theology as a dialectic of interpretation of history by the Bible and the Bible by history is enunciated here as it were programmatically to mature at the end of his career. His social concern is as evident as his internationalism. His lifelong concern for improving the quality of theological education is painfully laid out. And his hope is voiced that a long-suffering people, leavened by the Christian gospel, could witness against the *libido dominandi*.

The essay proceeds with an attempt to clarify concepts. Osuský first distinguishes between expansive or offensive and defensive war. The former, including acts of colonization and annexation, has its roots, theologically, in human sinfulness. But defensive war is not immoral. In fact, it is divinely commanded; a state that wants to be a state has to defend its governing power or sovereignty. As this distinction between just and unjust war slowly matures, we can reasonably hope that war between states will be overcome, as capital punishment is being overcome within modern states. 'If war is an armed solution of controverted questions by the same conflicted parties, we are still at the primitive state of development… in which barbarian remnants from pagan times prevail … and physical power and cunning win the victory instead of ethical properties' (4).

Thus Osuský gives voice, as he will throughout this early period of his authorship, to a teleological view of humanity's moral progress. The same scheme frames his attempt next to clarify the concept of religion. As noted in the Introduction, Osuský understands religion theistically. 'In religion we find two directions, one from above to below, from God to creation, and the second from below to above, from humanity to God'. What is decisive is the representation of this relationship, which is a matter of historical development and indeed the progress from primitive to enlightened religion. 'Man endeavours to approach God and His creation in such measure as he has a representation of God and His revelation to us' (4). It is by the light of representations of God in human consciousness that humanity moves forward ethically. The goal of everything in the history of religion is to find ways to unite with God, to return to Him. Paganism, Judaism and Christianity all offers such ways in confession or dogma, the cult and in morality. These mediate representations of God which, in turn, form human consciousness.

When we compare these two concepts, war and religion, however, we find that they are incongruent with each other. War is the means to defend a right

[17] In the *Gallery*, the question of theodicy takes the apocalyptic turn, in keeping with afflicted Israel's hope for the messianic kingdom (193, 259, 450, 454).

under attack, and religion, by contrast, is a way to salvation. From this clarification, theology must determine God's relation to war as a human act, and so also the stance which the religious person must take towards war. History is the mother of study. So Osuský will next study the New Testament's relation to war (8).

In a move that is characteristic but complex in Osuský, he thus declines to discuss war in the Old Testament. We will have occasion to return in the conclusion to this book to the problem of traditional Christian anti-Judaism in our discussion of his commentary on Job and of his frequent use of the trope of Pharisaic hypocrisy. His negative reasoning here for this distancing from the Old Testament is that war in the Old Testament concerned the conflict between God's chosen people and pagans. As such, this warfare is, he claims, neither precedent nor model for contemporary European warfare between Christian nations. His positive reasoning is that 'the rule of our evangelical, Christian life, faith and religious worldview is the New Testament, Christ' (8). Since there was no war going on in the time of Christ and the apostles, we will not find any direct stance on war in the New Testament. We can discern Christ's stance towards war only from His general view, spirit and tendencies. As a result, however, theologians divide into two great groups. One camp justifies war with Christ and the teaching of the New Testament and another smaller group does not.

Osuský takes the occasion to point to a hermeneutical error of 'our theologians': 'By bad interpretation of Holy Scripture we can prove everything and anything possible or impossible. Why, even the devil in the wilderness justified his way by Holy Scripture just as the devils also believe that God is one (Jas 2.18). To extract citations from the Bible apart from context, without consideration whether a certain citation can be used on a given occasion, is a very dangerous matter. So far as we justify just anything from the Bible we also justify sin …' (9). Osuský then enumerates passages which are used in a militaristic way, like the 'wars and rumours of war' of Matthew 24.6-7. Such a passage, torn from context, can be easily related to our contemporary war, but in context, as Matthew 24.29-31 shows, the reference is to the eschatological battle of the end times. Osuský asks sarcastically whether anyone today expects the angels to come at the trumpet's sound when this war ends; and he answers: 'Hardly'. When we use Christ's words in this way to justify the current war, then, we make of Him a deceiver. The statement that 'all this must be' in Matthew 24.6 to sanction war between modern nation states is bad interpretation, which also misses the true meaning of New Testament apocalyptic (10). Here the speech is not about modern warfare but about the battle going on above us, between God and the devil, between holiness and sin, in the framework of the family, not of the polis' (that is, by 'family' Osuský is referring to Lk. 12.52-3).

We know, Osuský continues, that 'in the present war every side says about itself that it is divine, holy and true. We can express this conviction as patriots but from a religious standpoint, if we want to be objective, we have to say that only the sovereign God can render a true judgment'. Thus, the theologians who do not justify war from a religious standpoint hold to Christ's teaching: 'Blessed are the peacemakers!' (10). They point to the general divine prohibition, 'Thou shalt not kill', and to the essence of Christianity, love. Opponents who still want to justify war call upon the Old Testament (11), and they invoke Paul's teaching about submission to the governing authorities in Romans 13. Osuský argues that this Pauline teaching about submission, however, is only a sober reckoning with reality and not the apostle's basic stance. In any case, the foregoing examination shows that, if we simply exchange proof-texts, all we do is fall into contradictions, mirroring war itself, from which we cannot extricate ourselves. But 'the best interpretation of words are deeds'. We must move on 'to deeds, to those expressions in life in which basic principles are actualized, hence to the vocation of the soldiers whom we find in the New Testament' (12). We will see that 'in reality Christ held the governing authority to be a divine work, as when he said to Pilate, "you would have no power over me unless given to you from above"' (Jn 19.11). But as the context indicates – Pilate giving sentence of death on innocent Jesus by divine permission – this is no simple justification of state violence.

Osuský next discusses the soldiers addressed by John the Baptist (Lk 3.14), the centurion from Capernaum (Matt. 8.5-13/ Lk. 7.7-10), the soldiers at the arrest, trial and execution of Jesus and the centurion from Caesarea in the book of Acts. In every case there is no demand to abandon the vocation of the soldier, but rather to fulfil the commandments of God within it. In historical context, that instruction means that soldiers should not exploit the poor and unarmed people of the land in a barbarian way but live within their means (13). Like John, Christ does not reject the centurion just because he is a soldier, but looks at the heart for faith. And, when Christ prayed forgiveness upon his torturers from the cross, he did not pray for them to be forgiven for being soldiers, but because they had neither love nor mercy (14). In every case, there is no call to abandon the military vocation. 'Everyone in his calling can live in a way pleasing to God' (16). This affirmation of vocation is also the teaching of the Lutheran Confessions, Luther himself and Jan Hus (16): when the community is in danger, it is the duty of everyone to sacrifice for others, only each must guard against sin such as rape, and when the enemy is overcome and submits, one must show mercy and make peace (18). These are, of course, the rudiments of the Western doctrine of just war, going back to Cicero and Augustine.

Bearing in mind that the empire of which Osuský is a subject is a member of the Central Powers and allied with Germany in the middle of a fierce and undecided war, the next section of Osuský's essay, 'What do German theologians say about the war?' is introduced by a disclaimer: 'I give their opinions completely objectively, historically for the sake of history. Judgment on them will be made by my entire work'.[18] This impressive series of citations, which I recapitulate here, forms a powerful picture of the war theologians.

Schultze of Greifswald: 'This war is equal to the war of Constantine the Great, here too the saying is fulfilled: *In hoc signo vinces*'. Bonvetsch of Göttingen: 'When God so powerfully speaks through war, we must be silent, "Lord, thy will be done"'. Wohlenberg of Erlangen regarding preaching during war: 'We must guard ourselves against opportunism; patriotism is not yet Divine Service. The sermon must be embellished a little by blood, because otherwise it would be utterly cold – but not by one's own blood, because the blood of Christ belongs in first place. The Old Testament provides the most appropriate texts'. (19). Ihmels of Leipzig:

> The task of the church is to cultivate innate patriotism with Christian virtue, which is rooted in God. With this let the church today serve its own. But if we think that also the church must make policy, that's ridiculous… [T]he decisive hour strikes. In place of war between Christianity and Islam war has come about in Christendom itself: mission is threatened… The task of the church is to discern the times, to serve by preaching the word of God. How? To enable the feeling of deep thoughts, that we live in extraordinarily serious times, when everyone must answer for himself, but also together have hope in the grace of the loving heavenly Father.

Uckeley of Königsberg:

> Many appeal only to the feeling of patriotism; the fate of the German nation is, they say, the fate of Old Testament Israel. This is an error. A German is not an Israelite. The Christian must stand on the soil of the New Testament… hope and trust is not founded on nationality but on the grace of Christ… The most serious task of the church is to teach prayer. War leads our people to be ready

[18] Osuský doesn't provide the sources for the quotations.

for prayer; our task is to catch this feeling, cultivate it, to hold up lifted arms in prayer, because without us they will soon fall into despair. A further task is to be Good Samaritans.

Bezzel, Chairman of the Bavarian Consistory:

> This war is called holy according to both reason and its origin: that France battles with us is understandable from the principle of vengeance; Russia, from the principle of the battle of darkness against light, culture and education; the English, from the principle of envy. All three motives are sinful, so our war is holy, holy also because social faithfulness binds us together... Our war is founded on three norms from Ps. 94.15: the right of the poor to pray, of the humble for help and of thanksgiving for strength. Being namely the poor, we pray; humble, that God helps us; and we are grateful for victory and that gratitude strengthens us (20).

Grätzmacher of Erlangen:

> War changes everything: the value of life, property, art, also religion... We have been too individualistic; war certainly shows the value of the individual, but we feel more the relative need of God for the whole nation. We have represented God only as a loving father, who does not know how to punish but guards against evil; war shows that God is also the jealous Lord, who returns iniquity. In peace we did not know how to understand that blood has redemptive value; war teaches us that... These times let us experience the truth: Christ poured out his blood for us. We did not believe finally in life after the grave. But war spurs us to consider: is it possible that so many fallen young lives would be without their eternal reward beyond the sufferings of war?

Dunkmann of Greifswald:

> Certainly war is a time of sacrifice and sacrifice is the peak of idealism, but Christianity is in part closer to war than idealism. War proclaims repentance, as also Christianity does. In war we learn to call for help, and Christianity also teaches us just that. But idealism seeks help in man and finally contains no comfort for the wounded and fallen, as only Christian faith does. See, our idealism fails in war in every way. War is an education for Christianity.

Bornhäuser of Marburg:

> War and repentance stand in a tight connection. How? We set out from the reason for this terrible catastrophe, which is the very existence and development of Germany and, as a result, the hatred of our enemies. Is that ... sinful? No, from this perspective we have nothing of which to repent. But many are not

> sufficiently thankful to God for His grace. We do not have the right to demand victory, but to pray for it repentantly, because this too is a gift of grace. (21).

Schaeder of Kiel:

> If we want to advance inwardly after the war, with the victory for which we pray to God, a healthy patriotism must march hand in hand with us. It will be healthy, if the relation between patriotism and Christianity strikes the right balance, which does not lie either in the invention of tribal feelings nor in meaningless, empty internationalism.

Stauge of Gőttingen:

> War teaches us to pray. But many abuse prayer, holding it as an instrument only to secure God's help … Prayer as conversation with God must have as its goal not our needs but rather that we conform to the Lord of heaven… This horror of war wholly changes our view of the world. We have thought that we stand on the heights of love, humanity and culture. And what do we see? War darkens everything, rights are not respected, power triumphs.

Hausleiter of Greifwald:

> Jesus brought the catastrophe of war into connection with the description of Jerusalem and equally with the last judgment. In every war the divine judgment on the nations involved plays out. War is the end of the preceding sinful life and the beginning of a new period of grace. Only the repentant heart understands grace and thus war is a teacher of repentance and faith, because we then feel that in distress no one else can help, only God.

Hilbert of Rostock:

> Before the war everything united against the church and there was a significant falling away. Here the powerful God spoke and by the voice of war He shook the hearts of men – and everything changed. In place of apostasy, return to Christ; in place of the jubilation of the atheists and monists, a great silence came about. Christ brings us a redemptive sword. A true paradox (22–3).

As mentioned, Osuský simply recounted these statements from German Protestant theologians without comment or analysis. They are not all of one piece. The statement by Hausleiter that war brings experience of the judgment of God that marks epochal change most approximates Osuský's own view that war in an apocalyptic event of *krisis* in the biblical sense of a judgment that divides. But the effect of this string of quotations is to show how little repentance was considered integral to the Christian message of the German war theologians.

Turning attention next to the pronouncements of Slovak theologians, Osuský scornfully writes about an article published at the beginning of the war, 'In Service of Merciful Love', that placed the work of the church 'in the hospitals', designating the task of the church as one of 'pouring oil on the wounded'. Such shallow, unquestioning counsel makes the article militaristic, Osuský charges, in effect encouraging war and giving no practical solution to the problem of it. The article gives only a general theological answer to the reasons for the war in our many sins, the Christian nations having forgotten the Lord and His commandments. Platitudes and prayers are offered, then, in place of real solutions. There are exceptions to such a piety that accommodates war. He discusses a published sermon of Pastor Michal Bodický (1852–1935), 'The Way of Peace', which rebukes those who blame only the enemy: 'Certainly the enemy sins, but neither are you without fault. The devil tempted your opponent to do evil, but you, instead of showing the opponent the way to peace, made yourself an instrument of evil. You cannot fight fire with fire, so also you cannot remove evil with evil'. Osuský also mentions with approval a Hungarian language article by L. Szebereny, 'God and War', which distinguishes Christianity from the state, the Christian God from the national God, Yahweh.

Osuský especially lifts up Martin Rázus's article, 'Religious Optimism',[19] which, he says, demonstrates in its very title the 'sophism' of the German theologians whom he had just reported on. At a pastoral conference, Rázus gave a lecture, 'War and Religion', which with logical arguments convincingly analysed the five arguments defending war from the religious perspective. He shows, Osuský claims, that the Christian God and war are opposing values and he designates the relationship of war to religion as a negative one. Osuský is somewhat critical though, complaining that in an unclear manner Rázus points to the determination of human will by the higher lords of this world. Always out of such ethical concerns a Melanchthonian defender of the moral freedom of the will against Luther's darker vision of the bondage of the will, Osuský writes that determinism prevails only where man does not have power to change that higher will lording over him. But we do not find this determinism in the case of Rázus, in spite of the misleading statement Osuský criticized. Rather Rázus correctly lifts up the 'divine passivity' in war. By this remarkable expression, Osuský affirms that God permits what God does not intend, that God creates and preserves a world for a blessed purpose that includes divine passivity

[19] Published in *Cirkevne Listy* [hereafter *CL*] XXIX/3. *Cirkevne Listy* is the theological journal of the Lutheran Church in Slovakia.

vis-à-vis actual evil that contradicts God. War, as an instance of such human sin actually contradicting God's will, is thus allowed reality in his theological thinking. God permits the evils that He does not will.

Osuský attributes the lack of theological clarity about this to the perceptive, subtle, rich, poetic soul of Rázus. He cites some of his wartime poetry: 'A soldier remembers the fifth commandment, which someone has posted by his bed. He sees the Lord's face so kind and divine, yet the visage is bitter and rebukes: "You too?!"' – that is, Julius Caesar's *Et tu, Brute*?. Another soldier recalls in the night his farewell to his fallen comrade: 'such shadows, such bitter pangs of soul. I would cry, but crying does not befit a soldier'. Rázus captures, Osuský says, the characteristic features of our patient, humble Slovak people, who have long known poverty and oppression. A woman cannot forget her man, and goes with the child to the grave. 'The child begins to cry and mother hushes him. "Hush, hush say goodbye, my angel beloved, hush, hush, they are angered by the cries of ladies". Another woman cannot remain faithful, a third is satisfied pitifully with welfare aid, a fourth suffers from dreams. Rázus's poetry paints a faithful and true picture of our nation's stance toward war, Osuský writes, citing the deep irony expressed in another poem: 'The nations, Forward for truth! In the name of the Most High! Into horror and flames of hatred, and flames of hatred' (26–8).

Many expect a return to God from the war or conversion of the soul to the better. 'Whether we will also be disappointed in this, as in much else, is hidden by a veil of mystery. We have already been disappointed in much, indeed totally; this war itself has brought with it surprises in every field' (25). The truly penitent judgment to be drawn from war is disillusionment. Osuský criticizes several articles which try piously to see the utility of war in varying ways. Such articles 'want to be comforting words for those whose loved ones have fallen in battle'. But as Osuský reflects on his own kin in danger and his 180 parishioners on the battle lines, he finds cold comfort in such sentiments. 'My heart protests in true reverence against the thought that God would want this horrible war'. It is one thing to say God wills this war and quite another to say that God permits it. In any case, it is hard to accept the claim that in this war the God of justice and love manifests His order. How is this to be reconciled with Jesus's words, 'God wants mercy, not sacrifice?'. In a statement that foreshadows Osuský's later commentary on Job, and his reliance on Leibniz to be discussed below, he writes: 'To represent God as a tyrant, to whom man is not able to draw close nor to question, whether He acts so cruelly because one deserved it, is not a Christian understanding …' (29).

Like his contemporary pastor, Karl Barth, Osuský wonders about the passivity of the church leadership. 'Where are our older theologians? The critical voices introduced above are from the younger theologians' (29). Osuský concludes this examination of European theologians on the war with a note about the devastating consequences for missiology. He cites a 'good article' from a mission magazine, *Light of the World*, 'Should Mission be National or International?'. 'Not only from a practical point of view is it impossible to conduct and thus to stamp a national veneer on Christian mission, but – and this is the chief thing – also it is impossible from the perspective of Holy Scripture'. With this final observation on 'our modest war literature' to show that 'also among us people are reflecting' deeply and critically on the problem of war and religion, Osuský now turns to his own analysis.

We have to divide the analysis into two parts, he says: God's relation to war, and the relation of humanity, and the Christian, to war. Since we understand God not philosophically but religiously and dogmatically, we cannot proceed from a general understanding of Him, but from the properties which fill His entire being. God's properties can be classified into three categories: physical, individual-logical and ethical. To the physical belongs God's omnipotence, including His omniscience and eternity; to the individual-logical belongs justice, and from it also holiness and wisdom; to the ethical, God's goodness, and from it also patience and faithfulness. If we emphasize one category at the expense of the others, we err. Those who emphasize divine power betray a pagan and Islamic stamp, such as contemporary German war theologians display. If we emphasize divine justice, we adhere to the Old Testament-Jewish understanding (of which, he adds, there are many adherents among us); and if on the ethical fundament we emphasize the goodness of God we stand in the group of New Testament-Christian theologians, representatives of which here and there speak out against the war. Of course, it is not possible precisely to separate these three.

Osuský now proceeds to analyse all three contemporary groups of theologians in their respective representations of God. As indicated, Osuský attributes the emphasis on divine power to a pagan and/or Islamic tyranny. Pagans offered sacrifices in order to overcome divine tyranny, or obtain its help for themselves by way of a bribe. Between humanity and God there is such a gap here that man cannot say 'Thou' to this God of Power nor approach It without mediation. Before Him man is a complete slave, and God determines human fate according to His own caprice. Everything must be accepted as it is, as God the Tyrant so wills. This God also often wills war to preserve the adherent's existence. Hence this God is ordinarily a local or national or particular God;

even if it attains to a universal claim, as in Islam, it is henotheistic rather than monotheistic, a violently conquering rather than a rationally persuading universalism. Such religion expands to universality by offensive war and conquest. With such a view, it is possible to sanction war. Elements of this view from the Old Testament, insofar as they depend on the divine property of omnipotence, survive in Christianity. But in Christianity we cannot one-sidedly emphasize omnipotence, because that curtails the other categories of divine properties and turns God back into one of the idols of the nations.

God's essence is the harmony of all the divine properties. So God cannot be arbitrary, but exercises omnipotence in justice and love. If one would argue, however, that God wisely wants to use war to educate to salvation, one would have to reason that God let Adam sin so that He could be saved. This is an excessively logical step! Let us not roll our sins onto God! When I do evil, am I to suppose that the Christian God wants that? Rather God gave humanity free will and passively permits sin; if we deny this we return to pagan capricious tyranny, where man is forever a slave. 'Therefore we do not name war God's revelation, we do not sanction war by saying it is God's will, sent for reasons of His own, nor do we say war is inevitable, lest we fall into Islamic fatalism' (33).

Through the Old Testament many pagan elements have passed into Christian thought. As we know from many Old Testament texts, the LORD is the originator of battles, He arranges military plans, He gives leaders instructions, indeed He Himself mixes into battle in order to save his chosen nation and – this is a purely Jewish thought – in order that the righteousness of the law unambiguously triumph. This notion comes from the representation of God as righteous. What is pagan is the idea that since God promised His chosen nation a land He arbitrarily destroyed all the nations previously existing in it. But the Jewish thought that corrects this pagan view adds righteousness as property that qualifies divine power. The extermination is because Yahweh punished these nations for their sins, just as He also punishes the Jews when they turn from Him.

The entire Old Testament religion is thus founded on the notion of theocracy, of which the middle point is the law of God and from the human side righteousness. Thus, while in the pagan perception omnipotence prevailed at the expense of the other divine properties, in the Jewish perception righteousness prevailed at the expense of mercy and love. Jews regarded victory in war as reward and defeat as the punishment of the LORD. But, as with omnipotence, righteousness also can be emphasized at the expense of the other divine properties. So it is also not possible to say that God does not send war arbitrarily but rather wisely and justly so that the just will be rewarded and the wicked punished. Such rigorous legalism does not square with the experience of war. Why must many innocent nations pointlessly shed blood? What sin did someone commit, that, as they say, they should be so punished? Where is that proven? Look where that leads us, if we put war into God's hands, whether for reward or punishment. In the final consequence, it is nothing other than sacrificing people to Moloch, so that the wrath is appeased. Is man so cheap, whom God created in His image? The one who in this way abandons trust in God is ready instead for every evil. The ethical element of goodness and love is lacking in the pagan and Jewish understanding of God. But here too we must be wary of one-sidedly emphasizing this property at the expense of others. That happens when we divide God into three and idolize one of the three as the right representation of God, as if these properties do not harmonize in Him as the living God who cannot be so readily contained in one basic idea (35).

The Christian God, Osuský argues, is, alongside His power and justice, also our loving Father, whom certainly we must fear as a child fears, but whom we can trustingly love. We can love God by trusting Him, because not only does He not want evil for us but also because He does not send evil from Himself or for Himself (36). Thus God neither sends nor wills war but rather allows it. War is the result of human free will. War is the natural consequence of sin. War is exclusively a human work, to which God relates as much as Pilate relates to Christianity in the creed. This passivity of God does not mean that God does not know about war; we cannot become deists! But God equips, begins and oversees war just in the same way that God left Eve to eat from the forbidden fruit. God is passive in relation to war. God permits and does not initiate war.

Of course, this solution of God's relation to war in the notion of the divine passivity of permission raises again a question about God as Lord of the universe, who also today destroys nations and raises up new ones. We have to affirm that the omnipotent God also today could intervene to stop war. But, as we see, He does not. Why? *Ignoramus et ignorabimus*: We do not and will not know. No one can penetrate these mysteries. But from that it does not follow that we can be self-satisfied and not try to solve what we can. Quoting from a hymn, Osuský recites: 'Why has the Lord God created you …? So that you may serve Him. He makes you alike to Himself; you have common sense, use its counsels and so you will come to salvation' (36).

It is the question in theological principle about Adam: why did God leave him to sin, when even then He foresaw the consequences? Because somehow the harmony of His goodness, wisdom and justice demanded it. Human free will comes from God's goodness. Man would not be man if he had not been exposed to the choice of eating from the forbidden tree in paradise. God gave an instruction that there would be sorrowful consequences if Adam were disobedient, that he would die. If God did not act this way, God would have proved to be a tyrant and not a loving Father. In His omnipotence God could have forced obedience, but the omnipotence of God is limited by God's goodness. So also with war. We know the commandment of God: You shall not kill. When nevertheless man transgresses, God permits the transgression to unfold with its natural consequences.

What determines God's omnipotence is not us but God's goodness and, further, His justice and wisdom. Once God has given free will to man, this wise counsel cannot be changed, because that would be infidelity to Himself and injustice in the eyes of man (I Jn 1.5, Jas 1.17). Well and good, one might object; so it is possible in general to justify God's passivity in war. But what about the particular fates of individuals: the repentant who survives, the hardened sinner who falls, the hardened sinner who survives and the repentant who falls. The third and fourth of these cases are the most difficult. Here we have to cry out with Paul, in Rom. 11.33-4, 'O the depths! How inscrutable are God's ways!' (37).

Osuský offers a comparison. We may imagine God in war like the father in a family where the children are fighting. The wise father knows that the children are punished most by leaving them to face the consequences of their actions so that when they experience its bitter fruit they will be convinced to seek the father and his wise counsel. So are we with our heavenly Father in this war. God seems passive, as with Adam, but in the fullness of time He can step in again. As the presence of God means blessing, so our poverty in this war points to the passivity of God. This is a powerful defence of God and the educational side of war. God, according to the Christian conception, does not want any to perish but all to come to repentance (2 Pet. 3.9). But the question about the loss of the repentant in war leads us to a new question (38). How does the Christian relate to war?

We have seen that God, according to the young Osuský, occupies a passive stance towards war so that war is a human work. We have seen that the New Testament does not opine directly about war. From this, Osuský draws the conclusion that we today are citizens in some land and state obliged to defend its sovereignty by such means as war. Furthermore, we see that wars are motivated by greed. All this extraordinarily complicates the question. From the foregoing considerations, we can state that, if we fight, we do not directly fulfil a religious duty but a patriotic one, and just so we are not free to sanction war religiously. A purely religious stance has nothing to do with war, because it is not a means of turning to God, nor does it aim at salvation. In war one sacrifices oneself, hence the question of duty to oneself arises; in war one murders the neighbour, hence the question of duty to the neighbour arises. Since these questions of duty are undertaken from the obligation of civil obedience, the question of the duty to the state also arises.

While it is frequently said that murder is forbidden by divine command, we must observe carefully that one who bases opposition to war on that basis alone does not always have to be an enemy of war. One can be motivated only by fear of the loss of one's life or that of dear ones. We hear also from our soldiers: all would be well, if only there were no heroic deaths. But if every Christian were really against war, because God's commandment forbids murder, so that it pains his heart to kill his neighbour, such rejection of war would be truly Christian and war would not exist. But this is often not the reason for rejection of war, but rather that we fear for ourselves and our own; this selfish fear is not in any case Christian, because not even war may tear the Christian away from his unity with God, as we see in Christ, and Stephen the martyr (39).

The Christian may not fear the one who can kill the body, but the One who can destroy both body and soul. The Christian has to know how to sacrifice his life out of love for others. It is the state which demands self-sacrifice from us, so from the side of the state the question must be weighed whether war is expansive or defensive, necessary or not. In unnecessary cases not even the state has the right to demand our life, but only in necessary cases. To determine the situation falls on those who govern, and for this reason they are responsible before God for the lost lives whenever the sacrifice of war is made unnecessarily. From the side of the common people, it is immaterial religiously whether the situation was necessary or not, because they will not have to answer to God for this decision of their governing authorities. The Christian does not mix into such machinations of the diplomats in the spirit of Jesus's saying in Lk. 12.14.

If God permits, but does not send, war, the death of the innocent and repentant is not God's will but the permission of God (40). Man does not sacrifice himself for God but for his neighbour. God's reward for such love can come only in eternity. Our human and philosophical reason cannot ascertain what the eternal is; so, for example, it cannot grasp how eternal life does not begin at the end of time but in Christ is already here. Temporal death cannot uproot it. This 'today' of salvation is a *novum* in Christianity. If we thus look upon eternity, if we are really repentant and innocent, if we trust God, the sacrifice of the fallen will not seem to us to be injustice on the part of God. God does not stop the lethal shell, shrapnel or grenade but remains the God of the deceased even in such graves. The Christian may not take bodily death so tragically. Not even in war does danger threaten the repentant, if he does his duty and guards his soul from stain. Love of neighbour and readiness to sacrifice self is the Christian psychological basis of a heroic death. Not pagan courage, nor Islamic fatalism, but self-sacrificing love, even in the extremity of war, is Christian (41).

Osuský now turns to the problem of murder of the neighbour who is the enemy as the inevitable consequence of the soldier's willingness to sacrifice himself to protect the neighbour who is threatened by that enemy. Reflecting a Troeltsch-like criticism of Luther's Two Kingdoms ethic, in the air in his times, he does not wish to make his argument on the basis of a strong distinction between private and public-official behaviour:

> To divide duties into individual and social categories, thus into private and official murder, as the Lutheran Confessions do, is an ember left over from Catholic ethics, echoing the morality of lords and slaves. Murder is murder, whether it is official or private, in either case it is sinful. Such a compromise, which already Luther proclaimed, is not possible. Nor is the distinction possible which Ihmels makes, that Christ's commandments in the Sermon on the Mount are the legal rules of the kingdom of heaven, and not a legal codex of civil law on earth. Why, the kingdom of God, according to the parable of the leaven, has to leaven all of the social formations, all of our life. Indeed, the kingdom of God has to be in our midst, as Christ says in Lk. 17.21. Christ did not for nothing teach us to pray, "Thy kingdom come!" The kingdom of God beyond the grave does not need commandments directed against sin, because there will be no sin there. In a word: we cannot leave the commandments of Christ hanging in the air. Here the question is on the table: whether the kingdom of God is something eschatological, transcendental or whether it is this-worldly, immanent. We accept both, because Christ so taught us to pray, "Thy will be done on earth as in heaven." From this it follows that the law of the kingdom of God and the commandments of Christ are valid also for the world, and so for individuals just as also for official bodies. In a word: on the one side we regard murder in any form as sinful. On the other side, we may not fall into sentimentality, into a sectarian spell of hyper-sensitivity (42–3).

We shall see how, later on, and certainly by the time of his final work, a better version of the Two Kingdoms doctrine directed against political Messianism on every side will become as important to Osuský as this protest against the dualistic version of the doctrine. Even now, in 1916, Osuský's next discussion of duty vis-à-vis the state shows the continuing hold on his thought of the Two Kingdoms doctrine.

Because war is murder, many Christian sects – Osuský mentions the Nazarenes, Mennonites, Quakers and followers of Tolstoy – one-sidedly explain the words of Christ and do not want to bear arms. But so far as sin is in the world it is necessary to fight against it. It is necessary to hate sin as Christ did; if sin reigns in someone it is necessary to punish this one. As we have seen, neither Christ nor the apostles demanded that soldiers cease to be warriors and lay aside weapons. The weapon itself and its use is not in and of itself sinful, but rather its abuse. The goal must be to improve things. With murder we improve no one, however, for in that case improvement is no longer possible. Accordingly we cannot regard a state as evil if it wants to accomplish its morally justified goal, even when it uses instruments of war that are today technologically inevitable. Yet these must not be decisively destructive.

The Christian has to help in the achievement of the moral goal of the state, also in war. So his Christian convictions must also dictate the method of warfare. That same one whom one has to regard as the opponent and political enemy also has to be seen always as one's neighbour from the religious viewpoint:

> War is the outpouring of sinfulness, the fruit of brokenness. But to oppose war in a general, even in a revolutionary way and not to care about the correction of brokenness, means to want to remove the consequence and leave the reason for it. Whoever opposes war and not its reasons does not reckon with reality, with people as they are, but inconsequently hallucinates about how they ought to be. We may not try to heal the wrong side of the problem. First we must try to improve people, to educate, to remove sin and war will then of itself and without us cease to exist (44).

Osuský concludes this discussion of duty towards the state with a discussion of whether military chaplains should bear arms. Because Lutherans hold to the priesthood of all believers, purely from a dogmatic point of view they could not reject this possibility in principle. It is rather a functional question. If we sent medical doctors into the flames of battle, whom would they then heal? Osuský tells the following story by way of conclusion. A German church superintendent sent a telegram to Kaiser Wilhelm asking that he allow the chaplains, also, to help the war effort, by arming them. The Kaiser thanked him for the willingness to help but denied the request because of the heavy burden the chaplains have in care of the wounded and in comforting the families of the fallen. Osuský observes: the representatives of the church requested weapons because that seemed to them to be the greatest need. But the supreme commander of the army for the same reason recalled the church to its religious duties. 'Who of these two knows better the mind of Christ and the will of God?'

As Osuský draws his little book to a conclusion, he reveals explicitly the target of his reflections. Many, he writes, expect from the war that human beings will become angels and the world a paradise. 'But let us not be such optimists' (45). Sin is a great power and it is not easy to overcome it. Signs of religious revival are superficial. People are humble now only from fear and selfishness. As soon as the fear goes away, the humility also will fly away. The positive effects of war are few. The tasks of the church while the war lasts are to mitigate the sins of war, to help the abandoned by good works, and to comfort the sorrowful. But the church fails in many places on all three counts. It is hard to comfort when we have erroneous views of the relation of God to war. Where war is represented as a work of God, comfort is impossible; then only a rotten quietism or a revolutionary resistance can be demanded. 'We can comfort in the way that the old Christians comforted: We have to suffer if God permits; we know how to suffer, if we have faith in God; we can suffer, that is our Christian boast; we want to suffer, that is our confidence in victory'.

We have to overcome the illusion that this is the war to end wars. Wars are inevitable until we lead people to another way of fighting (46). Not even Christ lived in such illusions, as if peace had already come, when he predicted the war of good and evil before the coming of the Day of Judgment. The kingdom of peace has to endure forever so its development goes very slowly. Let us not despair. It goes slowly but matures to the harvest. In the meantime, the wheat and tares grow together. Wars will be year after year more and more rare, as also the death penalty:

> World peace will not be brought to us by wars, as many paradoxically say, nor by revolutionary uprisings, as socialism proclaims, nor by the visions of Plato, Danto, Augustine or philosophy, as Kant demands, nor by the thought of European equality in value or the American pacifism without religion. That humanity, cultural ideals, civilization, internationalism, and reason have disappointed us – of this we are sufficiently convinced in this war.

It is true that the enemies of religion use war to their advantage as also they collect material from it as proof that this war of Christian nations refutes the possibility of God and exposes the church as something passé, as a now unnecessary social organization. Many mock us as they did Christ on the cross:

where is your God? Does He sleep? Where are the results of two thousand years of Christianization? (47) Especially socialism, with all the varying shades of materialism, prepares for war against Christianity, just as it claims that this war shows the bankruptcy of the church. But the truth is the opposite.

Never has chaos dominated in the camp of the socialists like today, since they gave up their cherished internationalism, defence of the weak, and their own thought of peace, to join the warmongers! They pick the speck from eyes of Christianity but ignore the log in their own. It is easier to take a political stance in socialism than it is in Christianity. Their field, I would say, is only ethical, while Christianity's is dogmatic as well. In ethics it is much easier to orient oneself than in dogmatics, just as it is much easier to know the state of the body than of the soul. Socialists already have precisely articulated principles, but Christianity is life and development. Among us it is even today an open question, even a riddle, what stance Christ takes towards war. Yet if we set out from the fact that the socialists have not remained faithful to their own principles, just so, we cannot regard their beautiful program as bankrupt, any more than we can regard Christianity as bankrupt because of the preachers who become war propagandists (48). The main thing is that whoever judges Christianity itself on the basis of the war does not know the essence of Christianity or the goal of Christ's coming. What the war proves is that materialism runs the world, not the patient spirit of the Christian religion.

Christ did not come to the world to revolt. He did not teach us to fight evil with evil but with God. He did not want to be a judge in worldly matters, but taught us in the first place to seek and realize the kingdom of God on earth. Neither war nor revolution leads to the kingdom, but rather the constant preaching of love, the constant leavening of the old, sinful way. That humans have not become new creatures is not our fault but the fault of those who attack us, who agitate our people so that they leave the churches and thus lead people away from the gospel of Christ.

Although, as Osuský maintained, it is not Christianity's fault, he acknowledges that the spirit of the world has prevailed in much of Christ's church. Certainly, the wounds of Christianity are painful. Many of its sons exceed the ancient pagans in cruelty and bloodthirstiness; but what drives them to this? Christianity or the gospel of Christ? Did Christ teach Judas to betray or Peter to deny? What war teaches is not that Christianity is overcome but that sin is a great power and that repentance is the most needful thing. Back to the sources! *Ad fontes*! In that case the way of the future will lead to the separation of the church from all state enchantments (49).

The great evil in man does not prove the fault but rather the need of Christianity. But we have to take into consideration that Christianity does not have armed power with which to enforce its principles. It has only one sword, the Word of God. The Christian world view brings peace to us, for it does not acknowledge higher interests in the world than to live in a way that is pleasing to God, and to believe in eternal salvation. Some theologians think that the task of religion is to take on a nationalistic form in place of internationalism. Osuský denies that. Precisely international Christianity will help us towards peace. We may not be either Jew or Greek.

We will aim for this when we put all our theological work under the viewpoint of love. If we study history, we see that now we must become the epoch of Johannine love after Pauline faith. We have to revise dogmatics, that is, the theology that serves to determine what has to be believed into the faithful mirror of what is believed. Theology in this way must become practical and social and the lives of the preachers must become a weeklong sermon more beautiful than their Sunday sermon. It is precisely bad exegesis that leads us to nationalize Christianity, leading us back to the soil of the Old Testament, back into polytheism, where every nation has its own god and chauvinism again grows. The true task of Christianity is and will be to teach a love of humanity, a better patriotism than one which draws from hatred of other nations (50). The internationalism of Christianity does not mean to uproot people from their national life but to leaven it with the good, so that in relation with other nations and states it behaves according to the commandments of God. So the book concludes with a prayer that God would grant from the precious blood poured out from the Slovak fathers a blossoming of a better future for their children (51).

Several features of this final peroration are worthy of special note. First, the concluding demand for the 'separation of the church from all state enchantments' is a rare instance in the history of European Lutheranism of the actual teachings of the final Article 28 of the Augsburg Confession on the difference between the swords of steel and of the Word of God.[20] That the church of Christ may stand only on the Word of God, hence powerless vis-à-vis the state in terms of the sword of steel, is the price paid for the authenticity of its proclamation, uncompromised by the state's patronage whenever the two swords are institutionally fused. This kind of institutional separation, however, has nothing to do

[20] Wilhelm Mauer, *Historical Commentary on the Augsburg Confession*, trans. H. George Anderson (Philadelphia: Fortress, 1986), 59–84.

with a sectarian abandonment of the world to the devil. Second, what it does have to do with is a sharp focusing on the 'leavening' of society with the spiritual mission of preaching the gospel of Christ – the long, slow, patient slog through world history that Osuský sketches – which forms the church in the world as an international society that can speak prophetically to the world of nations. Third, Osuský sees the need for profound reorientation of the discipline of Christian theology, away from an abstract and idealistic theorizing about what must be believed to a practical – I would say pragmatic – discipline that understands, with Dietrich Bonhoeffer, 'the social intention of all the basic Christian concepts'.[21] The radical nature of these youthful stances will emerge again with clarity only at the end of Osuský's career, with his experience of the collapse of European Christendom.

The History of Religion (1922) and the Legacy of Liberal Theology

The critical and prophetic edge of Osuský's wartime intervention is lacking in his next book, a textbook he prepared for use in the Lutheran schools within a world opening up to newfound, post-war Czechoslovak possibilities. To be sure, the positive task of nation-building as a Christian social responsibility after the disaster of war motivated Osuský, and the fruits of his education in Germany and Prague are on display in this work, as they were also in *War and Religion*. But there is a discernible shift in orientation. The biblical theology in its tacitly Reformation-Lutheran construal of *disillusionment* fades into the background and the *optimism* of the liberal faith in history as a progressive movement towards perfection takes its place. The demand for the modernization of the old tradition of theological orthodoxy is nowhere more pressing than in the discovery, now inescapable, of the vast world of the religions. In fact any kind of dialectic of retrieval and modernization in theology requires facing the challenge to an insular European Christianity of the massive existence of other, prima facie, rival formations of religion.

In the opening pages, he acknowledges that Holy Scripture does not answer the preliminary question, what is religion? So he has readers listen to what some significant thinkers have had to say about this concept. His list indicates his educators in the ethical idealism of nineteenth century Germany, even as

[21] Dietrich Bonhoeffer, *Sanctorum Communio* (Minneapolis: Fortress, 1988), 21.

his final entry comes from 'our deep thinker, President Masaryk'. Plato said that religion is the greatest possible resemblance of man to God. According to modern German thinkers like Hegel, religion is the human consciousness of unity with God; according to Schleiermacher, religion is the feeling of unconditional dependence on the infinite; according to Kant, it is the respect for and following of the moral law as God's law; according to Fichte, it is faith in the moral order of the world. Masaryk adds that religion is life lived under the aspect of eternity. 'All of these characterizations are true', Osuský concludes, 'but one-sided in that either they relate only to the individual sides of religious life or only to some religions'. (6).

Masaryk is right that religion is life, and so relates to all three aspects of spiritual life: thought, feeling and endeavour.[22] Consequently, Osuský would supplement and expand the definition as follows: 'religion is the sum of all those phenomena of life which relate to the relationship of humanity to God, as to the higher power. And the history of religion, then, is systematic description of all those life phenomena which relate to the relationship of God and humanity'. Osuský, we note, echoes Luther when he next writes that there was never a time nor a nation in the world which did not have some kind of religion. To be sure, he continues, any religious worldview depends for its formulations of religious truth on the surroundings, where it exists, and the circumstances in which it lived, and so on. We would have to call our discipline 'history of religions' if we sought only to describe each and every religion without analysis or comparison or temporal ordering. But we want to investigate, compare, and, in a word, put descriptions into a unified system. As a discipline, the 'history of religion' is a systematic description that discovers the underlying representations of God.

We should take note of the singular number that Osuský employs in his historical account: 'religion', not 'religion*s*'. The use of the singular to interpret the world religions as various relations to the one, true God mediated by representations of God in human consciousness in their historical developments is both the (theological) strength and the (empirical) weakness of Osuský's approach in his second book.

[22] Gažik cites Osuský's critical appreciation of Masaryk from somewhat later in life (1930) as follows: 'Masaryk is a critical spirit and his reason does not come to a stop before theology. It is necessary to consider whether his critical judgments do not point at painful wounds where healing would be necessary. If we receive with satisfaction from him opinions that are welcome to us, we must accept also critiques with thanksgiving, when they well up from deep religious conviction and test, whether they are from the spirit of Jesus and act accordingly. Masaryk is a powerful individualist, and neither theological or ecclesiastical places suffice for him. He merits a thorough analysis'. Gažik, 24.

As religion is about God and the human relation to God, Osuský continues, so religion develops under God's direction from the less to the more perfect, from the primitive to the more complex, from the bodily to the spiritual. While there are cases of decline and degeneration, it is not possible to accept in principle a theory of the fall of religion, according to which there was a perfect religion in the beginning which was then damaged; rather, we have to receive the theory of development (evolution), which is that in general the direction of the development of religion proceeds forwards, not backwards. The significance of science consists precisely in that it teaches us to know the extent of religion in all the world, its great past from the beginnings of humanity. Just so, it delivers us from superficiality and teaches us correctly to judge that religion is a motivating power in the life of nations and epochs. It teaches us to compare our religion with others and to think through its individual phenomena. It teaches us that our Christianity is the peak of all religions and, in this way, it teaches us to defend our Protestantism, which is the blossom of Christianity. Thus, it teaches us to defend the inheritance from the fathers. (8)

Osuský's presentation in this book of primitive religions and their development into the great world religions is of little contemporary interest, since the teleological scheme in which he organized the data and the theological definition of religion that he employs find little critical support in religious studies today. In fact, what can be seen is that in his comparative 'science' Osuský hardly ceases to be the evaluating Christian theologian. In context, this pioneering work, executed in a textbook, can be appreciated for opening up new vistas on the hitherto impoverished horizon of his audience. But it is neither instructive for us today nor is it particularly helpful for understanding Osuský's turn to the Bible, which is the special theme of this book and its investigations.

Rather, what cries out for understanding is how the prophetic disillusionment with the nineteenth century's faith in historical progress sounded in *War and Religion* is now muted, and with the new task of post-war nation-building is rather renewed in the opportunity, so to speak, 'to get things right' this time. Hand-in-glove with that task comes renewed expression of the 'optimistic' liberal theology Osuský had learned in pre-war Germany as a student.[23] In this respect it is interesting to see how Osuský concludes the textbook with the argument that, out of the conviction of a faith deeply grounded in historical science, we today can assert that Christianity is the most perfect religion. Yet

[23] Gažik, 82–3.

there are some, he concedes, in the contemporary educated class, who are in doubt about this conclusion, following from an attraction to Buddhism (134).

Ever since Schopenhauer, we may note, the Buddhist alternative has functioned as something of a trope among the literati for inward rejection of the modern capitalist regime of desire and its organization of religion. It is instructive, here, to recapitulate the book's concluding polemic against Buddhism, not as any kind of adequate account of Buddhism, but as a clue to the young Osuský's 'scientific' account of the 'perfection' of Christian religion over an emerging competitor.

We do not have to compare our Christianity with other religions for the sake of its defence, Osuský confidently begins, except in the case of Buddhism. For Buddhism is responsible for a lot of propaganda among the educated. Let us look and compare. It is true that between Christianity and Buddhism there is much in common, but also much that is different and that will be found to be to the detriment of Buddhism. It is true that the life, conception and work of Jesus Christ is mixed with legendary representations, as is the Buddha's. It is true that both walked, talked, preached and had disciples. It is true that as Christ grew up on the soil of the Old Testament Buddha grew up on the soil of Brahmanism; that as Christ condemned pharisaic ceremonialism Buddha rejected Brahmin wisdom. Both went out as prophets, redeemers of humanity with a claim of salvation.

But to mark the differentiations, which are deeply rooted, we must see that Christ stands for a higher power. Buddha is a teacher only, a prophet, who teaches maxims, while Christ is much more. He not only teaches but also fulfils His teachings, indeed helps us, also, to fulfil the commandments, when we make them our own through faith. And there is more. Let us present both figures next to one another and ask which is more acceptable. Buddha lives without God, Christ constantly with God (although this very atheism of Buddha is what pleases contemporaries attracted to Buddhism). Nothing fills Buddha with joy, he is constantly cold. Christ is satisfied, he has peace in God. There is no prayer in Buddha; while prayer, fervently remembered, fills the Christian sweetly with joy. Buddha proclaims a physical redemption, a redemption from life as such. Christ proclaims a spiritual redemption, redemption from sin, from evil. The goal before Buddha is Nirvana, eternal sleep, eternal night, and so eternal death; the goal before Christ is eternal awareness, the eternal kingdom of God, life. Buddhism teaches how to die, Christianity how to live.

There, a cold love, a sympathy with all suffering creation from a selfish foundation, but, here, a warm love from the foundation of religious consciousness that we are all children of a gracious and loving Father. There, the motto: do not harm another, so that you do not harm yourself by that act of harm. There, a selfish and negative morality. Here, a generous, positive love, also of enemies. There, self-salvation; here, salvation by the help of Christ. There, a sense of superiority; here, a praiseworthy humility. There morality has one rule for monks and another for common individuals, thus a double morality: of lords and of slaves, as in Nietzsche. There, the family and social life are a barrier to Nirvana; here, everything is the object of sanctification of the kingdom of God. Buddhism is against culture, the world, and is life-hating; our Christianity is the source of education, pleasure in life, for it is also self-sacrificing. Buddhism is only for the spiritually able, Christianity (well understood!) is for everyone. Buddhism knows how to overcome evil, poverty, which stand in the way, only by self-destruction, while Christianity battles against evil. Which is more acceptable? (135) Thus Osuský ends this textbook with an altar call: 'Let whoever is a friend of education, of work, of the battle of morality and for heartfelt human satisfaction arise, not in blind faith, but with evangelical conviction on the side of Christianity' (136).

If ever there was an exemplar of the contemporary complaint[24] that the very category of 'world religions' is an invention of triumphalist nineteenth century Protestant theology, by which it continues in a new key its quest for hegemony, Osuský's little book could contend for the title. It breathes the spirit of nineteenth century optimism and triumphalism, so unlike the 1916 tract, *War and Religion*, which breaths apocalyptic disillusionment. In Osuský's post-war mind, the outcome of the world war has given Christendom a new chance, and the new Czechoslovak Republic has given the suppressed and marginalized traditions of Hus and Luther in the Czech and Slovak lands respectively a new opportunity to assume the spiritual leadership of culture, taking on the role of the Christian conscience of the nation. This is eminently clear in the alliances Osuský tried to forge with Ragaz's religious socialism and Masaryk's democratic socialism, powerful streams of influence which he had imbibed during his study at Charles University in Prague in the immediate aftermath of the war. While social democracy was attractive to most of his co-religionists,[25] the liberal theology was not always welcome, as the following episode illustrates.

[24] Tomoko Masuzawa, *The Invention of World Religions* (Chicago and London: The University of Chicago Press, 2005).

[25] For a compelling account in English of this attraction, see John Palka's description of his father's 'utopian socialism', in John Palka, *My Slovakia, My Family: One Family's Role in the Birth of a Nation* (Minneapolis: Kirk House, 2012), 206–21.

A Fundamentalist Challenge

We might have noticed how, in passing, Osuský acknowledged that the gospel accounts of Christ, especially of his conception, are overlaid with legendary features, just as are the accounts of the Buddha's life. In spite of Osuský's increasing prominence in his church as one of several leading intellectuals, this reserve regarding an article of faith did not go unnoticed, and in the course of time it became the occasion for a public controversy.[26] It happened like this.

Osuský's church journal published a report with commentary on an article by a professor, F. Linhart, of the Hussite Theological Faculty in Prague, 'Free-Thinking and Religion'. Linhart, says the anonymous editorial writer, attempts to engage with Czech freethinkers. In this engagement, he correctly guards against the slippery slope objection to such dialogue, that criticizing out-dated features of religion entails rejecting religion itself. We no more thus reject religion than we reject science when we reject the geocentric science of the Middle Ages, or reject philosophy when we reject Aristotle's metaphysics, or art when we reject an outmoded style. The free-thinking critics err when they presume to reject Protestantism as such, since, if they looked carefully, they would see that we modern Protestants are ourselves critical of that which merits criticism. We are not blind to our own errors and inadequacies. 'It is', so Linhart writes according to the report and commentary, 'in truth necessary to distinguish religion from religion just as it is necessary to distinguish science from science and art from art, et cetera'. As we have seen from Osuský's *History of Religion*, there would thus far be little if any distance between the Slovak Osuský and the Czech Linhart.

After this sympathetic introduction, the anonymous editor continues his coverage of the Linhart controversy by reporting on Linhart's answer to a question that was put to him as a member of a churchly community and a teacher on its theological faculty preparing future preachers: Did he believe in the Apostles Creed? Linhart did not waffle, the report continues, quoting his words: 'In order that you have a precise and definite answer, as you desire: I do not receive the Apostles Creed because it is an expression of the mythical worldview of ancient times that is completely overcome by the scientific developments of the modern period. I stand on the foundation of modern science and I acknowledge the singular merit of truth also for religion, which science

[26] The following exchange between Struhárik, the anonymous editors, and Osuský is drawn from *CL* XLI 53–4, 72–4, 94–5, 107.

must also acknowledge. On this foundation all of modern Protestantism stands: experience and reason' (53). To this frank confession, the anonymous editor then registers an equally frank question: *Quo vadis*?

He next points out how the eminent Czech professor and future leading theologian, Josef Hromádka, had recently rebuked his fellow Czech Protestants because they did not know what they wanted and where they stood.[27] He also recalls a Slovak Lutheran pastor, J. Struhárik, who in 1923 had argued that even the healthiest of the Czech Protestant churches are but 'a conglomeration that is ideologically a free zone for all the various spirits'. What is concerning to the editor in reporting this controversy between Linhart and Hromádka is that the church should take care to proclaim the great truths of Scripture, the revelation of the living, personal, transcendent God, sin and grace in Christ Jesus, so that the one thing needful should be done, to lead all people without distinction to Christ. Or, are we to become a society of free-thinkers?

In the next issue of the church journal, the aforementioned J. Struhárik published an essay, taking up the editor's question, '*Quo vadis?*', that had been put to Professor Linhart's frank rejection of the Apostles' Creed as scientifically outdated. 'It seems to me', writes Struhárik, 'that the report about this controversy and the commentary was incomplete'. The question can also arise here in Slovakia. We send our students to Prague for study and we recommend the Hussite Theological Faculty. Indeed, our church, or rather its leaders, seek closer relationships with the Czech churches, which do not express any word of judgment on such manifestations of infidelity. Furthermore, the reported stance of Professor Linhart is new proof that in the Czech Brethren church there is a powerful stream of liberal theology; that is, that there is a churchly or religious circle of free-thinking alongside a positive stream of Calvinism, and that each of these circles lives in brotherly fashion next to the other. And for this reason, Struhárik writes, it is alarming that our Lutheran Church in Slovakia in 1923 entered into a federation with this Czech church.

'Why? For what?', Struhárik asks. We pitched this federation among ourselves as nothing but a defensive alliance against outside forces – that is, against Rome. But in the constitution of this federation the goal enunciated in the first place is to manifest the 'essential spiritual unity' of the uniting churches in spite of

[27] An intervening report in *CL* told how Prof. Linhart's lecture was subject to criticism also in Czech Protestant circles. The most significant dissent is that of Hromádka, who faulted Linhart for speaking so vaguely of 'what in the Creed is mythical' and thus 'overcome by science', and not saying openly what survives this sifting for faith on the basis of Linhart's sole criteria of experience and reason. Such vague and shifty language does not attest very well to intellectual seriousness (*CL* XLI 95).

differences in doctrine. This clearly indicates that doctrine or confession has become something inessential, secondary; and that the first purpose of the federation is to cultivate confessional indifference. If this were accomplished, Stuhárik insinuates, the real agenda of union would be within reach. And we can read in the official journal of the Czech Brethren church that the federation is expressly considered to be a step on the way to union. Other magazines of this church, too, make it clear that union with the Slovak Lutheran church is the goal. For this reason the fact that precisely the Czech Brethren church was the initiator of the federation is a weighty one.

Struhárik thus played out his cards as a Slovak patriot and Gnesio-Lutheran. The two were unified in the nineteenth century disciple of Ĺudovit Štur, Jozef Miroslav Hurban (1817–88). In the nineteenth century the same political pressure for unification of Protestant churches came from the side of the Hungarian Reformed Church during the time of the empire. Hurban rallied the Slovak Lutherans to resistance on both religious and nationalist lines and in the process led a 'confessional revival' which accented the anti-Calvinist features of the 1580 Book of Concord. At this time, the pastor's wearing of the ornate white surplice over the black Geneva gown became the symbol of true, that is, Gnesio-Lutheranism. As with Struhárik's opposition to the Czechs, Hurban's 'confessional' Lutheranism was overlaid with Slovak resentment towards the Hungarian overlords. Needless to say, something like the 'ecumenical intention of the Augsburg Confession'[28] that has come to light in the years after the Second Vatican Council was far from consciousness. While the indigenous Slovak Lutheran confessions of the sixteenth century were ecumenically more open, as they were written by students of Melanchthon, with Hurban's nineteenth century confessional revival came for the first time an assertion of the decidedly anti-ecumenical features of the 1580 Book of Concord.[29]

Struhárik continues in his protest to argue that the goal of drawing closer together by coming to know one another through the federation is being interpreted in the Czech lands as coming together in 'common doctrine'. But we have already seen, he argues, that for the Czechs common teaching really means a common doctrinal indifference. He offers further citations from the literature of the free-thinking Czech Protestant circles to show that they regard the Slovak

[28] See *The Role of the Augsburg Confession: Catholic and Lutheran Views* ed. Joseph A. Burgess (Philadelphia: Fortress, 1980).

[29] Friedrich Mildenberger, *Theology of the Lutheran Confessions* trans. E. Lueker (Philadelphia: Fortress, 1986), 151.

Lutherans as victims of 'dead churchianity', 'confessionalistic jealousy', and so forth.

Struhárik now pivots in another direction. 'To show ourselves worthy of swimming in the great stream of contemporary world ideas', he writes sarcastically, 'we Lutherans should also accept the sects like the Methodists and the Baptists'. The goal is clearly doctrinal indifference. And the consequence will be to invite these sectarian missionaries into our congregations. Their sheep-stealing is intolerable. We have the right and the duty to block them, but we will not succeed in blocking them by buying into doctrinal indifference. Why else did the Baptists and Methodists join the federation? Certainly not like the Czech Brethren for the sake of a union in liberal theology; why, the sects regard us Lutherans as an unconverted *massa perditionis*! Joining the federation is only a mask of friendship to cover their expansionist ambitions at our expense.

'I don't know', Stuhárik acknowledges:

> how many of us will agree with my deductions, but it is sinful to be silent about such matters. I ask our "new reformers," you who are pushing religious development and progress with Professor Linhart, to acknowledge sincerely that you do not intend to stop until you achieve union. Only do not forget that as long as you are still members of the Slovak Lutheran Church you have a duty and a task that cannot be put up for sale. The task is the understanding of the Bible in accord with our Lutheran Confessions, which understanding does not justify you but rather is in conflict with your endeavours (which is just the reason why the modernists reject the confessional writings). I mean that you must subvert the confessional subscription of our Lutheran church on the basis of the prophets and apostles (not scientific or philosophical reason). This is your duty: to demand that the church leadership ask the believing Lutheran people whether they agree with your endeavours, since according to our church constitution, all power in the church derives from the congregation.

Stuhárik adds one last thought, but in the process reveals by it the individual who has been his domestic target all along. He asks whether our professors in the Slovak Lutheran Church confess the chief articles of Christian doctrine. He mentions Jesus's divine Sonship, saving death and resurrection from the dead in a glorified body. 'Why', he concludes, 'Dr. Osuský already in 1922 made clear without any concealment his disagreement with the Apostles Creed – if I remember well, in the question of the conception of the Lord Christ from the Holy Spirit. Osuský is a friend of the "new reformation," which intends to repair the old creeds, and has given expression to this intention also in writing. So what is alarming in the Czech churches must also be alarming in ours. We also have to ask about ourselves: *Quo vadis*?'

People could and did regard the crudeness of Struharik's intervention as evidence enough of the need in the Slovak Lutheran Church for a 'new reformation', that is, a contextually appropriate modernization of the old orthodoxy. Indeed, the anonymous editor of the church journal appended a comment on Struhárik's article under the Latin motto: *quo bene distinquit, bene docet*. He argued that if we apply this rule we see that Struhárik takes more than a few illogical leaps in what he has written. What an exaggeration to condemn an entire faculty because of one or two professors! We would have to put all the theological faculties on the Index, beginning with our own – as Struhárik indicated by his comment about Osuský at the end of his article – but continuing on from there to even the most orthodox faculties in Europe and beyond. Furthermore, to listen to liberal or even unbelieving professors does not mean to appropriate their stance. Nor would it be correct to want to cordon theological students off hermeneutically from the thoughts of liberal theology. If we want to stand firm in the battle with various currents of the times, we must know them. We cannot be ostriches putting our heads in the sand of orthodoxy and think that, in blinding ourselves, everything around us is in good order. In regard to relations with other churches, much depends on how we explain words like 'relations' or 'drawing together'. Struhárik constructs a bogeyman: federation. 'I certainly do not see', the editor concludes, 'in our Czechoslovak federation of Protestant churches a covert preparation for union'. Who would deny that Struhárik has some truth in much else that he has written? Yet we minority Protestants do need a common defence against Rome even as we cannot be indifferent in matters of doctrine. But in regard to the article's concluding comment on Osuský, the editor closes, 'I will not reflect. I do not feel called to Osuský's defence, whether Struharik's rebuke is justified'.

Osuský replied several months later under the title, *Quo Vado*? He begins by confessing ignorance regarding Struharik's purposes. Does he want to call forth a necessary and fruitful exchange of thoughts on the somnolent field of our church's theological life? Or does he want to confuse the concept of religious conviction with the concept of a theological stance, and so does he want, in a return to the evil spirit of an epoch of religious intolerance that we have since exorcized – and in contradiction to the doctrine of the freedom of conscience of the Christian person, the great outcome of the Reformation – to anathematize every theological stance that does not agree down to the last letter with his own? If the first, Osuský declares, I welcome his intervention with sincere joy. Otherwise I must think of his essay as an alarming phenomenon that has not up until now appeared in any seriously orthodox and confessional circles nor from even one of our regional Protestant churches. Since Struharik's intervention is alarming in this latter way, in that it would elicit in readers the idea that, if I am not sheer unbeliever, I am at least more or less a heretic, I regard it as necessary to reply, therefore, not to Struhárik, but rather to indicate my basic stance before our Protestant audience. In this way I won't imitate a priori the dishonourable procedure of Stuhárik in making an insinuation by way of a parenthetical note in passing.

Osuský's *apologia pro vita sua* is worthy of a lengthy citation:

> I have been trained by the spirit of the gospel of Christ and the principles of our church thus far that which I do not hypocritically conceal, but openly and sincerely confess before God and before people: I try to fulfil the command of Christ not only on the field of works but also on the field of thought, "Seek first the Kingdom of God." I try to keep the command of the apostle Peter: "Be ready always to give an account to anyone…" I try not only by my life but also by my intellectual views to be running the race with Paul the apostle, saying, "Not that I have arrived, or that I am already perfect, but I press on." I am thus not satisfied that like a Catholic I would believe just anything that is presented to me for belief. I want to live through beliefs, to logically work them out in myself, so that they become in me a grounded conviction, which I could defend both to myself and to others, and thus be able to give an account of them so that a doubting and seeking soul can gain God and His Son, Christ. I seek, I run. I have not yet found everything, I have not yet finished the race – as has Struhárik – I am not yet at the goal, perfect in my views – like Struhárik – but some things have troubled and trouble me still. I fall here and there into doubts – all this I do not conceal. But let someone who is perfect cast the first stone at me… But anyone who sees what is happening around us, if he seriously has the interests of our church in his heart, does not poke his head in the sand like an ostrich in today's difficult times! I pray with the publican, "O God, be merciful to me the sinner,' but I do not demand, as does Struhárik, either for divine examination of "kidney and heart," nor for papal inerrancy, nor for haughty judgment, nor for medieval inquisition, nor for loathsome pharisaicism! If Struhárik intends to anathematize in the name of his confessionalism, let him also anathematize the apostle Paul for his views expressed in Phil. 1.18 and Eph. 4.13.

Osuský's co-religionists found this defence convincing;[30] six years later they elected him one of the two regional bishops of their church. As bishop, he preached in Bratislava's Great Church for thirteen years, from 1933 to 1946.

[30] Gažik writes that the Dean of the theological faculty and Osusky's bishop 'testified that "professor Osuský sincerely believes in all the chief articles of our doctrine but wants to bring them near to reason …" The polemic between Struhárik and Osuský eventually clarified, also between them personally' (93).

So we arrive at a definite irony from the review thus far of the early Osuský's path: although Osuský was remembered as a philosophical theologian, he is not particularly interesting as a philosopher. What is interesting is his reserved, yet undeniable, Biblicism and Christological commitment coming increasingly to the fore. True, in the spirit of nation-building with an eye to a modernized and renewed Christendom, he excavated for the first time in his young nation the thinking especially of the nineteenth century Lutheran pastors led by Štur in the national awakening of the Slovaks. One contemporary philosopher rightly describes the slant of this work as follows:

> Philosophy often came and comes into opposition to theology and Osuský also makes the difference between the histories of philosophy and theology plain. He wanted to write a history of philosophy but he made it clear that he is a theologian. Thus his history visibly arose from the position of Protestant theology – even citing the old Czech Bible in places. This theological position is not, however, bigoted dogmatism, although it is hard to obtain from it a relatively reliable picture of the development of philosophy. Theological concerns influenced the choice of themes (philosophy of religion was very much emphasized) and he so lifted up the significance of certain authors and on the whole diminished the significance of the products and of figures who were atheist and revolutionary. The revolutionary significance for example of Galileo and Newton, deism, enlightenment – which are in the end important also for the history of theology and the understanding and interpretation of the concept of God are not sufficiently appreciated.[31]

Despite these deficiencies from today's perspective in what at the time was a pioneering work, this scholar professes admiration especially for the final chapter of Osuský's book on the history of philosophy with its detailed description of thought in Slovakia. He calls this the most precious part of the book, whose value is enduring. It served and still serves to awaken cultural awareness in Slovakia.

Osuský also wrote in this period another pioneering textbook, the first Slovak language *Introduction to Sociology* (1930), which in many places touched on philosophical questions, especially where, when and how the human race originated. While he allowed for an ancient origin of humanity, perhaps as long ago as three million years, he was reserved regarding the Darwinian theory that humanity evolved from lower life forms.[32] While he did not expressly

[31] Ján Kocka, 'Odkaz Osoského "Prvých Slovenských Dejín Filozofie," *Filozophia* 49/9 (1994): 585.

[32] Already, in 1909, Osuský had written an essay, 'Darwin and Humanity' on the 100th anniversary of Darwin's birth. 'According to Osuský', Gažik writes, 'it is incorrect and pointless to compare

reject Darwinism, he was manifestly concerned with the ethical implications, not only of the principle of the survival of the fittest but also of racialist possibilities in theories of polygenetic human origins (the date, let us recall, is 1930!). Osuský wanted to uphold the theological view of monogenesis from the book of Genesis, reiterated in Acts 17, that endows the entire human family as the image of God. He held that the oppressed classes and nations will always, and rightly, appeal to natural and indeed supernatural right against social Darwinism. His philosophical and ethical idealism held that humanity had developed from primitive collectivism to ethical individualism in the sense of personal freedom and initiative, so that the social task today is to foster the cooperation of classes rather than class warfare. In the end, spirit, ideas, views, feeling and will, and not matter, will reign. Economic relations are created according to ideology, not the opposite.

Thus Osuský the sociologist wanted Christians to be more socially oriented in order that socialism become more religious, as Ragaz had first maintained.[33] He regarded democracy, in the sense of universal voting rights, as the best form of the state, together with parliamentarianism and political parties, despite the vulnerability to demagoguery. Nationalism emerges in the modern age as a by-product of human self-awareness and dignity. But a nation that thinks only in terms of its battle against oppressors acquires only a negative consciousness and produces an unwelcome chauvinism. Osuský tries in this way to deal with ethnic others, not only in regard to Czechs but also to Jews and Romani: 'It is not possible to solve the Jewish problem with hatred or arrogance, but with objective knowledge and arrangements informed by that'. But this stance, too, was ultimately grounded not in social science or philosophy but in Christianity, which is in essence international, although it also implies nationality in the sense of creating a community of nations. Christ loved although he also criticized His own nation, and emphasized that he had sheep in other folds. Nationalism is thus qualified by the Bible's proclamation of the international kingdom of God.[34]

Darwin with the Bible. Darwin's theory and faith do not stand on the same level'. Gazik comments: 'Osuský's approach to Darwin is correct. This approach, however, was in fact not always respected by materialists either, who used Darwin in their battle against faith, and it was not respected by the church, which occasionally condemned Darwin'. Gažik, 33.

33 But Osuský was also sharply critical of utopian features of Ragaz's theology, such that his own position could more be likened to Reinhold Niebuhr's Christian realism. Gažik cites from Osuský's essay, 'Ragaz' Religious Socialism', that 'he does not sufficiently reckon with the weakness of sinful humanity and thus with the greater need of divine grace'. Gažik, 46.

34 Münz, 470.

Defence of the Truth (1946): Ethical Idealism's Last Hurrah

This line of ethical idealism in Osuský culminated in his 1946 *Defence of the Truth*; this apologetics, written to confront the rising tide of Marxism-Leninism arriving with the defeat of Hitler, the fall of the Slovak rump state and the reunification of Czechoslovakia, attends to the basic questions of religion and philosophy. As one philosopher today describes the work *qua* philosophy: 'In his views Osuský agrees in almost everything with Catholics, especially with the neo-Thomist stance. He depends on many scholars and philosophers and tries to resolve in brief many problems. The work has thus a popular character and accordingly its argumentation tends also to popularization'.[35] *Defence of the Truth*, in other words, is an altogether conventional work. It was not convincing to the Marxists' opponents. Nor did it meet the deeper challenges demanded by the times: 'Just like the neo-Thomists, Osuský did not know how to coordinate the freedom of the human will with divine omniscience and providence… He got no further than the Catholics',[36] that is, in the attempt to defend either theologically or philosophically the modern liberalism of the bourgeoisie.

This is not a trivial failure in a work that purports to refute the alternative account of human social evolution being made by dialectical materialism. The book takes an unsavoury turn in the end with an acutely partisan defence of Protestantism, which faults Catholicism, namely, the same Christian Platonism on which Osuský is otherwise fully dependent, philosophically, for the discrediting of Christianity in recent European history. This inconsequence aside, the book is even less interesting philosophically, as we must next review.

There are features of this book that are of interest in the present study, in other words if only to show that Osuský is not remembered at his best if he is remembered solely or primarily as a philosopher. The very first sentences of the Introduction indicate this:

> The Second World War has now finished, but those would err who think that its ending will also be the end of every conflict. The conflicts of the battlefield between nations and states now pass into the life of nations, communities, families and souls … Experience teaches that after such wars, as the present one, great earthquakes and revolutions come about, not only on the field of politics but also in spiritual realm, thus also in the moral and religious field (5).

[35] Ibid., 471.
[36] Ibid.

These introductory words cannot but remind us of the polemic with which Osuský had concluded his work of thirty years previously, *War and Religion*, warning against the Marxist-Leninist revolution that would take place after the First World War. In the interim, Osuský had given an extended analysis of 'Bolshevism' in his prescient 1937 lecture, 'The Philosophy of Fascism, Bolshevism and Hitlerism', which we will discuss in the next chapter. It suffices here to note that in the 1946 book, *Defence of the Truth*, Osuský tried in the same way to fight philosophy with philosophy. This last stand against Bolshevism realizes the underlying motive of his entire philosophical research, namely, the idealistic endeavour to replace the role of force in social life with spirit and reason.

Everyone who has survived the war is asking why he has suffered, Osuský begins. What ought we change, and how can we go forward? Examining the reasons for which we had to suffer and to sacrifice lives, and finding these reasons in the flaws of existing institutions, causes us to turn against the existing order and seek to remove it. So the flames of war pass over into the quiet villages, families and souls. The soul aflame looks for new ideas and ways, a new starting point for a better life. These reflections are laws of social life against which it is not possible to object. Who would not want, after the storm, the coming of fresh air? But it is necessary to take care that in the birth of a new, more beautiful life worthwhile things are not also destroyed (5). Osuský quotes a village proverb about the risks of heating highly flammable wood houses with thatched roofs: 'Take care, light and flame, that you do not harm the human'; he wishes the proverb to be applied also to the fire of the spiritual revolution that is now approaching. Let us protect and preserve what it is necessary to protect! We have watch towers guarding against forest fires and I would like, Osuský announces, to be such a watchman in this book over one little section of our little Slovak world, namely the field of morality and religion. Moral and religious life are firm only as their foundations are firm, founded on the rock of truth. Only a fool denies the significance of this foundation or says that a flower can live without its roots. Let us not uproot this root but rather come to the defence of the truth!

In a conflict where there are aggressors, there must also be defenders. In military terminology it is said that defence is not only permitted but is a moral duty. How much more that applies to matters concerning the truth of genuine moral and religious life. This is all the more necessary in our nation because our thousand year history reveals two basic principles: religion and nationality. God have mercy! Religion in the most recent time of the Slovak fascist state was terribly abused, politicized in a partisan way and also clericalized. When it comes to religion, the defence must take place on both the right flank and on the left flank. Listen to the martyr's voice of Jan Hus: 'Seek truth, listen to truth, teach truth, love truth, speak truth, hold to truth, defend truth to death'. So Osuský proposes to write in defence of truth.

By what method will the truth be defended? Osuský divides the subject into two audiences. Since the unbelievers and the indifferent do not believe the reasons of faith, it is necessary to answer them with scientific and rational reasons from experience, history, logical judgment and appeal to the opinion of significant teachers, thinkers and actors. Thus in the first part of the work (that is, the part being summarized in this chapter), Osuský intends to fight fire with fire, philosophy with philosophy. When superstition or the misuse of faith attacks, by contrast, there he will defend the truth by the reasonings of genuine faith, the experience of religious founders or geniuses, especially the biblical prophets; this will occupy the latter two parts of *Defence of the Truth*. He will thus proceed from the widest circle of concern to the narrowest: from religion in general in Part One, to Christianity in Part Two, and finally to Protestantism in Part Three. The times are urgent, he writes, and he cannot delay publication further. 'I expect another to take my place as a similar watchman. Much that I write in this book is only an indicator so I will be happy if some future writer completes and also corrects what I write. May God help defend the great legacy of the fathers!' So Osuský concludes the Introduction.

As already indicated, in what follows we will find little more than a conventional reiteration of the philosophical tradition of Christian Platonism simply contradicting the materialist alternative on the Marxist horizon without freshly solving the conundrums of the idealist tradition, as we shall now see in detail. Osuský draws regularly on the existential focus given to the tradition of Christian Platonism by Luther's 'pro me' principle. 'Truth is truth for us only when we actualize it alongside confessing it' (10). At the same time, he is well aware of the sceptical turn from the nineteenth century under the influence of Kant in regard to the objective pole of knowledge of God. This agnosticism regarding the knowledge of God has cultivated a definite indifference to divine truth, since Kant convinced many that the supernatural world is unknowable. This attitude is very comfortable and widespread, Osuský observes, but shallow, arrogant, cynical and empty. It is the worst reflection of the creature made in the image of God. Nevertheless, the empty soul of modern man cannot remain empty; in place of the lost God, it will seek and find some idol.

Osuský surveys other contemporary attitudes towards religious truth besides that of the agnostic and indifferent. They are 1) the untroubled pious believer; 2) the half-believer who professes with lips but denies his faith by his life in the body; 3) the formal believer who accepts religion as an inherited custom; 4) the seeker who painfully questions. Such questioning and doubt on the part of the seeker is not altogether bad. Christ himself accepted the questioning of John the Baptist (Mt. 11.2-6). Questioning can lead to a deeper understanding of truth, if it does not end in the sceptical denial of truth. Yet another type is 5) the rationalist, who is dissatisfied with faith as a principle of knowledge and rather tries to create a suitable religion by reason. This fifth type would include deists and pantheists. Finally, 6) complete unbelievers who do not acknowledge God in any form, believe in nothing and regularly attack religion. They are called atheists. Characteristically, given the 'pro me' principle borrowed from Luther, Osuský concludes this opening survey by demanding of his reader: 'Examine yourself. To which group do you belong? How do you stand in relation to religion? And for what reasons? What motivates you to a stance of disbelief in one or the other?' (11)

Many adopt a stance towards religion solely on the basis of the spirit of the times. Others are awakened from slumber by the crises of life, whether in time of war or in peacetime by personal problems. Behind all these serious reasons for adopting a stance lies the problem of suffering: Why does the fate of a person not square with his morality? The immorality of half-believers only compounds this problem for many seekers and strugglers. So also does the superstition of the pious. When religion transgresses the borders of its activity, Osuský now argues drawing on the very Kant[37] whom previously he had faulted for modern agnosticism in regard to the knowledge of God, it enters the field of science in such a way that it does not acknowledge the actual truths science has obtained. Superstition is the result. This does not have to happen, certainly not in biblical religion, according to which in the beginning God determined that humanity should have dominion over nature, which cannot happen without scientific investigation. By the same token, however, science cannot transgress its boundaries and pass into the field of the supernatural, metaphysical, religious, denying

[37] As Gažik sees, Osuský's relation to Kant is ambivalent to the point of being self-contradictory. On the one hand, he employs Kant's regionalism to separate faith and science into different spheres and calls this act of separation the work of 'Protestantism's greatest philosopher' (35). On the other hand, he blames Kant for the dualism of spheres which removes faith from life and especially ethics: 'In [Osuský's] works we will not find any sign that ethics and morality could have any other foundation than a religious one. For Osuský morality was equally religious morality' (68). The most important difference, as Gažik puts it, is that 'in distinction from Luther Kant in his philosophy of religion does not start from revelation and the gospel but from anthropocentric moralism' (76).

the latter's truths. Good science knows that it is not omniscient but forever progresses in knowledge (12). When a scientist philosophizes, he speaks as a human being, not as a scientist, giving reasons not proofs for this or that belief.

To think something and to know something scientifically are two different things. Believers believe that God exists and unbelievers believe that God does not exist. Thus both are believers. The real question is which of these two beliefs is more rational. Even more deeply, however, reason and true faith can join hands and thus form a genuine whole, as also head and heart together form a complete human being. Reason seeks God but the heart finds Him (13). Quoting Emil Brunner, Osuský continues, 'If reason is the highest principle for someone, they have become "autonomous, their own lord, their own god"'. The deeper truth is, then, why 'people do not believe is not because they cannot on account of reason, but because in their will they do not want to believe'. The unwillingness of the heart to believe has various pretexts, but, as the Russian philosopher Nicolaus Lossky has written: 'When a person brings reasons against the existence of God, you will see that the subconscious basis of unbelief is hatred of God and opposition to the thought that there exists a being infinitely higher than he is' (14). With this move, things get very personal.

Religion, universal in human cultures, is about God, Osuský insists. The modern critics of religion, that is, of a basic and ineradicable human orientation towards God, are only modernizing the old objections against a priestcraft that intoxicates the common people for profit or social control. But true religion is neither clericalism nor caesaropapism; it rather gives to Caesar what is Caesar's and to God what is God's: 'it is a misfortune for religion when worldly and spiritual powers are mixed or identified' (15). Osuský briefly discusses Feuerbach's theory of the religious illusion created by the projections of alienated humanity's own misplaced essence onto a blank screen, that is, that man creates God in his own image, not the opposite. How would that explain primitive religions that worship plants, animals and heavenly bodies? How do you explain the figure of the devil? These would be terrible ideals! Surely the psychological explanation that primitive people, out of fear of mysterious natural occurrences or in thanksgiving for natural blessings, personalized natural forces is a more serious explanation than Feuerbach's. But even this does not explain the fact that among modern people, who, with the availability of scientific explanation, no longer fear such natural mysteries, religion continues.

Osuský now comes to the real challenge before him: historical materialism. Marxism advances beyond Feuerbach by attributing the origin of religion not only to powerlessness before the forces of nature with their threats of death but also to the human conflict between economic interests. This conflict brings about the division of society into the classes of the oppressors and the oppressed; the result is that the primitive family gods retreat before the new concept of God as the All Powerful One, who holds the reins over the oppressed by sacralizing the oppressors. But if we take this theory seriously and put it to an empirical test it would require that in conditions of economic equality there ought to be the same religion, and that different classes should have different religions. But that proves not to be not the case.

Deists also object, however, because of the plurality of religions. That they are disunited, they say, proves that they are not true. A weak objection and a weak reason, Osuský rebuts. For also scientific, philosophical, legal, social and economic truths are diverse. The philosophers of the Enlightenment, dissatisfied with the plurality of religion, invented a religion of their own, which they called 'natural'. They called it 'natural' religion in vain. It was not natural and it died soon after it was born, from its own artificiality. Natural and eternal religion is really only the first of the commandments: 'You shall have no other gods before me'. Yet the objection of the Enlightenment deists continues today in the claim that religion is the fruit of a naïve and childish human age; that only children and simple grandmas believe such things; that faith originated from superstition and is superstition, which science overcame and is overcoming. But in reality faith like science develops and never ceases to modernize. Howsoever science or philosophy progress, so also does faith. There is religion because there is God; there is God because there is religion (16–17).

From this promising broadside, with its intimations of a genuinely post-Kantian (James and Hamann are mentioned as thinkers teaching the historicity of reason) engagement with diverse viewpoints on the levelled playing field of post-modernity, the rest of the book unfolds with competent but not particularly compelling argumentation that is, in fact, 'modern, all-too-modern'. Osuský discusses next the traditional proofs for the existence of God, which he affirms as offering reasons for believing in God, not proofs for the existence of God. Osuský's concern with theodicy, the law of sufficient reason and the Melanchthonian tradition of the Lutheran theology of culture, makes mention more than once of Leibniz[38] as a precedent for the right relationship of faith and reason or theology and philosophy in modern times. Faith is affirmed in the Augustinian sense of the 'utility of believing', which attends all supposedly purely rational philosophies, which cannot ground their first principles in

[38] Gažik demonstrates this dependence on Leibniz in several connections, 59–62, 67.

demonstrable knowledge but rather assume them in faith of some kind or another. Faith thus constitutes the principle of knowledge that corresponds to divine revelation, whether in nature, history or miracle. Faith's knowledge consists, however, chiefly in the interpretation of historical human experience, just as its self-knowledge in doctrinal theology undergoes a corresponding historical development in refining representations of God.

At this juncture, Osuský asks, 'What are the signs of true revelation?'. He answers: 'a) revelation must be from God, that is, it must reveal God's will regarding the stance of man towards God and thus it must lead to good, to God; b) it cannot be related to selfish, small-minded goals; c) it must not be against reason, but rather beyond reason'. This articulation is said to concur with Emil Brunner's judgment that the goal of the entire Bible is the revealed Word of God, 'so far as it speaks of Christ', who most perfectly reveals God and the relationship of humanity to God. In words that anticipate his final work, he writes: 'It is true that God speaks in the Bible by the lips of human beings and that there is thus also in the Bible a human side. In the Bible we do not see God Himself, or His photograph. But of the many photographs in the Bible the most perfect is Jesus – the same must be said of the photographs of God in the holy books of other religions' (26). Jesus represents God to us most perfectly – a reprise of the position a younger Osuský took *vis-à-vis* rival Buddhism.

All such 'photographs' are representations in some aspect of God as Spirit, essentially beyond representation, on the basis of which we come to conceptions of God by reflection on things in time and space regarded as effects of God, especially productive of the representations of God. From these conceptualizations various properties are ascribed to God, for example that He is the *eternal* source of the temporal order, the *immense* ground of the spatial universe, and the *powerful*, *wise*, *just* and *good* Creator of the world. From these reflections, we garner the notion of a perfect person and, its being such, of the highest being. 'Only such a God can be the true God, the rest are only gods with a small "g" – idols' (26-7).

There is, as already indicated, an interesting dependence on Leibniz here,[39] as Osuský goes on to argue that the perfection of God consists in the living *harmony* of various divine properties, which can be recognized in hindsight but never fully anticipated:

> Perfection does not mean only rational perfection, nor only the highest degree of all the individually mentioned properties, of every individual spiritual

[39] On Leibniz's place in the history of Melanchthonian Lutheranism, see Paul R. Hinlicky, *Paths Not Taken: Fates of Theology from Luther through Leibniz* (Grand Rapids, MI: Eerdmans, 2009), 17–42.

> activity of thinking, feeling and desiring, but also the mutual relation and again the coherence of all these properties and activities in harmony. Otherwise there could be conflict between them, but in harmony with perfection that cannot be... Each property by itself would not be perfect, if it were not perfect also in relation to the others and to the whole. Just in relation to the others, and of all to all, do we know about perfection... Accordingly, omnipotence in omniscience cannot mean caprice, but the power or ability to do everything that omniscience recognizes as right. Omnipotence does not mean, for example, that God would be able to declare evil to be good and good to be evil, or that he could declare that something which exists at the same time does not exist (29).

So by the principle of harmony, love is not against justice, but finds a new way beyond justice, just as wisdom is not against power but finds a new way beyond power. The echo of Leibniz here continues with an explicit mention of the problem of theodicy: 'various possibilities of suffering do not exclude God's omnipotence, nor His omniscience, nor justice nor goodness and love'. Objections can be met by pointing to the freedom of the human will and the divine permission of the evils that humans freely will, as well as to similar phenomena in nature such as storms alongside sunny days, weeds growing in the wheat, day and night, life and death.

Leibniz is mentioned by name in a following section, subtitled, 'Why the morality of humanity does not square with its fate', with the observation that 'evil must always be evil, and in the time that it happens it certainly looks evil, but in the future it can be changed to good, or again, that evil is evil only in the narrow perspective of the individual, while in the perspective of the whole it is good, so that by one's own suffering and oppression we redeem others, perhaps the whole – as did Jesus Christ' (30). In thoughts that at this juncture point to his work on Job, The *Mystery of the Cross* (to be discussed below in Chapter 3), Osuský affirms that we can suffer not only for reasons but also for purposes; for example, when God tries us to show us and others that our piety is not selfish or calculated, or that we were good only so long as things went well. Or again, when by suffering we learn a deeper compassion for others or how to rise to God in faith. Nietzsche's claim that God is dead, then, does not stand on the basis of human suffering: without pressure there would be no progress, without storms no clearing of the air, without evil no good because good is the overcoming of evil (31).

On this basis of Leibniz's theodicy, Osuský contends against the pantheistic identification of God with the world as in Leibniz's antipode, Spinoza. 'It is illogical that modern man in excellent ways has examined nature in order to have dominion over it and nevertheless becomes in pantheism its slave. The consistent pantheist must subject himself to the law of nature when he sees God in nature' (32). The ethical implications of pantheism are ominous for Osuský: if nature is God, everything must thus be just as it is. It is impossible to do anything new. It makes no sense to distinguish between the world as it is and the world as it ought to be, as ethical idealism requires. In pantheism, there is no free moral will. As was the case with the ancient Stoics, pantheism leads to resignation. 'Thus it is impossible to identify God with the world. We have to separate Him, as we divide the product from the producer. God is above the world, above nature, above thought, transcendent and immanent equally… It is better to say that God is in the world or that the world is in God'. So Osuský affirms theism, by which he means belief in the personal God, not an impersonal fatalism. Pantheistic fatalism is 'antireligious, anti-progressive and dangerous from the moral perspective' (33).

Osuský now tries to reconcile the divine sovereignty of a personal God with human freedom; he does so by the Lutheran argument, already lodged against Calvinism in the Book of Concord, that divine foreknowledge does not entail foreordination.[40] The question, Osuský says, is poorly posed: whether man has free will. The better question is to what extent he has free will. He has free will insofar as he is responsible for his deeds. Believers are dependent on God, to be sure; they, like all people, are determined by inheritance, weaknesses, sin, circumstances, even though in all of this they have freedom: true, moral freedom not the freedom of caprice. Who is free and who is capricious? Free is the one who can rule himself with a view to what he really wants. People become free to rule themselves when they submit to God's will in prayer, which is the living nerve of any religion.

God relates Himself to people by revealing His will and transforming desire. Religion is life with God and in God. To be sure, the new deists deny that God

[40] *Book of Concord*, FC XI, 640–55. The Lutheran teaching violates the venerable principle of divine simplicity that had driven Zwingli and the orthodox followers of Calvin by logical necessity to the doctrine of the eternal divine reprobation of the wicked. Divine simplicity means that God is simply one in knowing, willing and doing. So if anyone is damned, God has known it, willed it and done it. Against this principle of divine simplicity, the formulators demand that we 'carefully note the difference between God's eternal foreknowledge and his eternal election of his children', the first understood as an act of divine intelligence which knows all things in advance, but the second as an act of divine love by which God determines Himself towards creatures in one way and not another. The formulators say there is a difference here, that God is not simply one in knowing and willing. Thus according to these early Lutherans God can know and permit that Adam will sin but not properly will it, just as God can foresee and determine that Jesus will be crucified but not desire or author the malice and injustice of His crucifiers. According to the doctrine of simplicity, however, this Lutheran distinction is quite impossible. There can be no real difference between God's knowing and God's willing; in God both are simply one and the same. God knows what he wills and wills what he knows, otherwise He would not be God.

can connect with this world, filled with so many imperfections as it is. But evil consequences flow from this view that it is not necessary to pray, to relate oneself to God, but necessary only to admire Him from a distance. It would be unworthy, they say, for God constantly to mess with the world and intervene in events in order to repair and arrange things. People come to such views because by reason alone they see in God conflicts between individual divine properties. But God is both immanent and transcendent, thus omnipresent and also beyond conception; those to whom these properties are apparently contradictory are right, but they must understand this correctly. God is above the world but in relation to it. He created this world and also further forms it, preserves it and arranges it. We therefore do not speak of fate but of divine providence (36).

Osuský continues on this basis to affirm the possibility of miracles that transcend the boundaries of scientific knowledge, in an argument that is once again reminiscent of Leibniz. Natural laws are not objectively understood literally as laws or instructions, but rather they are fallible human descriptions of certain relations and phenomena in nature, which researchers observe as regularities and thus generalize into working or warranted hypotheses. Scientific laws are not some kind of mystical divine powers, idols, which all of reality and thus also humanity have to worship (37). Miracles are not against the laws of nature, but against such a human description of nature, that is, against a view making natural laws into idols. Furthermore, we have to ask if it is scientific to regard any present view of the laws of nature as complete and perfect. There will be no miracles when we know everything. There are no miracles now to the omniscient God. Miracles are just the consequences of still unknown laws. Thus, the more human reason reveals the laws the more we will know, the more we will rule nature, but always again and again unknown forces will set us on the way of new research. The reality that there are many laws unknown to us guarantees on the one side the possibility of the progress of science and on the other side the possibility of miracles. As eternity does not contradict time, nor immensity space, so also miracles do not contradict the laws of nature. The miracle expresses the freedom of God, just as the moral freedom of man contravenes the law of causality when human beings spontaneously do the good against their own natural inclinations.

Osuský next takes on materialistic and monistic views of God. According to materialists, from all eternity everything is matter or its motion, also the soul or spirit, which are then actually just a more subtle form of matter, or a manifestation of its motion, or a product of its properties. There is no God at all, and religion originates from fear. 'What?', Osuský protests, 'Matter is afraid – of matter? Isn't that a terrible contradiction? Matter by necessity is driven to its effects and so comes to fear itself'. Put otherwise: everything is only matter and yet that same matter is held to have such various and contradictory effects in the world and in life (39).

But if spirit is a product of matter, how can spirit battle against body, or rule over the matter of the body? The assertion that matter is eternal is nothing but a flight into the unknown, because the concept of eternity, like the concept of God, transcends reason. Where does motion or energy come from? According to the law of conservation, matter does not move itself. According to the law of entropy, motion will one day cease. But what has an end also has a beginning. How does life arise from matter? Matter can only work mechanically. How do goal-oriented behaviour, spiritual life, perception, thought, language and so forth arise from matter? If someone says that organized matter is only an instrument, we have to ask whether an instrument does not need its inventor. From all this we see that to want to derive everything from matter is to make matter an idol which requires more faith than to accept a rational, spiritual, perfect being, God the Creator.

In fact, honest materialists who say they believe in nothing but science soon have to admit in response to these arguments that they cannot resolve every question by reason but must complete the knowledge of science with philosophy. And the philosophy of choice is monism. And if we ask where this leads, the honest materialist monist answers: to the boundary of the unknowable. Thus we end in the best case with agnosticism and in the worst case with superstition (41). The entire materialist worldview thus betrays itself as equally religious, but also superstitious insofar as it makes an idol out of matter.

Here the question of the origin of the world and humanity arises. Christians confess that God created the world and humanity from nothing at the beginning of all that exists in the six days in sequence, as it is written in the first chapter of the Bible. The objection is that here we have a miracle with which science cannot deal. It certainly is a miracle, indeed the greatest miracle. But how can science say that either the world or matter is eternal, when science itself asserts that everything has its beginning and end, also the whole. We do not remove the wonder of the origin of the world when we say it arose by accident, but we increase it beyond all understanding. No, the question of origin places us before the great wonder as such.

Again, no science may pass beyond the boundary of temporality to either prove or deny God. God is absolute, the eternal being. Besides Him in eternity there was nothing at all, so God who creates the world creates it out of nothing. Certainly human reason does not know how to comprehend either the absolute God or absolute nothing. Thus also the absolute beginning is not in time but the creation of time; the world and time originate simultaneously. As for the theory of evolution by natural selection, it surely sheds light on many riddles, but God's creative power cannot be reduced to it. In creation, God's creative power hides itself behind all the creatures put into motion. God arranged, arranges and will arrange the origin and also the progress of all creatures and these creatures in turn are manifestations of God's power (43). God's creation is continuous.

The Bible is not and does not want to be an astronomical or natural science textbook. The Bible presents creation with the origin of the world, and humanity in it from the perspective of the pious heart. What matters is not how it happened but who here works. Yet how great is the concurrence between the Bible and the progress in knowledge brought about by modern science! The Bible does not, of course, present us with the transformation of life-forms from previous forms, but it does see the evolution of forms from the least to the greatest, from gas to liquid to the solid state of bodies, from chaos to cosmos. Life evolves in the Bible too: from plants to water-animals to flying animals and finally to humanity. Is this evolution self-originating and mechanical, or intentional? Can accident create order? That takes more faith than to receive the rational plan of the all wise Creator as in Christianity. To be sure, the Bible does not speak of transformation of life forms from one to another but of an ascent from lower to higher, not one *from* another but one *after* another (44). The believer can easily accept evolution; it is the sole mechanism of natural selection that is problematic.

Osuský now lists a number of standard objections to old and new versions of Darwinian theory, but it becomes clear that his supposedly rational and scientific objections are animated by the ethical catastrophe the world had just experienced in Nazism's Social Darwinism.[41] He cites, again, Emil Brunner: 'Whoever thinks that man is an animal will also thus live like an animal. The proverb applies: You are what you believe about yourself'. Or, as Osusky adds, 'Man makes himself into an animal when he makes himself into a god. The truth is that upright walk, articulate speech, work, abstract reasoning, culture, moral free will, and religion all erect a Great Wall of China between humanity and the animals, but sin erects another such wall between God and humanity. We are

[41] In this connection, see the useful review of the evidence in Richard Weikart, *From Darwin to Hitler: Evolutionary Ethics, Eugenics, and Racism in Germany* (New York: Palgrave MacMillan, 2004).

neither gods nor animals but we both bear the image of God as mirror and are dust like the animals' (46–7).

Once again Osuský draws on Leibnizian arguments for organism over mechanism; thinking of the story in Genesis 2, where God breathed life into the figure formed from dust, Osuský affirms that the soul is something distinct from the body, by which we distinguish a corpse from an animated body. The soul is something unchangeable in essence which provides for the unity of consciousness through the body's temporal passage. The corresponding desire for immortality in the soul and the belief in the soul's survival of death cannot be explained from the battle of the oppressed, as the Marxists think, since this faith already existed before the division of society into classes. Plato, for example, and Cicero and Seneca after him, tried to prove the soul's immortality. But the true ground of this belief is theological: the soul is from God, and as such is immortal, because whatever is God's cannot decompose but is eternal. The soul is a special, life-giving power breathed from God. If it were otherwise, it would contradict not only God's spiritual essence but also His justice, goodness and perfection.

Faith in immortality is the greatest motive power in history, moral life and of mutual love. It overcomes many difficulties, encourages morality, warns against despair and makes dying easier. Like faith in God, faith in eternal life is not, thus, a question of the head, but of the heart, longing for its mysterious object of desire. But the immortality of the soul alone is not enough. For how can we live after death should the dead body decompose? We do not believe in resuscitation of this decomposed body, but in the resurrection to a glorified body. This is needed, for the immortal soul can live on only with such a body (49) with which to relate to God and others in the heavenly community. Just as the rational reasons for the existence of God do not suffice, neither do these reasons for immortality suffice as proofs, because they surpass reason; but these reasons do support faith in immortality and also prove that this faith is not against reason.

Osuský's defence of religion as a reasoned belief in God thus comes into a certain confrontation with 'modern man': it is said to be undignified if modern man must obey God. But Osuský replies: if someone does not want to obey God, he will obey the devil. True morality, consequently, must have absolute, superhuman laws, which recommend as good what is also good for others, not for the individual alone, and good under all circumstances. The dependence on Kant, we may note, is once again evident in this formulation as is the ensuing and corresponding attack on modern ethics, like utilitarianism, which are founded instead on the basic selfishness of human nature, so that it becomes unthinkable to love another as oneself. By contrast, obedience to God is not slavish, in that it is voluntary and in the interest of good for oneself as also for others.

If someone objects that religious morality makes man weak, when it points to God's help and grace, a fatal error has taken place, because the kernel of religious morality is love, and love is the greatest of powers. Were Christ, Paul the Apostle, Jan Hus, Martin Luther and other giants of Christian history weaklings? Were the martyrs weaklings? Religious morality makes people great heroes. For in morality it is not only a firm principle that matters but even more so the power to live according to it, which the faith that moves mountains brings. Moreover, in morality it is not only individual life or life in time that matters, but the whole moral order of the world and of eternity.

The objection arises here that religious morality is neither realizable nor progressive, insofar as it is based on unchangeable laws of God's will. While it is true that God's will is unchangeable, because of the progress of theological science, people understand God's word better and better, so that, while humanity has not yet reached the divine ideal, it all the same makes suitable progress in both understanding and realizing it. Another objection is that religious morality is in fact immoral, because it threatens hell. And it is true that for immature believers heaven is a reward, indeed a merited reward, and that punishment is feared. But for the mature believers, heaven and hell are only natural consequences of the ethical lives undertaken in life, and righteousness is only truly undertaken for its own sake, never for ulterior motives.

So we come next to Marx's famous objection, that religious morality diverts attention away from this world to eternity. We can admit that at times, as in monasticism, this happened, through an inadequate understanding of the kingdom of God. But Christianity does not only proclaim God's kingdom eschatologically, that is, in eternity, but also in this life, on the earth, in time, as when we pray, *Thy kingdom come*! Ragaz wrote well: 'It is a tragedy when Christians believe in God but not in His kingdom on earth and when socialists believe in the kingdom on earth, but not in God'. All morality tends to the end that man should abandon evil, and be born anew, so that his body becomes the temple of God's Spirit and human society a society of children of God living in love. The intention is to transform this life. So, if primitive religions have also a primitive morality, there is in both religion and morality nevertheless progress. The Kingdom of God grows and leavens the whole world.

A final objection urges that individual religions cultivate intolerance in people. But is there not also intolerance in various scientific and philosophical trends, and in schools that do battle among themselves? Let us only consider whether atheist morality is more tolerant than theistic. Philosophers like Hobbes argued that faith in many gods would be more tolerant. But is that actually so according to present experience, when individual nations, states and classes have their own gods? Is not a safer foundation laid in the Christian worldview that as children of the one Father we have to love one another mutually? (53)

Osuský turns now to the imminent practical question about education in a society where the churches had fostered whatever schooling existed, but, now, on the Marxist horizon looms the threat of the state's monopolization of education. We cannot forget, he argues, that schools not only instruct but also train, not only the mind but also the heart, not only filling the head with information but also filling the heart with ennobling feelings and impressing on the will desire to do the good. There are some who do not oppose this kind of religious education but oppose only making it obligatory. They argue that religion is a private matter. This is a baseless objection; if we let the children decide, they would decide not only against religious instruction but against any instruction, against school itself (53).

This debate depends upon how we evaluate the subject of instruction. Should this value judgment be left to individuals? Does not society, too, have to evaluate, not only for me but for others who may have different interests, not only for today but for all times and for society as a whole? We cannot forget that human culture is the product of the work of many social elements, including religion. What would we replace religious education with? Undoubtedly, with the opinions of some philosophical tendency. That might seem persuasive, if we think that religion is identical with morality and morality can be taught by philosophy too. But in this world of relativity, of physical, intellectual and moral weakness, insufficiency and perishability, religion gives man the feeling of absolute liberation, redemption and satisfaction that philosophy cannot.

Religion is not a private matter. Every great founder of a religion gains adherents and forms a new community, often in conflict with older ones. This has social significance and so cannot be the private matter of an individual. Of course religions belong among the most inward, intimate, subjective and subtle values, and no one has the right to take that away or interfere with it or force anyone to believe anything. Indeed, we know from history how the demand for privacy arose as a reaction against religious coercion when the slogan was *coge intrare*, 'force them into', the church, outside of which there is no salvation (56). To this extent, privacy in religion is understandable and correct. By the same token, however, the extension of this would not be correct if someone wanted to force us not to believe in anything. Rather, the state has to determine its basic relation to the values of religion. The ideal relation is a free church in a free state with precisely delimited fields, neither an ecclesiastical state nor a state religion.

Even though the state needs moral, peaceful and content individuals, there are in fact people from today's educated and progressive circles who doubt religion's contribution to civil life. But every religion not only orders the relation of the individual to God but also relations between people. Can it be a matter of indifference to society when Christianity teaches that there is no difference between slave and free, Jew and Greek, male and female? That we are all children of the one God, brothers and sisters who have to love one another? To the objection that these ideals have been realized very slowly, Osuský replies that the realization of these ideals does not depend only on the proclamation of the church, but on many other factors. The church has only spiritual power, not physical. It cannot force its ideals. But for society it is remains important what ideal a religion sets before society.

Look at the social difference that results when Buddhism proclaims flight from the world and submergence into Nirvana, while Christianity teaches the kingdom of God, a spiritual kingdom of love, justice and peace, not only eschatologically but also already here on earth, fighting against sin. How can that not have a great influence on culture and morality? (57) Finally, society bears with many broken lives that need internal, spiritual strengthening, encouragement and comfort. Today's state cannot be only a military power collecting taxes, but must be also a cultural, moral and many-sided social unit that cares, and has to care about all the needs of its citizens, including their pastoral needs.

Osuský concludes this first part of his apologetics in defence of religion as the human relation to God with the question of which religion is the most valuable – just as he had concluded his textbook of twenty-five years earlier on the history of religion. Of course, every religion regards itself as best. So, also, we Christians assert about our Christianity that it is best. Osuský presents his credentials for proffering a judgment here. He has dedicated a quarter of a century of his life to the study of the history of individual religions. On this basis he once again asserts that only Buddhism (and, to a certain extent, Judaism) are such that they can be considered comparable to Christianity in value.

But Buddhism is actually a religion without God, and without God there is no true religion. Buddhism is a religious philosophy of death, rather, while Christianity is a religion of life. Osuský denies that he says this out of bigotry; it is, rather, a fact that Buddhism understands this life as a mirage and illusion from which we are to be delivered by way of strict asceticism and cold compassion for suffering beings. But for Christianity, with its social ideal of the kingdom of God, the way to salvation is new birth, abandoning not the world and life, but evil and sin. As to Judaism, which rejects the Christian Trinity in the name of a purer faith in the one God, its rejection assumes that Christianity teaches tritheism. But the accusation can be reversed: ancient Judaism, in fact, was not monotheistic but henotheistic, acknowledging not the singular 'one true God of all that is not God', but only one god among many as its own particular, national god. Isn't that the very nationalist idolatry that has just wrecked Europe in the recent war? Judaism exalts the righteousness of God as something more valuable than Christian love, but, as said above, Christian Trinitarianism harmonizes God's properties and does not set them against one another. So God is not the God of one nation only but of all; He is just, but also loving; wise, but also powerful (60). So the first part of *Defence of the Truth* ends.

In conclusion, we can safely judge that Osuský's philosophizing is ad hoc and eclectic and altogether articulated in the service of his theological agenda. In another vein, we could argue that just this engagement with the thought world of his own time, in which the most pressing contemporary questions are raging, delineates a better theological method than either the systematic apologetics of merely liberal theology or the wagon-circling of conservative reaction. There is little chance that Osuský knew of his near contemporary, the American philosopher and friend of William James, Josiah Royce. Despite the tendentious apologetics, it is clear that in his more curious and less defensive moods he would have much appreciated Royce's statement concerning a proper hermeneutical method in theology. Royce justified 'philosophical' exploration of Christian creedal themes on the grounds that, 'familiar as these… ideas are, they are still almost wholly misunderstood, both by the apologists who view them in the light of traditional dogmas, and by the critics who assail the letter of the dogmas, but who fail to grasp the spirit'.[42] What is needed, Royce argued, is an approach to Christianity as a 'problem', that is, 'at least provisionally, not as the one true faith to be taught, and not as an outworn tradition to be treated with an enlightened indifference, but as a central, as an intensely interesting, life problem of humanity, to be appreciated, to be interpreted, to be thoughtfully reviewed, with the seriousness and the striving for reasonableness and for thoroughness which we owe to every life-problem whereupon human destiny is inseparably interwoven'.[43] Royce thus sought a method, that is, in distinction

[42] Josiah Royce, *The Problem of Christianity* (Washington, DC: The Catholic University of America Press, 2001), 74.

[43] Royce, *The Problem*, 61.

from partisan apologetics and equally partisan polemics, which would investigate hermeneutically just what it was that creedal Christianity was trying to communicate. I see this quest less in Osuský's ad hoc 1946 apologetics, still redolent with themes from liberal theology that are in continuity with the text book on the history of religion, but from his new theologizing out of the Scriptures provoked by the double plague of fascism and Bolshevism, to which we now turn.

2

Resistance to Fascism and the Turn to the Bible

Institutionally, Osuský gave thirty years of his life to the establishment and cultivation of what is today called the Protestant Theological Faculty of Comenius University in Bratislava. This was always a struggle for recognition as also for its material existence. For sixteen eventful years during this academic work, Osuský was also the bishop of his church's Western District and thus a regular preacher at the Great Church, as it is still called, in Bratislava. But his passion was for theological education. In 1946, at the age of fifty-eight, he voluntarily resigned from his episcopal duties in order to dedicate his remaining years to the theological school, only to be forced into premature 'retirement' and made *persona non grata* a short four years later.

One student, who later went on to become bishop of the church's Eastern District, remembers him as a teacher, in this way:

> In the courses at the seminary Dr. Samuel Štefan Osuský awoke in me the greatest interest. He taught us the history of philosophy, psychology, sociology, disciplines that stick tightly to life. In the history of philosophy he led us on from the most ancient times and also noted individual philosophers according to their religious profile. He also pointed us to the fact that one who wades through the waters of philosophy and science cannot be an atheist. In him faith and reason were not in opposition, because true science and biblical faith complement each other and thus stand in a mutually harmonious relationship. He lectured by memory. He knew the doctrine of individual philosophers accurately and wrote for us *The First Slovak History of Philosophy*. This work is very valuable for it is written in understandable language and we very gladly and easily studied and learned difficult things from it … From Dr. Osuský I learned to put philosophy into the service of religion and to understand religion and to interpret it practically in harmony with science. So he placed the emphasis

> not only on metaphysics but also things of social and ethical significance. I am grateful also to the professor and bishop, Dr. Samuel Štefan Osuský, for many practical stimulations for preaching and oratory. Osuský was an outstanding thinker, a Christian and Protestant theologian, and also a captivating speaker. Neither can we forget his Slovak patriotic profile, which was not chauvinistic, but in tune with the spirit of Slavic mutuality and brotherly cooperation with the Czechs in the fields of religion, culture and politics.[1]

Inspired by Osuský, this student, Július Filo, Sr., went on to publish a number of studies in philosophy ranging from John Locke to Tomaš Masaryk. He was father to Július Filo, Jr., who later became the general bishop of the church (1994–2006) and still works as the chair of the department of practical theology in Bratislava. The elder Filo's testimony to Osuský as teacher gives us a vivid profile of his public persona.

In this chapter we will trace Osuský's resistance to the rising tide of fascism. Domestically, he resisted the 'political Catholicism' of the Hlinka National Slovak Party, which culminated in the wartime regime of an autonomous and authoritarian Slovak state allied with Nazi Germany. Of special interest in these events is exploring the occasion for Osuský's turn to the Bible in the struggle under and, finally openly, against fascism. 'Turn to the Bible' may be, however, a somewhat misleading phrase. As we have already seen, Osuský was never far from the Bible as the matrix of his faith. He speaks sweetly of learning his Bible stories as a child on his mother's knee. He was a pastoral preacher from the beginning of his career in a church tradition in which preaching *is* the exposition of biblical texts. As we have seen in *War and Religion* and *Defence of Truth*, both in ethical analysis and in apologetic writing the faith of the Bible, as understood in Osuský's tradition of moderate Melanchthonian Lutheranism, is always presupposed and often explicitly articulated. And difficulties in professing that faith, as in the matter of the birth of Christ from Mary the Virgin, are owned and not denied.

So, by 'turn to the Bible,' I have in mind instead a disciplinary shift, neither abandoning all that he had learned from philosophy and modern science and history, nor a retreat to the kind of dry, scholastic dogmatism still alive at his time in orthodox Lutheran circles, let alone to know-nothing fundamentalism. Instead, by 'turn to the Bible,' I refer to his seeking and finding an exposition of scriptural texts to speak in their own voices, yet at the same time theologically, to the dire circumstances in which he and his audience found themselves. It is

[1] Július Filo, Sr. *Spomienky a úvahy: Láska zraňovaná aj uzdravujúca* [Reminicences and Essays: Love Wounded and Love Healing] (Prešov: Vydavatestvo Michala Vaška, 1998), 67–8.

important to bear in mind, then, that Osuský's 'turn to the Bible' entails neither a repudiation of his secular learning, nor a return to an idle form of theological discourse that is incapable of speaking to current events but constructs ivory towers by deliberately ignorant proof-texting.

An excellent illustration of the foregoing claim, and in fact the text that marks the point of Osuský's turn to the Bible, is the lecture he presented at a theological conference to an assembly of pastors in Ružemberok in 1937, that being when the Czechoslovak democracy palpably felt itself pressured on either side by Hitler's Nazi Germany and Stalin's Soviet Union. Using the skills he had acquired from secular disciplines, Osuský undertook an examination of the modern secular movements of Leninism, Fascism and Nazism at face value as 'philosophy', or 'worldview', which, if followed consequently, would entail predictable behaviours. While this analysis of the twentieth century ideologies is in itself impressive, Osuský's analysis shows the additional power of a straightforward, traditionally Lutheran, theological critique of these movements as pseudo-religions. While a contemporary student enjoys the luxury of knowing the outcome of previous events, what is striking, moreover, is the prescience, in 1937, of Osuský's analysis. As a Slav who had read *Mein Kampf*, Osuský knew exactly what Hitler intended for him and his kind.[2] Slovak fascists, including a handful of Lutherans, were blind to this, and this blindness has an arguably theological explanation which Osuský laid out for his auditor in the lecture. Osuský's theological commitment, via the Czechoslovak leader Tomaš Masaryk, to democratic governance and liberal principles, and his Christian, that is, non-Marxist, socialist commitment by way of the Swiss Leonhard Ragaz (1868–1945),[3] cries out through the decades for contemporary appreciation.[4]

In this chapter we will take note of this public intervention in 1937 as well as Osuský's 'Pastoral Letter on the Jewish Question' (1942), co-authored with General Bishop Vladimír Pavol Čobrda (1880–1969). We must be engaged, on the way, in considerable reconstruction of little known history to lay bare the

2 On 'intentionalism', such as Osuský might be charged with here, see Lucy S. Dawidowicz's response to her critics in the 'Introduction of the Tenth Anniversary Edition' in *The War against the Jews, 1933–1945* (NY: Penguin, 1987), xvii-xxxiii.

3 Vasil Gluchmann, *Slovak Lutheran Social Ethics*, Studies in Religion and Society, Vol. 37 (Lewiston, Queenston, Lampeter: The Edwin Mellon Press, 1997), 58, 70.

4 At the conclusion of his ground-breaking study, Robert P. Ericksen, *Theologians under Hitler* (New Haven and London: Yale University Press, 1985) pointed to such non-theological factors (187): 'We can best avoid the Nazi error by heavily stressing the values of the liberal, democratic tradition, humanitarianism and justice, and by conscientiously probing history with a view towards its significance for contemporary decision making' (191).

actual occasion, and thus the actual import, of each writing. In conclusion, we will also examine the third part of Osuský's post-war *Defence of the Truth* on Protestantism. Osuský's diatribe in this final section of the 1946 apologetics against Roman Catholicism is a regrettable act of theological revenge following the catastrophe of 'political Catholicism's' alliance with fascism. Consideration of it is a wholly unsavory experience for those raised on the ecumenism of the Second Vatican Council, renewed now under the reforming papacy of Frances. But it serves today as a needful reminder of how almost the entire pre-conciliar European Catholic world opted for authoritarianism in varying shapes and to varying degrees in the 1930s and 1940s. So a preliminary word on the rise of Slovak Political Catholicism as a fascist phenomenon is next in order.

The Hlinka Slovak People's Party and Fascism

The Roman Catholic Church hierarchy in Upper Hungary had been officially allied with the imperial Hungarian regime until the time of the empire's dissolution in the aftermath of the First World War. This transformation demanded a quick and dramatic shift; Jews on this territory, for a counter-example, had learned the Hungarian and German languages to negotiate their precarious way during imperial times, but rarely had they learned the language of the common, working people, the Slovaks. This alliance with the old power-structure, reinforced by a language barrier ever present in daily relationships, served Jews ill, as we shall see, during fascist times. But Slovak Roman Catholics were quick to realign themselves after the decline of the Hungarian Catholic hierarchy. 'A powerful movement for Slovak autonomy within Czechoslovakia grew, championed by Andrej Hlinka [1864–1938], a charismatic Catholic priest whose influence became so profound that the party he founded and led was officially renamed Hlinka's Slovak People's Party [after his death]. Starting in 1923 it was the most powerful Slovak political party… The Slovak National Party, led by the Lutheran minister and much admired writer and poet Martin Rázus [1888–1937, whom we encountered earlier in Osuský's *War and Religion*], also espoused an autonomist position but was much smaller and less important' than Hlinka's party, which was often called the Ľudáks (that is, perhaps, etymologically deriving from the Slovak word for people, *l'ud*, hence, the 'populists').[5]

[5] Palka, 17. Palka's maternal grandfather, Milan Hodža, was a Slovak Lutheran and the single Slovak to serve as prime minister in the first Czechoslovak republic at the time of its dismemberment by

'Autonomy', in this inter-war period, refers to the creation of a Slovak parliament for the eastern third of Czechoslovakia, which would legislate in all matters except those concerning Czechoslovakia as a whole, along with a Slovak judiciary and with Slovak as the official language.[6] Hlinka was a fervent Catholic with 'conservative' social and political views against the liberalism of democratic capitalism, building on the policy of industrialization promoted during his youth in the Hungarian empire as the way to progress and modernization.[7] For a rural and agricultural land centred on village life, this policy was massively disruptive socially and brought in its wake all the well-known ills of exploited workers, alcoholism, crime and prostitution. Already, in 1906, Hlinka fell out of favour with the Hungarian church hierarchy and was imprisoned by the state authorities on charges of sedition for his priestly agitation on behalf of the oppressed Slovak common people of his parish. A massacre of pro-Hlinka parishioners at the consecration of a church building, whose construction the then imprisoned Hlinka had supervised, led to a European-wide scandal.[8]

Hlinka was a major player in the wartime and post-war negotiations that led to the First Czechoslovak Republic. From there he went on to serve in the Czechoslovak Parliament, during its twenty years, as leader of the democratic opposition, as he opposed the secular tendencies of the predominant Czechs. So it is intelligible how this hard-working, socially conscious, Slovak patriot and populist priest rose to prominence, although he was not very well educated, and given to crude demagoguery, especially targeting Jews.[9] It is probably a mercy that he died in 1938. After the fall of communism, rehabilitators had his portrait as 'father of the nation' adorn the 1000 crown paper currency, although not without controversy. It was Hlinka's disciples and followers who lived to play out roles of naïve or willing collaboration with Nazism.

By the end of his life, Hlinka, like many Catholics in the 1930s, was seeking a third way, between liberal and democratic capitalism on the one side and Soviet Bolshevism on the other, which would conform to Catholic teaching on social solidarity. And, like many Catholics of the time, Hlinka saw models for such a third way in authoritarian figures like Salazar in Portugal and Dolfuss in

Hitler. Palka's excellently researched study provides an indispensable perspective on this to the English-speaking world. On Hlinka's 'charismatic' leadership, see Palka, 255.

6 Palka, 49; see also 261.

7 Palka, 235.

8 Palka, 245.

9 Linda Osyková amply documents this demagoguery in her 'Protižidovská Agitácia v Druhej Polovici 30. Rochov 20. Storočia na Slovensku', in *Riešenia Židovskej Otázky v Spojeneckých Krajinách Nacstického Nemecka* [The Solution to the Jewish Question in the Allied Regions of Nazi Germany] (Banská Bystrica: Múseum Slovenského Národného Povstania, 2012), 30–46.

Austria. The chief of his political disciples who carried on after his death was another priest, Jozef Tiso, who, as leader of the 'moderate' wing of the Ĺudaks, became first prime minister and then president of Slovakia as it was being split off from Czechoslovakia by Hitler. Vojtech Tuka and Alexander Mach, prime minister and minister of propaganda respectively when Tiso became president, were leaders of the 'radical' pro-Nazi wing of the Hlinka party. This difference in miniature between Hlinka radicals and moderates reflects a difference akin to the Hitler-Mussolini differentiation, that is, between the virulent, biologically based racial 'science' of Nazism and the ethnic chauvinism and populist authoritarianism of Italian fascism.

In October of 1938, Hitler had approved of autonomy for Slovakia as a way of intensifying pressure on the Prague government of still intact Czechoslovakia to surrender to his demands for the Sudetenland. When this Slovak autonomy within Czechoslovakia came about, the Hlinka party ascended to power in Slovakia, with Tiso as prime minister. Its first aim 'was to build a monopoly position in the political, economic and cultural life of Slovakia by destroying the existing political structure'. The Communist Party was banned in October, and the Social Democrat Party in November. Echoing fascist and Nazi rebukes of the 'chaos of parliamentarianism', the 'voluntary simplification' of political life which the Ĺudáks initiated culminated in the merger of all the smaller agrarian and nationalist parties with Hlinka's Slovak People's Party.[10] Trade Unions were reorganized on a religious basis, while other units of civil society were abolished, and in their places came the establishment of a paramilitary force, modelled on the Nazi SA, the Hlinka Guard and thereafter the Hlinka Youth, reflecting Germany's Hitler Youth. 'The process of building an anti-democratic authoritarian system contained all the usual features, characteristics, methods and procedures of similar developments in other authoritarian and fascist countries, with some nationally specific features'.[11] Here, as elsewhere in Europe, 'the antidemocratic measures were more or less tolerated or accepted by the population, because the achievement of a "united front" and the calming of the political scene were regarded as priorities'.[12] That process and acquiescence included the cultivation of enemy images, especially of erstwhile brothers, the Czechs, and longtime neighbours, the Jews.[13]

[10] Valerián Bystrický, 'Slovakia from the Munich Conference to the Declaration of Independence', in *Slovakia in History*, 161.

[11] Ibid.

[12] Ibid., 162.

[13] Ibid., 163–5.

The Ľudáks organized elections with a single list of candidates, beginning with a plebiscite held in December 1938 'with only one question, "Do you want a new free Slovakia?"'.[14] In February of 1939, Germany informed the Ľudák government in Slovakia that if they did not declare independence from Czechoslovakia they would be reabsorbed into Hungary in the new order of Europe that the Nazis were planning.[15] The central government in Prague tried to intervene in March, even dismissing Tiso from office.[16] Summoned to Berlin, Tiso then negotiated Slovak nation-state autonomy in exchange for a military defence treaty with Nazi Germany.[17] Tiso, prime minister from October 1938, was now elevated to the presidency of the so-called First Slovak Republic, and in 1942 received the official title, *Vodca*, the Slovak language equivalent of *Duce* or *Führer*.[18] In Tiso's own words: 'The party is the nation and the nation is the party. The nation speaks through the party. The party thinks in place of the nation'.[19] Mimicking the Nazi policy of *Gleichschaltung*, 'coordination' of existing sub-cultural entities with the National Socialist worldview, the Ľudáks instituted a policy of 'unification', with, as mentioned above, the 'Hlinka Guard and the Hlinka youth… modelled on fascist organizations abroad'.[20]

One historian accurately characterizes the church situation under Slovak fascism in this way:

> The Christian churches in Slovakia had a specific and somewhat contradictory role in the internal system of the state, which proclaimed its allegiance to Christian ideology. The Roman Catholic Church held a dominant position among them, with more than two million inhabitants declaring Catholicism as their religion. The Catholic Church had close ideological and personal connections to the new state and its regime. The prime minister was a Catholic priest, and dozens of other Catholic Church dignitaries and laymen held positions in the Diet of the Slovak Republic, State Council, structures of the ruling state party, Hlinka Guard, Hlinka Youth and so on. The official representatives of the Protestant Churches [which would include Osuský] were in the position of a sort of loyal opposition to the regime, which often transformed into a kind of resistance.[21]

14 Ibid., 169.
15 Ibid., 171,
16 Ibid., 172.
17 Ibid., 174.
18 Ivan Kamenec, 'The Slovak State: 1939–1945', in *Slovakia in History*, 177.
19 Cited by Kamenic in ibid., 178.
20 Ibid.
21 Ibid., 179–80.

The same historian informs that 'the regime was based on three ideological pillars: a Christian world-view, Slovak nationalism and corporate solidarity', although in practice only the nationalism 'prevailed'. But herein lies a great irony.

Much to the incomprehension of the Ľudáks, another kind of patriotism grew to fuel the 'anti-fascist, anti-German resistance'. Just as problematically for the Ľudáks, this historian maintains, the 'Christian world-view' from the papal encyclicals that the Slovak state invoked in fact 'clashed with the national socialist ideology imported from Nazi Germany'. Furthermore, the fascist 'corporatism', allegedly a conceptual twin of Catholic notions of community and solidarity, was opposed in Slovakia by the small but influential *Deutsche Partei*, which had Nazi Germany's ear; the German enclaves feared that 'corporatist arrangements would erode their privileged status in the existing order'.[22] All such entanglements and cross-currents must be borne in mind, as we shall see, when sifting through Osuský's end-of-the-war attempt to disassociate Christianity and Protestantism from deeply compromised Roman Catholicism.

The moderates and the radicals among the Ľudáks were in any case 'conservative-clerical' and 'radical-fascist' respectively. This is not a distinction without a difference. The intervention of the papal nuncio in the summer of 1942 convinced Tiso that the Jews he was then deporting to Poland for resettlement were in fact headed for mass liquidation, and so the shipments ceased until the Nazi occupation of Slovakia in the autumn of 1944.[23] There is evidence, too, as we shall see, that it was the Tiso government's intervention that led to the release of Osuský and Čobrda from Gestapo imprisonment and interrogation in the winter of 1944. Ironically it was Tiso's 'priestly dignity' and the popular support it lent him and his populist regime that thwarted the efforts of the radicals under Tuka and Mach to 'complete the national socialist revolution'. One could say with some justice that the Tiso wing mitigated greater evils with lesser ones.[24] Yet, prior to 1942, both wings 'fully agreed on the necessity to build a totalitarian system, on the closest collaboration with Germany and on the need to

22 Ibid. 183.

23 Ibid., 188–9, though Kamenic does not mention the intervention of the Vatican and accounts for the survival of Jews from 1942 to 1944 in other ways. On the Vatican intervention, see Yeshayahu A. Jelinek, 'The Catholic Church and the Jews in the period from spring 1942 to spring 1944 in Slovakia', in *The Tragedy of Slovak Jews: Proceedings of the International Symposium at Banská Bystrica, 25th to 27th March 1992* (Banská Bystrica, Datei, 1992), 125–42; for a much sharper judgment against Tiso, see Viera Kováčová, 'Dr. Jozef Tiso a riešenie Židovskej otázky na Slovensku' in *Riešenie Židovskej otázky*, 46–54.

24 Ibid., 185.

"solve" the Jewish question'. After the war, Tiso was tried, condemned and hung by the neck until death for his disastrous misjudgments.

One final note remains on the 'Jewish question' in Slovakia at this time. Jews had long lived in the territory of Upper Hungary, and indeed Bratislava, then named Pressburg in German and Pozsony in Hungarian, was something of a centre for Judaism. In modern times following legal toleration Jews had prospered under the Hungarian Empire; emancipation in the course of the nineteenth century saw a blossoming of creative energy, especially into entrepreneurship under the capitalist development policies of the empire. As elsewhere in Europe, this combination of massive social change and Jewish economic success led to the perception, laden with resentment, that the Jews had allied themselves with foreign interests and profiteered off exploited native workers. In this context, Tiso's 'Christian' solution to the Jewish question was to expropriate the unjustly accumulated wealth of Jews and to send them into 'labour camps' where they would learn to work for a living, just like the native workers whom they had exploited. When Nazi Germany demanded the shipment of Slovakia's Jews to Poland – many already interred in such labour camps – for 'resettlement', fascist Slovakia actually became the one and only European nation to reimburse Germany for the transportation costs. Yet, as mentioned, when the true fate of the deported Jews was learned, the shipments stopped. The behavior of the Tiso regime makes sense when we grasp that, for them, the 'Jewish question' was neither racial nor religious, but an economic and class problem. The revolutionary-fascist solution to a perceived problem of economic injustice was expropriation of unjustly acquired wealth and retraining of the privileged in labour camps. This treatment of the Jews as class enemies was coupled with distrust concerning Jewish loyalty to the new Slovak state as a result of the Jews' traditional Hungarian sympathies.

'*The Philosophy of Fascism, Bolshevism and Hitlerism*' (1937)[25]

Osuský's prescient analysis in this lecture on political philosophy is in keeping with his disciplinary specialization, as he notes at the outset, in philosophy and

[25] My translation of this lecture appears as the Appendix in Paul R. Hinlicky, *Before Auschwitz: What Christian Theology Must Learn from the Rise of Nazism* (Eugene, OR: Cascade, 2014), 193–220. All the citations from Osuský's lecture are taken from this translation, as are some of the contextual data from my introduction to it there. Osuský's lecture originally appeared in *Styri Prednasky* [Four Lectures] (Mikulaš: Tranoscius, 1940).

the social sciences. But his lecture was one among others in a collaborative effort with colleagues from the theological faculty. Thus it helps to learn a little about his co-lecturers on the occasion of the November 22, 1937 gathering of the pastors. Dr Jan Jamnický (1878–1967), professor of Pastoral Theology and Church Law, lectured on the 'The Essence of Preaching the Word of God and the Contemporary Problem of Exegesis', in which he engaged knowledgably with Karl Barth's new summons to theological exegesis, while also refusing to separate pneumatological from historical understanding. Appealing to the Luther rule of *tentatio, oratio, meditatio,* he connected scientific-historical exegesis with Luther's description of preaching in the church, where 'nothing else will take place but that God will converse with us in His Word and we will converse with God in hymns and prayers'.

Dr Ján Beblavý (1898–1968), professor of Systematic Theology, lectured on the Faith and Order meeting that had taken place earlier that year in Edinburgh, interpreting in a Lutheran way its consensus statement on the doctrine of the church. He claimed that, similarly to Jamnický's acknowledging of the new impulses coming from Barth, the anti-doctrinal liberal theology[26] of the previous century had committed a great error in regarding the church as a human work. Beblavý called his auditors back to Luther's teaching of the church as the creature of the divine Word; this summons had as its background Beblavý's claim that 'the majority of German liberal theologians supporting the new regime have betrayed the church of Christ and entered into the service of German racism'.[27]

We meet again on the podium of the theological conference Osuský's old nemesis, pastor Juraj Struhárik (1893–1969), who lectured on the 'Battle of the Spirit against the Flesh in the Church and in Church Life'. Here he took up Luther's insight that the Pauline battle is not the Platonic-Stoic conflict between emotion and reason, but between the spirits of human self-reliance and of reliance on God. He applied this principle not just to the individual Christian but to the visible Church in history as a field of battle: 'the Church becomes flesh … by a collective divinization of the body, the blood', so that 'the chief

[26] Beblavy's indictment – that the German Christians' ranks were filled with liberal theologians – has been justified by recent historical research; cf. Doris L. Bergen, *Twisted Cross: The German Christian Movement in the Third Reich* (Chapel Hill, NC: The University of North Carolina Press, 1996); Richard Steigmann-Gall, *The Holy Reich: Nazi Conceptions of Christianity, 1919–1945* (Cambridge: Cambridge University Press, 2003); Susannah Heschel, *The Aryan Jesus: Christian Theologians and the Bible in Nazi Germany* (Princeton, NJ: Princeton University Press, 2008). See further the discussion in Hinlicky, *Before Auschwitz*, 14–43.

[27] *Four Lectures*, 74.

virtue is the preservation of a pure race and the chief sin the mixing of races'.[28] Stuhárik and Osuský had reconciled by this time, alike recognizing the overarching threat coming upon them from Germany. Like Osuský, Struhárik was imprisoned in 1944; and again, by the communists, in 1962–3.

In short, a collective appeal to Luther and protest against the race theory-theology of the German Christian movement characterized the lectures surrounding Osuský's that were presented on that autumn day in 1937, forming with him a united front against the gathering storms. So when we turn to Osuský's analysis of the sources that inspire fascism, and Hitler's race-biological variant of fascism, we cannot be in doubt about the specifically, indeed traditionally, Lutheran theological front in which he stands with his colleagues.

Osuský traces the sources of fascism back to Machiavelli, whose work, *The Prince*, he calls 'the first teacher of Mussolini and his fascism. It is only necessary to insert the word, "Duce", in place of the word, "Prince", to see this'. The trend to replace the church with the nation or its political sovereignty, as the object of human veneration arose in the Renaissance, but its crystallization in modern fascism is articulated by the 'official philosopher of fascism, Giovanni Gentile'. Osuský sees Gentile as starting out from Hegel's idealism, but 'over against the speculative and intellectual characteristics of Hegel, it is also voluntaristic and actualistic' like Bolshevism. The 'foundation of Gentile's metaphysics is the act of knowing in the sense of action and this, furthermore, in the sense of a creative act of mind'. Only this is 'alive', according to Gentile: 'the ego in its act of consciousness. Reality is only comprehensible to the extent that it is really thought. Thinking does not comprehend reality, as it is, but creates reality. Philosophy then is and ought to be a creator of reality'. This is the logic of the 'knowing subject in its activity of knowing… Truth is not the identity of things with reason, nor the identity of sensations and reason, but the identity of reason and will. To know means to think and to desire and that means to act. The one and only truth is the one that I create'. Gentile, who was Mussolini's ghost-writer, is thus exposed, and exposited by Osuský to lay bare the roots of fascism in the modern doctrine of the sovereign self. [29]

[28] Ibid., 102.

[29] In this author's systematic theology, an excursus was devoted to 'Augustine, Luther and the Critique of the Sovereign Self' to set my own theological project off from the 'profound Cartesianism of the modern project, on which philosophically the triumphs of Western political economy in technology are predicated and its hopes nourished'. I continued there with the thesis that 'Augustine would teach us that technology cannot save us from our greed, *concupiscentia* in his language, nor deliver us from the fatal dynamics of political sovereignty, the *libido dominandi*. Technology rather enables those dark forces'. Paul R. Hinlicky, *Beloved Community: Critical Dogmatics after Christendom* (Grand Rapids, MI: Eerdmans, 2015), 99–100.

If Osuský is right about the sourcing of fascism in the doctrine of creative knowing by the modern subject who resolutely decides for his own reality in the very act of subjugating material to comprehension, then fascism is an endemically modern possibility. While Osuský did not probe further than this basic observation about Gentile, focusing instead on the anti-democratic features of fascism, with its idolization of the state, he did note another root of fascism in the metaphysical view that war is the deepest nature of things. 'According to the view of fascism, life is motion, conflict, war. Death awaits whoever does not fight'. Or, again, 'life is not a game, fun, but a hard, merciless struggle. It demands work, sacrifice, heroism, physical and mental youthfulness'. Osuský quotes a fascist writer, whose statement he takes as something of a capsule summary of the spirit of fascism as he has exposed it: 'The light of a sublime myth shines in us aristocrats, in beings whose visage is frightful, who breathe freely in a world freed from Providence, teachers and reasons for things, but now looking into the shadows where there is no God and where they themselves are his creators'.[30]

The fascist appropriation of these philosophical themes for purposes of political sovereignty and imperialism is not ill-grounded, just as the Nazi appropriation of Nietzsche is likewise plausible.[31] Osuský's philosophical response to this state of affairs amounts only to his discernment of its horrific ethical implications and a protest against them in the name of the tradition of Christian Platonism. Osuský, that is to say, does no more than counter-assert in the fashion of a theological *obiter dicta* the transcendence of God as the foundation of an absolute morality. As we will see, this protest in the name of the collapsing Christian synthesis of European Christendom is not nothing; but neither was it, nor is it, adequate to the depths of the challenge.

Perhaps sensing the chasm yawning open up here, Osuský spends the remainder of his discussion of Italian fascism on the mutual accommodation that has been worked out between fascism and Roman Catholicism in Italy. He worries that under different conditions from those of his present day multi-ethnic and democratic Czechoslovakia, Slovak Catholics too would become

[30] In a book co-authored with the Deleuzian philosopher Brent Adkins, we argued that this 'plane of immanence', that is, the 'the world freed from Providence, teachers and reasons for things', in which nothing whatsoever is or can be transcendent, is, minimally, the philosophical reality of our times: the descent of the modern sovereign self into the dark night of post-modern nihilism. The metaphysical claim, of course, is even stronger: immanence does not merely seem to be our reality, but *is* reality. Brent Adkins and Paul R. Hinlicky, *Rethinking Philosophy and Theology with Deleuze: A New Cartography* (London and New York: Bloomsbury Academic, 2013).

[31] Steven E. Aschheim, *The Nietzsche Legacy in Germany 1890–1990* (Berkeley, Los Angeles and London: University of California Press, 1994). See also my discussion in *Before Auschwitz*, 117–24.

such fascists as the accommodating Italian Catholics. So he quotes the slogan on the party's battle flag: 'We go with Andrej Hlinka, the dictator of our hearts, souls, desires and hope'. Osuský allows that 'from the standpoint of the doctrine of Christ' the Catholic 'brothers' would have grounds to object to fascism. While he considers a nod to fascism understandable for Catholics, Osuský expresses astonishment at 'some Lutherans' who also greet its coming, 'either of ignorance about the essence of fascism or because the feeling of Lutheranism in them has completely perished'. This allusion is carefully to be noted; it gives the underlying rationale for the anti-Catholic diatribe that we will examine at the end of this chapter.

When Osuský in his lecture next turns to Hitlerism, he quite cogently zeroes in on the so-called Neo-Darwinian synthesis that arose with Mendel's work on genetic inheritance. The science of the matter aside, Osuský rightly sees the inference that fascists made from this scientific discovery: 'inherited human properties cannot be changed by internal means. This in particular supported the opinion that was everywhere being [simultaneously] introduced that there are gifted and less gifted races'. This inference from genetics leads us to the first of the two principles of the National Socialist worldview: *Blut*. As with fascism's doctrine that life is struggle, the Nazis now specify the nature of the struggle as racial: 'if in the struggle of natural selection the strong triumph and if the Germans are the higher race, so the race must go to war with the less valuable races and triumph'. Osuský traces the antecedents of this biologized Nazi view of the sovereign self of modernity to Fichte, Nietzsche, Spengler and Feder; he finds the synthesis of these sources in a careful examination of Hitler's 1924 *Mein Kampf*. He locates Hitler's central doctrine in the following quotation from it: 'The strong drive away the weak, because the life instinct always crushes the ridiculous bonds of the so-called humanity of individuals and in its place introduces the humanity of nature, which destroys and devours weakness, in order to grant a free field of play to actual strength'.

Humanity becomes great in this eternal struggle. This law of war in nature justifies the policy of conquest. As nature has laws, so also does the nation. The life of nations works by the law of race. 'The stronger must reign and must not mix with the weak and thus sacrifice their greatness'. Race creates everything on the earth: culture, technology, science. There is no equality of races. There are races which create culture, and races which appropriate culture, and races which destroy culture. The Jews are such destroyers of culture. Hitler regards it as a great deception to take Judaism as a religion. To the Jew religion is nothing else than a system of teaching about how to maintain the Jewish race and its material benefits. In order for the German nation to triumph in the struggle, then, it is necessary to preserve its racial purity by purging the Jew from its midst.

Thus we come to the second principal doctrine of Nazism's philosophy: the principle of *Boden*. 'If we want to acquire soil in Europe', Osuský quotes from *Mein Kampf*, 'there is nothing else to do than to conquer it at the expense of Russia'. 'The German Reich, as a state, has to take in all Germans', to subjugate other nations, 'not to Germanize the people but to Germanize the soil'. Osuský fails to note explicitly the correlation here with *Blut*, as a reflection of the Darwinian science of the interplay of genetic inheritance and habitat in the process of natural selection. But he rightly sees that the conquest of land represents for Nazism an 'agrarian imperialism' and in this agrarian sense names Nazism as 'the conservative revolution'. He explains what he means by this as a 'return to the old Prussian ideals [of the emblematic modern despot and enlightener, Frederick the Great!]' and he comments, 'many German ideas may be thus characterized as the actual Prussianization of Germany'.

Osuský devoted the remaining discussion of Nazism to refuting its anthropological science, which of course regarded Slavic peoples as 'uncultured, valueless, half-savage, with no right to exist on European soil'. He tried to demonstrate with scientific counter-evidence that 'black skin is not connected with a black soul', and that in Europe today there 'are no longer any pure races'. Moreover, racial mixing in fact advances culture as 'Europe itself, North American and even Germany itself' sufficiently prove. Neither 'science nor statistics prove that the Nordic race is the most valuable'. As Osuský drew to a close he cited Nazi propagandist Rosenberg as saying that to 'acknowledge freedom today for Czechs and Poles means to be wed to racial chaos. If he writes this way about us', Osuský infers, 'we can imagine what he writes, for example, about the Jews'. Although the concentration camps in Germany contain not only Jews, but also Christians, what matters is not religion but race. 'Look and see where Hitlerism is going!'

Osuský finishes the lecture with the same threefold schematization that later structured his book, *Defence of the Truth*: Religion, Christianity and Protestantism. 'In so far as bolshevism is atheistic and materialistic, we cannot accept it from a religious standpoint; so far as Hitlerism is naturalistic, we cannot accept it from a Christian standpoint; so far as Fascism is Catholic, we cannot accept it from a Lutheran standpoint … terror [and] the denial of individual freedom, we cannot accept either as Christians or as Lutherans, and Hitlerism we cannot accept either as Slavs'. In the lecture's very last sentence Osuský made an ominous allusion. He repeated his earlier expression of astonishment in the lecture in regard to fascism, with a further specification: 'how anyone from the Slovak Lutherans could sympathize, preach and write sympathetically about the philosophy of Hitlerism'.

We shall shortly see that this is a reference to a specific individual. For the moment, however, let us gather together the following analytical observations regarding Osuský's 1937 lecture which not only prophesied 'where Hitlerism [would be] going', but arguably stated why the predictable initiation of total race war would have to follow. First, Osuský has used the critical thinking skills acquired by his philosophical labours to analyse the thought of the powerful social movements of his time. Second, Osuský has used his theological inheritance as a vantage point from which to expose the pseudo-religious motive of these movements in filling the European spiritual vacuum created by the abandonment of Christianity. Third, Osuský has acted ethically to warn against the catastrophe that is aborning. As we shall see, his warning was sounded not entirely in vain.

Interventions in 1939 upon the Formation of the Slovak Republic

After the Second World War, Osuský published a record of the terrible times recently endured in *Service to the Nation II*, which included several of his essays from the time of the beginning of the autonomous Slovak state allied with Hitler, along with the 1942 Pastoral Letter on the Jewish question co-signed with Čobrda. Here we will consider two of his interventions from 1939, 'The Spiritual Import from Germany in the Past and Today',[32] published on the occasion of the Reformation remembrance, and, from earlier in the same year, 'Eternal Leader',[33] a critique of the posthumous cult of Andrej Hlinka. Both essays reveal Osuský moving away from his earlier theological liberalism towards a more classic Reformation commitment to the Christ-centred reading of Scripture.

Osusky begins the essay, 'Eternal Leader', with a citation from a newspaper. During trying times, the newspaper put it, 'the nation had also its Leader, who moved his nation and suffered for his nation, and offered the highest sacrifices for it: Andrej Hlinka'. Today, Osuský notes, the name of Hlinka is everywhere

[32] Samuel Štefan Osuský, *Sluzba Narodu* II [Service to the Nations II, hereafter *SN II*] (Svaty Mikulas: Tranoscius, 1947), 74–8. This volume is a collection of documents Osuský preserved from the period 1938–45 to record the memory of his church's opposition to fascism; the entire collection deserves serious study and historical-theological interpretation.

[33] Ibid., 79–82.

and the picture of Hlinka even appears on Lutheran altars. When Masaryk died, the Ĺudák magazines coldly, if correctly, reported on it with a few dry lines because they did not want to fall into the error, they claimed, of deifying Masaryk by calling him the 'Eternal' or 'Immortal' Leader with a capital 'L'. But these magazines commit the very error they criticized in the case of Masaryk. The chief of the Hlinka Guard, in an article published in their magazine, is cited as saying: 'He, Andrej Hlinka, does not live within the boundaries of past time. By his sincere faith he flew above time and remained eternally young. Hlinka Guard: On your guard! It is possible still to march forward on the way! Let Jesus Christ and Andrej Hlinka lead us onward on this way'. This bundling of Christ and Hlinka, Osuský, observes, has become typical: Christ and Hlinka arm in arm as equal with equal, and the Hlinka Guard following close behind.

Although we have many pictures from the life of Jesus and his disciples, everywhere it is the same: Jesus *leads* and disciples *follow*. This is certain: we human beings can *only* follow behind Jesus. So we could only affirm something like, 'With Andrej Hlinka but following Jesus Christ!'. Anything else borders on blasphemy. Another article in the same issue of the magazine formulated the matter differently. Here, it was said that 'they will march onward in the spirit of Hlinka'. But they, too, write of Hlinka as 'the Immortal One'. If that were not worrisome enough, Osusky notes how even the Lutheran pastor, Jozef Struhárik, conceded the need for a Leader, in an article in the Lutheran journal: 'The great armed nations today have leaders, men endowed with full power, dictators, who represent the nation, speak for the nation, decide for the nation, whom the nation obeys. Also our little and unarmed nation would need a leader, a great one similar to Moses, who led the nation through the terror of the Red Sea to the promised land where righteousness would dwell and the ancient desire of the people of God for justice and peace would be fulfilled'. Thus, also, Slovak Lutherans, on the model of Moses, are looking for a Leader.

Osuský asked: 'Does our nation have such a leader? Who is and who ought to be such a leader? One thing is very strange. We seek such a leader among the dead. Someone dead ought to be the "eternal Leader of the Slovak nation." So the newspapers write and that is also what we hear on radio broadcasts. Do we have to receive that without qualification? Can we agree with that?' Osuský answered his own question: 'We are a Christian nation. That fact binds us to resolve the question about a leader according to the will of God revealed in Scripture … does it accord with the doctrine of Christ to proclaim a mortal, or dead man, as the eternal leader of the nation?' According to Christian doctrine, the attribute 'eternal' belongs only to God Himself. When we transfer this eminent quality of God onto a human being, it is robbing God; it is blasphemous idolization of a creature. In fear of God and for the sake of conscience Christians cannot participate in such idolatry. In the Transfiguration story from Matt. 17.5 we hear the commandment of the heavenly Father concerning Jesus the Son: Listen to Him who calls you to take up your cross and follow!'

'I write this,' Osuský draws to a conclusion, 'so that it is clear to us Christians that the question of the Eternal Leader has been resolved for us long ago and by God Himself. Jesus Christ is the Leader fully authorized by God whom according to God's command we can and must blindly obey. There is salvation in no other name. The Eternal Leader is Jesus Christ alone. Only this Leader can lead the nation through the valley of death to resurrection. Do not seek for the nation a leader from among the dead. Only a dead nation can be satisfied with a dead leader'. But what has this 'Leader', Hlinka, actually said about himself? Osuský quotes him: 'My struggle is not national but religious'. And again, 'Only that which rests on Catholicism and breathes the Catholic spirit has true and enduring value, while everything else is here today and gone tomorrow. That applies for all our life and politics. Never forget that Andrej Hlinka told you that and that according to this you can judge and explain all of my political activity'. The quotation is a double-edged sword. It is an affirmation of the primacy of religion over against politics and it is also at the same time a warning to Lutherans and other non-Catholics of their precarious place in the nation that idolizes Hlinka.

As for Osuský himself, the same Barmen-like confession of the sole Lordship of Jesus Christ appears in his Reformation essay later in 1939. 'A standard piece of traditional Catholic polemic against the Slovak Lutherans', he begins, was that they are traitors to the nation because their faith comes from the German, Luther, and that their pastors consequently get their education in Germany. The Catholic propagandists say that our nation, and in the first rank its own spiritual leaders, should be on guard against such foreign imports so that the nation is not leavened by thoughts threatening its own profile and very existence'. 'The Western world of thought has always penetrated also to us in Slovakia', Osuský notes, either through neighbouring Germany or from elsewhere. He promises, however, that in this essay he will restrict himself to what came from Germany in the sixteenth century and what is coming from there today.

The sixteenth century Reformation was not in fact an innovation but rather a return to the apostolic foundation from which the Christianity of that time had departed. It was a critique of the ecclesial conditions of that time, not a negation of Christianity. It put Jesus Christ and His gospel back in the centre, in place of surrogates: in place of grace for sale by the purchase of indulgences it presented the grace of God, which God gives freely because God purchased it by the precious blood of the Lamb of God. The Reformation imported from Germany opened up, and made into the sole source of Christian faith, the Holy Scriptures, and made them known in understandable language. It set the thoughts of God against human speculation, the eternal Word of the living God against the word of mere mortals. It brought spiritual freedom, and together with that personal, individual responsibility before God, in place of conscience-tranquillizing collectivism.

This spiritual import came to us from Germany in the sixteenth century and found fertile soil among us, conquering in time almost all of Slovakia. Roman Catholicism did not know how to stop this advance of the Reformation with spiritual weapons but from the beginning sought to block it by secular power; even so, only after years of cruel Counter-Reformation did it succeed in the restoration of Catholicism in tandem with foreign rule. It was the good fortune of our nation that at least a minority endured faithful to the Reformation because the Reformation gave them the power to resist the attempts of foreigners to de-nationalize us.

But is it true today that all Protestants are fully faithful to the traditions and spiritual treasures of the Reformation? No, Osuský replies. But this is the consequence of an internal alienation from the Reformation, an alienation which is not influenced by religion but by an antireligious spiritual import, which has come to us not *from* Germany but by *way* of Germany, from the West; it contains the doctrines of nationalism, liberalism, materialism, those which exalt man and his reason in place of God, or matter in place of spirit. And this import from the West reaches to, and does its damage, in the ranks of the Roman Catholics. Indeed, precisely today, when Slovakia is politically friendly with its German neighbour, the danger of this spiritual import from Germany is greater than even before. The Ĺudaks explicitly declare that they take Italian fascism or German National Socialism as their model, even though they claim that their Catholicism guarantees protection from any strange and unchristian ideology.

We cannot deny, Osuský continues, the social achievements of German National Socialism, and indeed, on the social pole, there is much from which we can learn. But otherwise to copy its nationalist politics and to take over its state structures is dangerous. These are bundled together with its ideology, as soul is bundled together with body. And regarding this ideology no-one can claim that it is genuinely Christian, if only because one of its pillars is uncompromising antisemitism. If this were not so, resistance would not have arisen in Germany on both Catholic and Protestant sides. 'In my view', Osuský writes, 'Christianity and state totalitarianism are heterogeneous elements and thus not reconcilable. The continuation of National Socialist ideology cannot be realized without the accommodation of Christianity to it'.

'Even Catholics are not of one mind about Hitlerism, and some argue that, in the present crisis, alliance with Nazi Germany is the only alternative to nihilistic communism'.[34] But in response to this Osuský asks, *Tertium non datur*? As if we were forced to choose between these two antithetical political conceptions, although both make the state or collective the highest value. If the third way of Czechoslovak democracy is being rejected by political Catholicism today, Slovakia cannot escape being drawn towards fascism. The Catholic attitude towards Protestants is like the attitude of Germany towards other races: supremacy, lordship, humiliation. It is Catholic totalitarianism, state clericalism. So the real question is this: Why do Slovak Catholics not take a stand against today's spiritual import from Germany as they did in the time of the Reformation? Why today is the fear of Luther or hatred directed against him greater than to anyone else in today's German leadership? We can only conclude that there is indeed a formal, if not material similarity between Slovak Catholicism and German Nazism.

The 1942 'Pastoral Letter on the Jewish Question'[35]

By the time of May 1942, the Slovak fascist state had long been at war. In September of 1939, and in keeping with its military alliance with Nazi Germany, it participated in the invasion of Poland, reclaiming some smaller border regions that had been ceded to Poland the year before in the so-called Munich Arbitration. In June of 1941, several divisions of the Slovak army joined in the invasion of the Soviet Union. This action was not a glorious success, especially as the German invasion faltered. So many desertions occurred in the Slovak units that the Red Army was able to organize from their ranks Free Czechoslovak battalions to fight on its side. At home, the military leadership joined the

[34] For an alternative, Catholic, account of the terrible choice imposed on Tiso's regime, and of the eventual Catholic Christian resistance and support for the Slovak National Uprising, see Pavol Čarnogurský, *Svedok Čias* [A Witness to the Times] (1997: Bratislava), 83–107. In many ways, Čarnogurský's fate parallels Osuský's: both of them resisters to fascism who were later persecuted under communism.

[35] Pavel Čobrda and Samuel Štefan Osuský, 'Pastoral Letter on the Jewish Question (1942)' translated and introduced by Paul R. Hinlicky, *Lutheran Quarterly* XXIII/3 (Autumn 2009): 332–42 from *SN II*, 227–32.

conspiracy to rise up against the fascist regime, once the Red Army had broken through the Duklov Pass on the eastern frontier. But in May of 1942 all this was still on the horizon. The present reality was that in Poland during the winter of 1941–2, a state-of-the-art death factory had come on line in Auschwitz, a very short distance north of the Slovak border. Germany was demanding Slovakia's Jews for 'resettlement' in occupied Poland, and Slovakia not only willingly began to ship its Jews there but also, as mentioned, to compensate Germany for the trouble.

Because of the Nazi ruse regarding 'resettlement', it is difficult to gauge exactly what knowledge and what confidence in that knowledge actors in Slovakia had in the spring of 1942. Certainly, the question was layered over by the domestic tension between sceptical Lutherans and gullible Catholics regarding the 'political Catholicism' of the regime and its alliance with Nazi Germany. In this confusion, the form in which the 'Jewish Question' was being posed, in 1942, had primarily to do with the reportedly 'mass' conversions of Jews to Christianity then taking place – another sign that in Slovakia, where *religion* still mattered, Christian baptism might spare Jews the dire fate due to their *race*.

This matter of Jewish requests for Christian baptism was a question exclusively for the *Slovak* Lutherans. Much to the dismay of Osuský, the *German* Lutherans in Slovakia, who had lived together in church fellowship with Slovaks since the Reformation times, had separated to form their own Church, in accord with the spirit of 'German Christianity'.[36] Obviously, that realignment meant that no Jews would be seeking Christian baptism in German Christian congregations in Slovakia. Osuský bitterly lamented this decision of the resident Germans 'according to the contemporary political situation', since, he insisted, the Church should instead make all decisions 'according to the essence and spirit of the Church, the body of Christ', noting that in contemporary Germany the 'most faithful Lutherans' are those who 'are in suffering and concentration camps'. Their only defence is 'faithfulness to the gospel' (72). Yet in predominantly Catholic Slovakia, unlike in Nazi Germany, baptism could indeed provide some cover for increasingly desperate Jews, who had fewer doubts about the dire reports leaking back to them from Poland.

In this situation, the Slovak Lutheran Church found itself confronted with a question that it had never before faced: whether, and under what conditions, to receive Jews by baptism into its Christian fellowship. The Pastoral Letter

[36] See *SN* II, 69–73.

openly acknowledged at the outset that 'not even we Lutherans ourselves have been or are united in opinion about the Jewish question, and especially the question, whether or not to accept Jews into the Lutheran Church'. This now unavoidable question, too, was fraught with the tense domestic situation, as the Letter went on to note the 'unjustified and unjust attack' on Lutherans by the base innuendo coming from the Ĺudák media 'that the situation of the Jews is being used this way: to baptize those who can pay for it'. The political magazines thus accused the Slovak Lutheran clergy of opportunism, of baptizing Jews for financial gain. An important percentage, we may note in passing, of a pastor's income was acquired by the traditional practice of honorariums for pastoral acts like baptism, confirmation, marriage and funeral. Thus publicly questioned in regard to its integrity, the Lutheran Church needed urgently to establish a policy that was both a credible expression of its own convictions of faith and a refutation of the accusations of the Ĺudáks.

The Slovak Lutheran Church had taken a public, although more muted, exception to the 'racial theory' behind the Jewish Codex that had been previously adopted in Slovakia; hence it now called attention to those 'Jews who are already members of the Lutheran Church'. A 1941 memorandum had complained about the severity employed in gathering Jews into the labour camps, but accepted the policy of economic equalization, as it was pitched, as an action within the jurisdiction and competence of the state. It merely pleaded that this action proceed as humanely as possible. Yet the 1941 memorandum did insist, against the racial criteria enunciated in the Jewish Codes, that baptized Jews in the Lutheran Church should not have to wear the Star of David.[37] Given its reticence hitherto, the Pastoral Letter of 1942 now tells us that the General Presbyterium is taking the clear and 'principled position' that 'according to the doctrine and eternal gospel of Christ' it is 'impossible on national or racial grounds to reject Jews who present themselves to the Lutheran church'; hence, 'no legal regulation of the State exists which can forbid the baptism and reception of Jews into Christian churches'. Moreover, 'the social status or the material situation of those concerned may not be allowed to be decisive'.

The 1942 'Pastoral Letter on the Jewish Question', undersigned by the bishops Čobrda and Osuský, grounds this 'clear and decisive position' on the teaching of the Apostle Paul in Romans 9–11, arguing that the desire of Jews for baptism might be 'the inscrutable judgment and incomprehensible way of the Lord, by which he wants to lead all the unbelievers, including the temporarily rejected

[37] See *SN* II, 223–4.

people of Israel, to salvation'. Paul's theology of Israel is thus privileged over, say, Matthew's woes (in Matthew 23), or blood guilt (Mt. 27.25), or John's demonization (Jn 8.44) of the Jews. It is essential to note, accordingly, that the plight of the Jews is being framed in the Pastoral Letter not on general humanitarian grounds or by notions of human or civil rights. The latter, we have to bear in mind, do not legally exist in the fascist state; on the contrary, it is law, the 'Jewish Codex', that Jews have neither human nor civil rights. What do legally exist, at least on paper, are Christian churches with the right of free exercise in matters of faith. The vantage point, indeed the sole possible vantage point, from which the Pastoral Letter can see, think and judge the 'Jewish Question' in this situation is 'the doctrine and eternal gospel of Christ'. This vantage, moreover, privileges theologically God's irrevocable calling of the Jewish people in Romans 9–11 over against notions of irredeemable blood guilt and demonically hardened hearts. Scripture thus interprets Scripture, when Scripture itself is normed by the gospel of Christ; material criticism (*Sachkritik*) also of Scriptural passages that fall short of the gospel is standard operating procedure in theology as a (self-) critical discipline.

Since the vantage point adopted in the Pastoral Letter is accordingly interested in 'the Kingdom of God and the salvation of immortal souls', baptism must be regarded as a 'holy matter, a sacrament, a divine mystery with which we are not permitted unfaithfully to traffic'. Proper catechetical training for candidates by the pastor and examination by the elders of the congregation are prerequisite to reception into the church, the details of which the Pastoral Letter goes on to specify. With this policy now in place, the Pastoral Letter continues by stating disbelief that 'even one Lutheran pastor would use the situation of the Jews for booty'. But, to avoid any appearance of evil, the Letter announces the policy that 'it is possible to accept only a charitable donation for church purposes', that is, not for the pastor's personal gain. In the same breath, the Pastoral Letter goes on to lay the emphasis on gaining the newly baptized Jews 'for the local congregational societies and institutions… so that they do not want to be Church members only in name but want to work for the moral-religious, cultural and material elevation of their church'. Thus a positive integration of Jews into the Slovak Lutheran Church is not only envisaged but desired and actively to be sought.

The contemporary reader, fully aware of the horror of the Holocaust, may well be dismayed at this apparent exercise in 'churchianity', sifting gnats while swallowing camels. To be concerned with the proper procedures of church life while the ovens of the Nazi death camps are roaring only miles away seems not a little disproportionate. The detailed discussion of conditions for baptism seems to reflect misplaced priorities, given the enormity of the crime being perpetuated against the Jewish people, who desperately need Christians to cover them in their hour of need. But we must be wary here of the retrospective fallacy that imposes present knowledge and certainty onto past actors. The minority Slovak Lutheran Church's theological integrity has been called into question by the propagandists of an authoritarian regime engaged in war as an ally of Nazi Germany. The Pastoral Letter has to maintain the church's integrity and put on public display its gospel principles informing its principled decision to receive Jews in baptism, not on supposedly universal humanitarian grounds but on Christian theological ones. This stance, moreover, entailed rejection of a racial law intruding into its life and thus, from the state's perspective, an act bordering on civil disobedience. An appeal to universal rights under the conditions of fascism, on the other hand, would have been a purely utopian act. Appeal to the freedom of the Christian was both integral to the church's life and not altogether hopeless in a fascism that claimed also to be Christian. And in fact this churchly procedure bore some fruit.

Having acknowledged the political weakness of the church, we can now see how the Pastoral Letter in fact proceeded, on the sole basis of 'the eternal gospel and doctrine of Christ', also to speak against the 'transport of the Jews' that was contemporaneously occurring – the actual occasion for the Letter's production and communication. The Ĺudák propagandists had also been claiming that 'the Lutheran Church authorities have expressed agreement with the anti-Jewish measures'. But, the Pastoral Letter affirms, such 'reports do not correspond to the truth. No one requested the opinion or the agreement or permission of the Lutheran Church authorities. Nor did the responsible Church authorities, who alone are justified to interpret the general opinion of the Lutheran public, ever express agreement with the measures which have been undertaken'. So, to make matters utterly clear, the Pastoral Letter will now indicate the 'Lutheran position, faithful to the gospel of Christ' on 'the Jewish Question' and specifically on the deportations to Poland.

Before we turn to that, however, we must ask whether the Ĺudáks had any plausible grounds for the claim that the Slovak state had the Lutheran Church's assent to the transports that began in April 1942. Andrej Žitňan, in his 2008 dissertation, *The Lutheran Church in Slovakia 1938–1945: The Relation of Church and State in This Period*, has clarified the matter. The internal disunity to which the Pastoral Letter referred at the outset, and the incredulous and critical allusion Osuský had made to such Slovak Lutherans who could sympathize with

Hitlerism in the 1937 lecture, referred to Dr Bohuslav Klimo (1882–1952), a lawyer-politician who was both a member of the Council of State in the Slovak fascist government and the General Inspector of the Eastern District of the Slovak Lutheran Church, the highest lay position on the district level. Žitňan documents Klimo's antisemitism and admiration for Nazi Germany. Similarly, in an article that was allowed to be published during the Prague Spring, 'The Protestant Church and the Slovak State', historian Ján Ušiak wrote about Klimo:

> Dr. Bohuslav Klimo is very much on record in the papers of the Ministry of the Interior. There cannot be the least doubt about his devotion to the Slovak state and his fidelity to its leading ideology. The atmosphere of public and political life in the Slovak state completely harmonized with his spirit and character. Dr. Klimo already during the tumultuous times of the Munich Agreement declared at the opening of the assembly of the Eastern District [of the Slovak Lutheran Church]: 'For whether it is Marxism, or Bolshevism, or free thinking, or atheism, or freemasonry – it is all Semitism, only dressed in various robes.' From this citation it is clear that Dr. Klimo accepted the doctrine of Alfred Rosenberg and the thoughts of Adolf Hitler and publically proclaimed them before their official import into Slovakia.[38]

In a record of the session of the Council of State on March 26, 1942, which Klimo attended on the day before the beginning of the Jewish deportations, Žitňan finds a discussion regarding what the position of Klimo's church would be. 'Klimo expressed the view that it is necessary to look upon this problematic from a political rather than a religious perspective'. In this comment, Klimo drew on a dualistic reading of the traditional Lutheran Two Kingdoms doctrine. Klimo went on to recommend to the State Council, however, that, in harmony with his church's Memorandum concerning the Jewish Code, generous Presidential exceptions be granted to Jews otherwise destined for deportation. From the same record we learn that Alexander Mach (of the 'radical wing' of the Hlinka Slovak People's Party) warned the Council of State against 'intervening into the fate of Jews,' as Klimo had suggested. Klimo in the end supported Mach's stance. In turn, the Ĺudák media evidently drew precisely on this 'official' expression of a representative of the Lutheran Church. Thus the urgent need arose for the General Presbyterium to distance the Lutheran Church from

[38] Ján Ušiak, "Evanjelická Cirkev a Slovenský Štát" in *Kapitoly Odboja na Slovensku* [Chapters in the Resistance Movement in Slovakia] (Bratislava: Ustav dejín KSS, 1968), 24; see further, 29–30, where we learn that Klimo argued that under the protection of Nazi Germany Slovaks would gain the autonomy for which they had long yearned and that friendship with the land of Luther was natural for Slovak Lutherans.

Klimo and to discredit the claim that it supported the deportations. Authorized by the General Presbyterium 'after a long and serious debate' – which session must have included a face to face confrontation with Klimo – Čobrda was first drafter and Osuský the editor of the ensuing Pastoral Letter.[39]

Returning now to the analysis of the Pastoral Letter, we must note its assertion against Klimo's distorted reading of the traditional Two Kingdoms doctrine that the distinction between state and church by no means allows the State autonomy from the twofold rule of God:

> The Lutheran Church cannot and does not want to intervene into the jurisdiction of appropriate state offices and organs, which are called to resolve the [Jewish] question, but it is convinced that this question can be and therefore also must be resolved deliberately and consequently, justly, humanely and Christianly, conducting itself in accord with all Christian principles, founded on the eternal law of God and the teaching of Christ: acknowledging to all the right to life and the inevitably necessary material means and ways of making a living, along the entire way respecting the sacredness of family life, preserving also among the Jews human dignity, so that none of them would be able to feel injured on account of nationality, religion or racial membership.

Addressing its own constituency in the Slovak Lutheran public, where a litany of perceived grievances against the Jews made it possible for churchmen like Klimo to sympathize with Hitlerism, the Pastoral Letter conceded:

> The Lutheran Church does not turn from consideration of the fact that many Jews often and terribly sinned against the Slovak people and nation – in national political perspective as tenacious adversaries and enemies of all the Slovak national endeavours who always and in everything were ready instruments of violent Hungarianization;[40] and, in material, economic and social perspective as almost the exclusive owners of licenced bars and taverns, cunning middleman, businessmen and industrialists of every kind in whose hands, especially in East Slovakia, were almost all the business and heavy industry. The Lutheran Church is convinced that a better, more beautiful and more happy future for the Slovak people and nation in much depends on the wise resolution of the Jewish Question also in the Slovak State, because it is not possible that one, large portion of the citizenship, the Slovak peasants and workers, would have to work their hands to bloody, sweaty calluses all their lives while others live easily in all

[39] Andrej Žitňan, *Evanjelická Cirkev Augsburgského Vyznania na Slovensku v Rokoch 1938–45* [The Lutheran Church in Slovakia 1938–45] Phd. Dissertation (2008: Evanjelická bohoslovecká fakulta, Univerzity komenského v Bratislava), 147–8.

[40] The Imperial policy adopted late in the nineteenth century of suppressing indigenous languages and requiring in all public transactions and schooling the use of the Hungarian language.

> comfort and abundance, plundering the Slovak poor and living off the calluses of the Slovak people.

We can leave to the historians the relative merit of these perceived 'sins' of 'many Jews'. In politics, and in political interventions, *esse est percipio*. To gain its own audience, the Pastoral Letter had to acknowledge the perceived grievances against the Jews. More relevant, however, is the fact that Slovak hostility to the Jews in their midst was interpreted not along racial or religious grounds but on economic factors, deriving from the nineteenth century political alliance of Jews with Hungarian imperialism and industrialization policy. Yet, even if Slovak Lutheran antipathy had some such rationale, it did not exempt the Christian from the obligation of love, love also of perceived enemies.

Thus, the Pastoral Letter concludes with this contextually bold statement against the rationale of the antisemitic actions: 'For the race theory, as some proclaim it, opposes the Christian faith, which confesses with the Scriptures that the Creator of everyone and of all people is God ....'. On the basis of this spiritual opposition to Nazism, it testifies against the deportations:

> Unfortunately, we have had to be witnesses of such unnecessary, utterly ungrounded and unjustified blunders and crimes, which repel also purely human feeling and square neither with human righteousness nor with God's law, neither with doctrine nor love. And this would never have happened, if all had respected the pronouncement of the Minister of the Interior in his radio broadcast, which assured that Jews would not be injured and that they would deal with them politely, humanely and Christianly, because the only issue is that they, the Jews, have to work like other citizens. These lamentable swings of human passions,[41] witnesses of which we have been in many places, the Church cannot approve; it can only profoundly express sorrow over them and indict them. And if adherents of the Lutheran Church have committed these things, it must most decisively condemn them for it.

Striking is not only the willingness to accuse its own members of sin for support and involvement in the deportations, as we have just read, but also, impressively, the expression of the Church leadership's 'consciousness of its great responsibility before God and before the judgment seat of future generations', and accordingly its strict adherence 'solely to God's eternal law, Christ's gospel and the doctrine of our church, completely independent of any changing national or

[41] The apparent meaning here is that, in contradiction to the reasonable assurances in the radio broadcast, the decision of the Slovak Government to transport Jews to Poland was attributed to an irrational outburst of anger.

racial theories whatsoever, i.e., immature and unstable philosophical, political and social ideologies'. Žitňan rightly comments: 'Such an open, cutting, and direct criticism of the Slovak variation of National Socialism in the work of the document, which was directed to approximately 300,000 readers, was at least courageous, if not risky'.[42] What may seem questionable from a post-Holocaust perspective of human rights is in fact a demonstration of a particularly Christian possibility, by means of a traditional (but not dualistic) Two Kingdoms doctrine, no less, to speak concretely to and against a situation of legal criminality.

Žitňan comments that, after such an expression of protest against the policy of deportation, it is hard to imagine how the authors of the Pastoral Letter could credibly continue to declare their loyalty to the state. And, indeed, if it were not for the tensions within the Slovak state between its moderate and radical wings (Tuka tried to have Čobrda and Osuský removed from their episcopal offices in response to the Pastoral Letter), neither would the deportations have ceased by August of 1942 after the intervention of the papal nuncio with the Tiso regime,[43] nor would Čobrda and Osuský have escaped the fate[44] which finally caught up with them two years later after the suppression of the Slovak National Uprising. As it happened, however, both these Church leaders, and many of the 300,000 readers of the Pastoral Letter during these two intervening years, entered into the conspiracy to revolt, and overthrow the Ĺudák regime.[45] Žitňan discovered in the church archives an open letter from the covert Central Office of the Jews in Slovakia, dated in March of 1943, appealing for help from Christians. Osuský's correspondence and letter regarding this appeal shows that he recognized the despair of Jews who by this time knew precisely what fate awaited them if deported to Poland. It is not surprising then that Osuský and his people were increasingly turning towards insurrection as the only way actually to help Jews.

After the Nazi army in the fall of 1944 occupied Slovakia to suppress the uprising, the Gestapo arrested bishops Osuský and Čobrda. Osuský was held in isolation and experienced several intimidating interrogations between October 20 and December 24. After his release, he needed months to recuperate. Žitňan records the many attempts by his co-religionists to secure his release during

42 Žitňan, 149–50.

43 The Catholic Bishops in Slovakia also issued a statement in their church newspaper that similarly noted the economic grievances of Slovaks against Jews. While it did not, like the Lutheran statement, explicitly attack the racial theory of Nazism, it did invoke the Papal Encyclical from 1937, *With Burning Concern*, which condemned racism (Ibid., 153).

44 For a poignant account of a representative case of the suffering of Lutheran clergy for their support of the uprising, see John Palka's account of Pastor Jozef Bučko's martyrdom in *My Slovakia*, 66–71.

45 Žitňan, 151.

the imprisonment but, because Osuský was held by an occupying armed force, interventions with the Tiso regime were not immediately effective. Post-war testimony held that the greatest willingness within the Tiso regime to help secure Osuský's release came from the Minister of National Defence, a certain Haššik, who informed the Lutherans, however, that Tiso would have to concur with Osuský's release. The concurrence evidently came, and the Slovak regime intervened with the German ambassador to secure Osuský's release just before Christmas 1944.[46] We will pick up these events in the beginning of Chapter 4.

Defence of the Truth (1946): *A Vindication of Protestantism as the True Christianity*

In the years between 1942 and his imprisonment at the end of 1944, Osuský had been at work on his apologetics, *Defence of the Truth*, addressed especially to the Marxists, with whom his Lutheran co-religionists were joining ranks in the underground and then later in the uprising. We can now readily gather how part of this defence of Christianity to this audience under these circumstances was the need to sharply differentiate Lutheranism from Catholicism, which had virtually fused with the despised Ľudák regime in the eyes of Slovak Marxists. Osuský had not always been as hostile towards Catholicism as he will now appear. In 1939 he gave a public lecture, 'The Meaning of Slovak National History',[47] in which tried to correct the claims being made by 'political Catholicism'. He cites from a Ľudák author at the beginning of his lecture: 'The meaning of Slovak history proclaims an organic connection of Slovak nationalism with the principles of Catholic political science'. Against this claim, he argues, first, that the sense of Slovak national history must be drawn from the entire history of the whole nation, not only one part, even a large part, and not only from recent or short periods of that history. Second, the 'meaning' of history is a vague notion. What we are seeking is the ground or reason or goal of what is sought in the course of a people's journey. We can abstract such 'meaning' of what was valued and significant from the deeds and manifestations of the nation's chief or best sons, spirits or representatives. If we study Slovak history this way we see that the first basic idea is the religious one, the orientation on God:

[46] Ibid., 179–81.

[47] Samuel Stefan Osuský, 'Smyseľ slovenských dejín' [The Meaning of Slovak History] (1939) from the archives of the library of the Protestant Theological Faculty, Comenius University, Bratislava, accessed in 2014 with the aid of librarian Vlastislav Svoboda and Prof Dr Peter Gažík.

> Up until the 16th century the religious idea of Slovakia was the universal Christian one, and from then on it divided into Catholic and Protestant formations, and both created values and deposited them into the national treasury, each in its own way. If we begin imperialistically to lay claim to one at the expense of the other, we open the door, according to the witness of the past, to a war unworthy of Christianity and dangerous to the nation. In order to avoid that result, both have to be set alongside each other and seen from a higher angle of vision, namely, the battle for the doctrine of Christ and His work, because both have come forth from Christ. Thus the goal ought to be penetration of public life by Christ's Spirit – not Catholicism's.

Osuský can thus plead for the common root – a genuine Catholicism, in his mind – in Christ of both churches and argue that this common root clarifies Christianity's relation to culture, in one of his favoured metaphors, as leaven in the dough.

While, as mentioned already, to contemporary ears this writing in Part Three of *Defence of the Truth* is Osuský at his least appealing, it is understandable in a world in which the Catholic lands from Portugal to Hungary and Croatia, and from Italy to the German south, had endorsed fascism in varying ways and to varying degrees. Under Christendom, Christianity is as such and inevitably a political religion, as we noted above with the help of Peter Brown; doctrinal controversies are thus fraught with political implications. As decadent and outdated as such polemical theology is, and must be understood to be today, after the end of Christendom, in concluding this chapter on Osuský's theologically formed resistance to fascism we take note of his case that democratic socialism corresponds to the purest and best doctrine of Christianity in Reformation Protestantism. The shadow side of this claim is, unsurprisingly, the corresponding critique of 'political Catholicism' as the religious sanction of fascism.

The third and final part of *Defence of the Truth* is titled simply 'Protestantism'. But here especially we must bear in mind that the word being translated as 'Protestantism' is in Slovak (similarly as in German): *evanjelictvo*, meaning 'gospel Christianity'. The accent is not on protest but on the good news of Christ. Yet various 'Protestants' stemming from the sixteenth century Reformation understood this 'good news' sufficiently at variance from one another that they self-identified as 'Gospel Christians' according to differing official confessions of faith. Osuský is a representative, then, of the 'gospel Christians' of the Lutheran Augsburg Confession from 1530. Thus, as context demands, the word has been translated as 'Protestant' as in general signifying non-Roman

Catholic Christianity and as 'Lutheran' when Osuský is speaking specifically of church and theology that self-identifies with the tradition of Luther. Thus, at the outset of this third part he writes: 'Since we live in a period in which there is and probably also will be attacks on Protestantism among us, just as we have defended the truth of religion [as theism in Part One], and then the truth of Christianity [as the person and work of Jesus Christ in Part Two, to be discussed in the next chapter], so also now we will defend the truth of gospel Christianity' [as the Reformation's doctrine of justification by grace through faith] (95).

Osuský immediately assures us that he will make this defence of Protestantism with forbearance and without bigotry in spite of the attacks by Catholics, with love for the truth of God and all people. If in some instances the truth hurts, that cannot be helped and, in truth, what hurts can also heal. Osuský appropriates the concept of catholicity, taken as universality, as that which is spread across the whole world. He thus defines his Protestantism as 'evangelical-catholic'. To be sure, the attackers dispute this. They say that the founder of Roman Catholicism is Jesus Christ, the Son of God, while the founders of Protestantism are sinful men like Hus, Luther, Calvin, and so on. But this is a gross error, going back to the Lateran Council of 1215 concerning the saving nature of the church as such, by which the Roman church identifies itself with the church of Christ, indeed with Christ Himself. To be sure, there are Christian elements in Roman Catholicism, Osuský grants, but what is unbiblical, and of human, Roman, and papal origin is not from Jesus, and all this is designated by the word, 'Roman'. Citing 1 Cor. 3.11-13, Osuský asserts that, after a gradual slipping away from the true foundation, the reformers returned to the church its exclusive foundation in Jesus Christ, and thus renewed the old Christian church (96).

Osuský next invokes the formal principle of Protestantism, Holy Scripture, as the one source of faith and rule of life given with the canonical books. He cites a Catholic statement to the effect that the Bible does not have independent and decisive significance apart from the faith of the Church. Protestantism rejects this claim and educates Christians in faith and moral life only on the foundation of Jesus and the apostles. Protestantism demands the reading of Scripture so that in worship services the chief part is the witnessing of the Word of God (97). 'We don't have to look any further', he writes, 'than the Catholic translation of the New Testament into Slovak in 1913, where we read: "In Holy Scripture we do not have to search for the entire doctrine of faith nor regard Holy Scripture as the chief or exclusive source of articles of faith, or as the rule of faith... The Holy Church gives us the clear teaching of faith and morals, which we are bound to preserve in the reading of Holy Scripture. The Holy Church teaches us everything that God has revealed. Her teaching must be for us the rule of faith and life, because Christ left to the Church the duty and the right to decide about the correct sense of Scripture'" (98). Against this Catholic understanding of the Church above the Word, Osuský invokes Luther who 'correctly noted that the Church is given birth from the Word, so the Church is the daughter and not its mother'.

The concept of tradition in Catholicism, Osuský continues, is grounded in the claim that tradition is broader than Scripture, that tradition was first, and that in fact Scripture originates from tradition. 'It is true', Osuský concedes, 'that the gospel of Christ and the speech of the apostles were at first handed on only orally and only later were written down. Thus tradition has historical significance. But what was taken from tradition into Scripture is certainly more important than that which derives from Scripture … What was written in Scripture, collected and authorized, certainly stands closer to Christ and the apostles than that which originated later and was so hard to control' (99). 'What is written and preserved in Scripture is that which is fully sufficient for salvation. Tradition may be a broad powerful stream, but it is better to drink from the clear pure spring than the dirty, muddy river into which it flows' (99).

From the supposed authority of tradition come all the impossible and offensive claims of Catholicism: that it alone is truly Church and the others are not actually church; that Christ can be found only in it so that whoever wants God as Father must receive the Catholic Church as mother. Outside the Church there is no salvation. In this view, the Church cannot recognize tolerance; indeed, dogmatic intolerance is a moral duty. 'So it is evident that the Catholic Church does not distinguish between the invisible/ideal and the visible/real church' (100). The Protestant church is attacked for lacking the signs or properties of the true Christian church as one, holy, catholic and apostolic. But Lutherans affirm, following the Augsburg Confession Article VII, that the true church is there wherever the gospel of Jesus Christ is purely attested and the sacraments are served according to His institution. In fact Lutherans also receive these four signs of the true church. But in understanding what these signs or properties truly are, everything depends on the primacy of the gospel so that in the matter of the identity of the church we do not appeal to human merits but to divine grace.

By works it is impossible to obtain justification before God, but only by faith through divine grace. Moreover, by faith we do not mean accepting whatever the church preaches and teaches, but faith in the sense of trust, entrusting oneself to the will of God and the love of Christ, thus justification before God through the merits of Christ and sanctification by the Holy Spirit who calls believers to true holiness. Thus good works are truly good, not done to earn merit but out of duty and gratitude to Christ. Truly good works are not religious works seeking merit, special religious works like alms, fasts, pilgrimages or monastic vows, but living faith, as James writes in the New Testament, which manifests in deeds of love for others (102). Thus the unity of the church pertains to the invisible church, because visibly we all remain sinners; there are only greater and lesser sinners in the visible church. For this reason, we do not see either the unity or the holiness of the church unambiguously, but believe in the holiness of the church as an article of faith. They attack us Protestants for lack of unity. Really? Well, in all the Protestant churches there is unity in the founder, Jesus Christ, in Scripture and not in popes. Who stands closer then to Christ and the apostolic church? (103)

They declare that we are unchristian, in error, heretics simply because, as they say, only Catholics are right. But they replace the centrality of preaching the gospel with the unbloody sacrifice of the mass. Not that there is no preaching in Catholic services, only that it is not Scripture that is sounded, but rather only traditions and legends. And when the Word is preached, it has a secondary place. Where is it written that Jesus or the apostles served mass? (104) What do they understand by the mass? The mass repeats in an unbloody way, they say, the bloody sacrifice of the Son on the cross for sinners. Is that biblical? God once for all sacrificed His Son, as Hebrews teaches, but the Catholic priest puts himself above God, when every day he sacrifices Christ. But this is a continuation of pagan and Jewish sacrifices rather than divine service. Why do the priests sacrifice the mass every day except Good Friday? Are they saying that Christ's sacrifice counts only once a year and that the rest of time the priests must sacrifice? (105) No wonder that they offer mass in the dead Latin tongue that is incomprehensible, while we Protestants instead attest the Word of God in the mother tongue of our people (106).

Of the two sacraments instituted by Christ, we have only baptism in common with the Catholics. By baptism we become genuine members of the church catholic, yes, but members of the church of Christ, invisible, the true, universal church, not the Roman Catholic Church. The Catholic Church also has the Lord's Supper, but how many errors! Transubstantiation, even though Jesus teaches in Matt. 24.24: 'if anyone say to you, Here is Christ, don't believe him'. Another error is that they serve the sacrament only under one kind to the laity. What is this but a way of elevating the status of the priesthood at the expense of the laity? (107) Did Jesus teach that children be confirmed? They justify this by the biblical custom of the laying on of hands, but that is something else entirely. Likewise, oral confession was made mandatory only so that the priesthood could rule over the hearts of people. Private, voluntary confession, which the Protestant church also receives as it existed before 1215, is something else entirely. But a fatal error occurs by making marriage and ordination sacraments, as when they explain priesthood as marriage to Christ in His Church. Was not Peter married? Why would Paul have instructed Timothy that a bishop must be a man with one wife? (108). In fact, Paul warned against the diabolical time when they would try to prevent marriage. Is it more sinful to marry or to live immorally without a wife? Anointing with oil and the doctrine of purgatory are likewise harmful inventions of human tradition. If purgatory helps, what did Jesus die for?

They attack us because we do not have a head of our church. We do have a head, but it is not the pope. It is Jesus Christ. They claim that Jesus installed Peter after Himself as the highest head of the church. But the rock on which Jesus founded his church is not the person of Peter but rather his confession of Jesus Christ as the Son of God. If Peter was head of the church, why did he fall into error in his argument with Paul in Antioch? (110). When these Scriptural arguments are exposed as unfounded, they appeal to the beginning of the history of Christianity in the apostolic period and point to Peter's role as leader of the Twelve. But how then do they explain the story about the quarrel between the sons of Zebedee and the rest of the apostles over primacy? Indeed how can they reconcile this elevation of Peter with Peter's own testimony in 1 Pet. 5.1-4, where Peter protests against such behaviour? The only reason is to find a pretext for the papacy. They have no proofs even for their traditions, which are only legends (111). They claim that the Roman bishop has primacy over other bishops. But why then did the Nicene council in 325 expressly reject such a claim to papal primacy? If papists claim that the papacy evolved as an alternative to the violence of worldly power, hence from love, we reply: Yes, love for power.

Nor is the pope inerrant, as the Vatican Council in 1869–70 proclaimed at the peak of Roman Catholic errors. The keys of the kingdom are given to all believers, not only bishops, let alone only the pope. Only with violence can the words in Matt. 16.19 about forgiveness of sins be applied exclusively to the papacy. But Catholics themselves feel the weakness of the theory of infallibility and thus limit it to faith and morals, excluding scientific, philosophical, political and social matters, including even church discipline. What we know today about the history of the popes – filled with intrigue, theft, murder, and adultery – hardly gives confidence to the claim to papal inerrancy in doctrine and morals (113).

While Holy Scripture proclaims only one mediator, Jesus Christ, Roman Catholicism adds in practice another over Christ: Mary, queen of heaven, heavenly defender, Mother of God. The Marian cult is alongside the papacy the second most characteristic sign of Catholicism. They pray to her, thinking that Mary was not filled with grace as a gift but was worthy of grace by her merit. But in fact she also needed grace, and waited with the apostles for the coming of the Holy Spirit. It is possible to bow only before God, and pray to Him alone. Is it any accident that the Council of Ephesus declared Mary Mother of God in 431 where the great pagan cult of Diana was located? To hear our prayers, Mary would have to have two divine properties: omnipotence and omnipresence. Even Thomas Aquinas senses the danger here, but solves the problem in a naïve way (116). But in fact all this confession of Mary and the saints is nothing other than a pagan divinization of people (117).

That is why in Protestantism we do not find relics, statues, pictures, symbols, because they are forbidden by Moses. We do not sanctify things because all of God's creation is suitable for our use. We have but one symbol: the cross. It is an exhortation, 'Praised be the Lord Jesus Christ!'. Clericalism is foreign to us, that is, ecclesiastical power, not only over spiritual matters but over individual souls, family, nation, state and humanity. The Church is to be a Christocracy, not a clericocracy. It was precisely Peter the apostle who declared the universal priesthood of believers in 1 Pet. 2:5, 9. The Reformation was a return to the pure teaching of the gospel, and that is why it is called the gospel church; while it is Roman Catholicism which is human, and an innovation from the twelfth century, when they abandoned holy government to pursue worldly domination.

On the basis of the foregoing recitation of 500 years of Protestant polemical theology, Osuský now arouses himself to a concluding peroration. We are to judge people by their fruits, their works, their lives. They accuse us, saying that the evil effects of Protestantism are evident in moral and civil life. They attribute to us rationalism, liberalism, democratism, freemasonry, materialism, atheism, Bolshevism and so on. To this indictment, we reply: Just compare. Compare the Christian world to the non-Christian world. And within the Christian world compare the Protestant and Catholic lands. Compare levels of literacy, criminality, literary production and its value to people, industry, business and other forms of progress. When the church intervenes between God and humanity, God and Christ are overshadowed and the rule of the will of God, as revealed in Scripture, is replaced by the words of men. Where the worship service is mystified, people do not hear and understand, believe and obey the Word of God. They are falsely made to feel secure and do not take care for their salvation. They do not develop conscience through a serious process of self-questioning. They become passive before authoritarian clergy, which attitude of blind obedience is carried over into the civil order in authoritarianism. Where infallibility is claimed, there is no possible freedom of conscience, nor research, nor progress. Neither love nor tolerance is possible, only fanaticism (120). Osuský's concluding sentence: 'Finally it is possible to count among the evil effects of a bad doctrine how political, clerical Catholicism looks upon Protestantism' (121).

I take this sustained literary outburst to be the last, dying gasp of Osuský's liberal Protestant triumphalism, as if the Protestants, vindicated by history, would now be welcomed with open arms. The world-intending and transforming Pauline doctrine of the justification of the ungodly has become the self-justifying claim of Protestantism to spiritual superiority over against rival Christians. The newly arriving agents of change, the Marxist-Leninists, riding the wave formed by the victorious Red Army, however, would not, in the event, so judge Protestantism. A vindicated Protestant church would not be invited to link arms with the true forces of progress to work, once again, for new and better nation-building within the international family of socialist nations. Instead, as we shall see, an accommodated Protestant church would cling pathetically to the ever-shrinking cultural ground of its legacy in forming the nation in the hope of sustaining state patronage.

As we have seen in the case of Klimo, the 'feeling of Lutheranism', as Osuský had described it, seems to have been wholly displaced by a 'feeling' for National Socialism in a Slovak iteration. His own church, then, was not quite what he claimed it to be. In principle, Osuský by now knows better than to claim an evident superiority for the really existing Lutheranism of modern times, as we shall see in the next chapter. It is perhaps gratuitous to point out, but nonetheless probably still necessary to say explicitly, that Roman Catholicism has in the interim executed a painful, not yet thorough, but all the same significant and on-going self-examination, provoked by the positive correlation during the twentieth century of the Church and fascism. Yet the old Christendom hope of a symbiosis of Christianity and culture dies hard; and the pent-up resentments of rivals losing in the zero-sum game of identity politics dies even harder.

More significant for the purposes of our study is that fact that Osuský is manifestly no longer a liberal Protestant theologically. The 'formal principle of the Reformation' has reasserted itself in Osuský, regarding Scripture as the one source of faith and rule of doctrine and life, when the canonical Scripture is itself understood as prophetic and apostolic witness to the gospel Word of God spoken in raising the crucified Jesus from the dead to justify the ungodly. It is not the progress of religion that justifies Protestantism, then, but God's way to sinful humanity; and such protest against the structures of malice and injustice that cruelly dominate this world is not Protestantism as national religion but the leaven that indeed leavens the whole. The disaster of political Catholicism, seeking in its own more 'conservative' way a modern synthesis with nationalism at the cost of authoritarianism, has shown this failure to Osuský in principle. But, in the attack on Catholicism in 1946, he has not yet seen how the same search for a synthesis, albeit a more liberal one, afflicts his own tradition.

If Christianity is God's way to sinful humanity, it is not the religious desire for God seeking a cultural synthesis. If faith active in love is the Christian's way, through the apocalyptic battle of the Spirit and the flesh, then it is not nationalism-patriotism sanctified, or rather mystified. If the church is the creature of the Word – the peculiar people created by the particular story of Israel's God sending Israel's messiah in the form of a suffering servant to reach Israel's enemies at the cross of Jesus – then the church is not and cannot be the soul or conscience of a people in the contest of the nations for domination. It must be instead a fellowship of conscience conscientiously contesting idols ancient and modern. Only as such can a modest but true patriotism – the finite creature's love for its own finite people in their own particularity – be redeemed from the structures of malice and injustice in which it finds a modern habitat.

3

Speaking from the Scriptures to a World at War

In the course of the 1930s and into the war years, we see the theological profile of Osuský sharpen considerably. He has heeded his colleague Beblavý, who at the theological conference in Ružemberok in 1937 called the Slovak Lutherans back to Luther's teaching about the church as the creature of the Word rather than the supreme product of religious evolution. And Osuský has also, like Beblavý, correlated this theological move with anti-fascism and anti-racism. Osuský now sees – perhaps recalling his own, earlier prophetic critique during the First World War of the 'optimistic' German war theologians – that, as Beblavý put it, 'the majority of German liberal theologians supporting the new regime have betrayed the church of Christ and entered into the service of German racism', while it is those 'most faithful' to the Reformation who languish there in concentration camps.

In this chapter, we will examine Osuský's turn to the Bible to speak to a world at war. Despite an unconvincing undertone of historicist apologetics, this turn is no retreat to the kind of fundamentalism represented by his sometime domestic opponent Stuhárik, as we shall see. It is rather a knowingly post-critical and Christocentric reading of Scripture that answers the question that Dietrich Bonhoeffer was almost simultaneously posing in Germany: 'Who is Jesus Christ *for us today*?', that is, in a world filled with messianic claims about *il Duce, der Führer* or the eternal *Vodca*. It was the embrace of a theological method that refused to collapse text into context, as in liberalism, or to circle wagons around the text with no regard for context, as in conservatism. It was a method that exposited the Scriptural text to speak to the spiritual situation, theology in a new key as a kind of learned proclamation of prophetic criticism and apostolic reconciliation that exposed the human social plight before God in order to deliver the divine Word of empowering and renewing grace even in the human extremities of senseless and unjust wartime suffering. This divine Word, moreover, is the person, Jesus Christ, and thus the event of coming to repentance and faith in Him by the advent of His own Spirit to convince the world concerning sin, and righteousness, and judgment.

In this chapter we will follow Osuský's learned preaching in the two monographs that he published during the war. The first publication on the book of Revelation in 1941, titled *The End of the World*, brought this most difficult scriptural text to bear on the end-times presently being experienced; that is, not as speculation about a literal end of the cosmos, the supposed timetable of which is to be deciphered in present events as, Osuský notes critically, 'sectarian' and 'chiliastic' readers would have it (243). Rather, it is the end here and now of the European world of Christendom in the flaming ruins of the Second World War, in the maw – in 1941 – of the apparent triumph of Nazism, figured by the great beast of the book of Revelation. In this perspective, 'liberalism' in theology is now treated by Osuský by the figure of the 'lukewarm' church at Laodicea in Rev. 3.14-23, something to be spat from the mouth of the exalted Christ. Osuský thus characterizes liberalism in theology as self-satisfied doctrinal indifferentism; as the proverb goes, 'on friendly terms with God but not on such bad terms with the devil'. 'The time of religious indifferentism is the worst. The time of religious liberalism gives a thousand proofs of this' (69). But today we have, to our good, been shorn of liberalism's faith in progress. In its place we are regaining our faith in the God who battles evil for us and finally defeats it in us. We are re-learning hope, which is not rational optimism based on probable calculation, but hope in God who has possibilities beyond what mortals know or imagine. Commenting on Rev. 20.7-10, a passage he entitles 'The Defeat of the Devil,' Osuský writes:

> This passage shows how shallow and superficial is the view of the theory of progress in the sense that the development of humanity with the help of science, culture, civilization and technology has matured to such an extent that man has become so perfect in all good that the opposition of evil will no longer exist. It is not so! The devil and the servants of the devil, the godless, the unbelievers and the thieves will remain until the cruciform death of the world and so the battle will continue until the end (251).

The second wartime work, on the book of Job in 1943, bore the title of *The Mystery of the Cross*, already indicating thereby the Christocentric reading of this classic, though puzzling, piece of the Hebrew Scriptures. In the end, on the basis of scholarly exegesis and patient argumentation, Osuský takes Job as a type of Christ, justified by God for telling the truth about Him, praying in the end even for his 'unfriendly friends', who were simultaneously exposed as those who do not tell the truth about God. In Job, Christians can thus see their own sufferings in these present day end-times: not the end of time but the time of the end breaking in on them in the dramatic wartime events. They can also be strengthened thereby inwardly not to resign themselves to the Nazi representation of God as brutal and capricious power, but instead to find resources for resistance and true hope beyond the apparent triumph of such a deity in the present, by the mystery of the cross.

At the end of this chapter, we shall take up the middle part of Osuský's apologetics, published at the end of the war, *Defence of the Truth*, on Christianity as the holistic salvation of the kingdom of God at work in Christ by the Spirit's preaching of the gospel renewing humanity. We will use this section to synthesize the results of Osuský's two wartime productions of 'clear, pure, biblical Christianity', making a fresh and renewed claim for the truth of the gospel when the truths of experience seem wholly to refute it. Or, we have to wonder in light of our knowledge of the triumphalism of the *History of Religion*, or Part Three of *Defence of the Truth*, is it a claim for the perfection of Christianity as a religion? More precisely, the question will be whether Osuský yet fully comprehends the import of his own investigations into the cosmic, apocalyptic conflict of good and evil that he discovers no less in Job than in the Revelation, if I may say so, *after Christendom*, or, whether Osuský still hankers after the fleshpots of Egypt.

The End of the World (1941)

Dedicating the book to his 'good Mommy' (as adult Slovaks, men also, do not shy from saying) is not an idle or sentimental gesture. At the end of his commentary, Osuský tells us that he sees in his own mother all 'our good Slovak women and mothers who gather their children around the table and read to them from the Holy Scriptures and teach them to pray, to sing, read, heed and fulfil the Word of God'. He tells us that he has written this book because he wants to help them, so that they themselves understand what they read to their children, so that they know how to answer when a child asks about this or that. He naturally also wanted in the same way to help fathers and spiritual fathers, that is, pastors, so that according to their own capacities each would know how to clarify the mysteries of Revelation to the children of God. 'As we have seen',

Osuský further writes, in conclusion, 'Scripture is best explained by Scripture', 'intertextually' as we might say today (297). That kind of understanding is what his commentary on Revelation hopes to provide, by showing how deeply immersed John the seer is in the imaginative world of Hebrew prophecy and Second Temple apocalyptic.

In much detail, then, Osuský's commentary on Revelation traces back its array of motifs to sources in Old Testament scriptures. In this way, he massively makes the point that scholarly and theological exegesis of Revelation does not proffer a kaleidoscope of fanciful speculation but presents Revelation as a true culmination of Scripture as a whole. Its contribution is to open us to view – as an *apocalypse* – God's ultimate goal of human inclusion in His own divine and eternal life, giving a vision which powerfully transforms human desire:

> A diligent reader is convinced that the book of Revelation beautifully completes the rest of the books of the Bible, because it is the richest source of knowledge concerning the last things of humanity. It does not dwell on the tragic end of the world and time, but opens up a comforting window into eternity. Even though we shed tears in the valley of weeping, through those teary eyes we are consoled. We want to be of eternity, in order that eternity would be our own. Grant it, Lord God, that our good mommies lead us to it! (297)

Or, again, from the final pages of the commentary:

> The first book of the Bible begins a panorama by the act of creation, so the last book ends by the act of eternal glorification. The first is the beginning and the last the end and in between the Bible writes about life burdened with sin, suffering and death. The Bible is a book of life, a book, which is a powerful voice in the world and in the conscience of people on the way of life, to the effect that suffering will pass away, that God and the good with Him will triumph. Therefore, dear human beings: believe, hope, love! (285)

To come to this conclusion, Osuský urges what today we call, after Brevard Childs, 'canonical criticism' of the Bible.[1] This is a critical-historical reading which takes seriously the historical fact that the scriptural writings are written from faith for faith to address a particular historical challenge to faith. At the same time, however, being written down, these contemporary addresses immediately begin to transcend that occasion of their composition. As texts, that is, scriptures are preserved, and so passed on to form future faith; in the process they are tested in the life of believing communities and eventually

[1] Brevard S. Childs, *Old Testament Theology in a Canonical Context* (Minneapolis: Fortress, 1986).

selected from the range of alternative or even competing texts, and finally integrated with other such selected and tested texts into the developing whole of the Genesis to Revelation narrative. This canonical narrative in fact comes to tell of the One God who is freely determined to redeem and fulfil by the missions of His Son and Spirit the creation fallen prey to demonic powers of sin, death and devil.

Returning, now, to the Introduction, Osuský spells out some contextual presuppositions of his exposition of the book of Revelation 'in stormy times of war':

> Life is a difficult struggle, not only for bread, but as the Bible teaches us, it is a battle between light and darkness, good and evil, truth and injustice, faith and unbelief – which of these triumphs in the end? In war time such questions intensify and multiply. Terrorized by the circumstances, one asks more than once about what becomes of those who suffer for truth yet to whom injustice occurs. Does a reckoning come by force? Do the truths of Christianity triumph? What becomes of the promises of Christ and His apostles? What will be after death? (9)

More broadly, Osuský notes, we know that the human being is a creature that passes away, and the experience of this sad fact provokes more disturbing questions: what becomes of the earth, the world, the universe? Are they, too, passing away like human beings? Most of all the fate of our earthly home interests us. What kind of end, whether natural or supernatural, awaits it? Will the death of the world happen quickly or slowly? Will the earth again be covered with ice, thus extinguishing life? Or will the end be unnatural, even as some astronomers predict? And what will cause it? Are there immanent reasons, like a comet crashing into the earth? Will the moon crash into the earth, as the planets also fall into the sun, and thus burn up? Or does God's providence prepare for us another, unexpected catastrophe? And if this earth passes away, then what? What awaits us, the human race? (9)

Yet it is especially in times of war that human beings painfully ask: do not signs of the end, the Day of Judgment, come near and show themselves? So people look and look for such signs, and sometimes they find some prediction satisfying. But in the end they are disappointed. Can science answer these questions, then, or do we have a conflict, here, of faith and science? Or in the end do we confront an eternally shrouded mystery just like the mystery of the beginning, the origin of existence? Does the answer lie only in faith, or does faith, too, disappoint?

Like many others, Osuský continues in his Introduction, both out of natural curiosity and out of recurring unhappiness with the times, he has repeatedly taken an interest in this riddle-filled but also beautiful book of the Bible. As said earlier, this unhappiness emerges in times of war as well as peace, also for him as a Christian and a minister. Already, after the First World War, in similar circumstances as today's, he tried to publish an exposition of Revelation. Since then he has studied thoughts on Revelation from many scholars and theologians: Luther through Bengel, and Herder to Lohmayer and Lilje. As a historian of philosophy he has been interested in the mystical and numerical symbolism in the book, and also chief problems of the philosophy of history in connection with Augustine's treatise on the *City of God*. In 1936, Osuský reports, he had published an updated article on Revelation. And then this new war broke out. And when Osuský saw all the mystical tendencies and how many people fell into speculative errors, he turned again to Revelation, thus writing the current book. People today reach not only for scholarly literature but also for occult and spiritualistic books and legends. They interpret the book of Revelation in the most fanatical ways. All this forced him to return to the study of this book of the Bible. 'With God's help I want to understand this book correctly so that readers together with me in the battles of life will believe in the victory of light, good, truth and faith' (11).

For similar reasons relating to the liability of the book of Revelation to fanatical readings (thus Osuský concludes the Introduction), Luther actually did not accept the book of Revelation. But, because of the condition of exegetical science in his day, he did not have the resources to penetrate into the kernel of the book and understand it as we understand it today. After a long period of study, Osuský writes, he has come to agree with the German Hanns Lilje[2] that Revelation is a beautiful and congenial book, both from a theological and also from a philosophical-cultural perspective. It is neither subjective fantasy nor diseased hallucination, but a great collection of symbolic pictures which seeks to illustrate prophetically the secret things approaching. It is a book of riddles, yet understandable when we have the key to understanding it, namely, when we enter into the time and conditions under which it was written and so have in mind the goal that the book serves. The book arose in a period of persecution for Christians, introduced by the cult of Caesar; so it was necessary to build up, strengthen and comfort the persecuted. The secret things it thus wants to convey are hard to

[2] Hanns Lilje, *The Last Book of the Bible* (Philadelphia: Muhlenberg, 1957) English translation of German original, 1940. Hanns Lilje was a German theologian who belonged to the Confessing Church and later became the bishop of Hanover and a leading ecumenist.

communicate in words, so Revelation employs pictures. Accordingly, the reader is asked patiently to accompany John along the way by working through the text of Revelation passage by passage in the commentary following. The end of the world is a great drama. 'May God lead us to a saving end that is more than the body and more than time – to His eternal and victorious kingdom' (11–13).

Apt as Osuský's wartime admonition to his readers is, to follow patiently his scholarly theological exegesis of Revelation verse by verse, it would be tedious for us today to do so. In one sense, the battle for which he fought is, for those who read a book like this, already won, namely, with the historical-critical interpretation of Revelation as a fresh word spoken to persecuted Christians during the reign of Emperor Domitian when they faced the life and death choice of publicly confessing Jesus as Lord or denying Him with a curse and sacrificing to the image of Caesar. Rather than repeat Osuský's now familiar arguments for such historical interpretation (which is most of the book), in the following I will present instead a summary of the major themes produced by his commentary.

First, I will present the gravamen of his interpretation of Revelation as a new proclamation of the gospel under the specific circumstance of persecution. Second, I will summarize his literary observations about Revelation as a coherent and well-planned work. Third, I will note briefly his aforementioned historical observations regarding the occasion of the book's composition. Fourth, I will describe Osuský's theological harvest from his scrupulous and patient exegetical procedure which rejects eisegetical, allegorical or other speculative readings. Finally, I will take note of his sparse and reserved, but unmistakable, projections of the message of Revelation to his contemporaries living in a fascist state militarily aligned with Nazi Germany on the cusp of apparent triumph in a war of naked aggression. I will conclude with the claim that since, in theology, interpretation, formally speaking, is the cognitive act of a particular subject knowing a particular object for a particular audience, we find in Osuský's book on Revelation an exemplar of post-modern theological exegesis.

In the middle of the book of Revelation is the passage in 14.6 about the 'eternal gospel'. Osuský comments:

> We have seen with what kind of weapons the enemies of Christ do battle. Over against this, the army of God, represented by the angel, fights with a sharp, two-edged sword, which is the gospel of Jesus… What the Lord foretold [Mk 13.10] is fulfilled. The gospel is and will be witnessed, even though not everyone receives it. This verse is very memorable for us gospel Christians. On these foundations our church rests and we are named according to the gospel; at Luther's funeral Bugenhagen preached on this verse. The gospel gives birth to

> the church, it sustains her and as God's warriors we have to witness the gospel by word and deed (182–3).

What is the Revelation's eternal gospel? It is the gospel of the reign of God, so proclaimed by the angel: 'Fear God and give Him honour'. This was the message of John the Baptist, and Jesus too, that all repent and turn to the Lord who is coming soon. To bow before God is to fulfil the first commandment. Whoever transgresses this commandment transgresses all the commandments. Whoever has bowed to the devil and his beasts, let them repent even at the last minute like the thief on the cross. For believers and those who repent, this testimony to the coming reign of God is joyful and good news indeed; but the same message is terrible and a terror for the impenitent servants of the devil and the beasts.

The eternal gospel tells us that God is God and there is no other to whom the knee should bow; it tells thus of the Lamb slain before the foundation of the world, in whom this one, true and eternal God does the deed of love that gains hearts to bend the knee to God and the Lamb but not to the devil and the beast. Commenting on 14.12, Osuský continues, 'Christians according to these words are characterized by two properties connected to the Old and New Testaments. They keep God's commandment, namely, to have no other gods, and according to this, they have faith in Jesus also during battles and persecution. Such patience is correct'. Faith, as Osuský exposits it, is a kind of suffering, a patiency, a paradoxically active waiting on God who comes in time through the gospel promise and comes also in eternity's fulfilment of that gospel promise. John, the seer, Osuský says, is thinking here of the benedictions pronounced at the beginning (1.11, 19) and at the end (19.9 and 21.5) of the book. Thus the blessed are, above all, those who remain faithful to God's commandments in battle, persecution and suffering, and to the faith in Jesus which keeps and cultivates patience in suffering, even to the extremity of martyrdom (186).

Patience is the eschatological virtue of the hope in God that is not worldly optimism based upon the rational calculation of a positive outcome, but rather hope against hope in the God who has given Jesus the keys to Hades. This hope in Jesus's triumph over death is patient in conflict; it endures the world of malice and injustice that now exists and is active there in love, redeeming evil times. In this perspective of patient hope, the martyr who suffers death for the name of Jesus is the one truly blessed. The prophetic Spirit announces that already such martyrs rest from their labours and their deeds follow them. Such a promise of present vindication in heaven is not human but divine, from the Spirit of truth and comfort. 'This is the most significant passage in Revelation', Osuský announces, 'with which John comforts and strengthens his brothers in great battle with foes and in hard suffering' (187).

Understood historically, in other words, the fresh iteration of the good news of Jesus and the kingdom in the book of Revelation is that the souls of the martyrs do not silently await the future resurrection in Hades, but are already exalted to the presence of God in heaven, there to behold the coming victory; and further, there their cries before the throne of God sound out in intercession for the persecuted who remain in trial and testing on the earth. Commenting on 15.1-8, Osuský states: 'Those who have not served the beast, even if they have fallen in the persecution, nevertheless triumph and now stand in heaven… and sing to the glory of God' (193, see also 111, 248). Discovery of this new iteration of the gospel is the historical gravamen of Osuský's reading of Revelation.

Osuský comes to this reading methodically. He affirms the Reformation principle that Scripture interprets Scripture in the now historically enriched sense of modern biblical scholarship (78), so that scholarly interpretation, by showing how John the seer lived in the world of the Hebrew prophets and seers, demonstrates that he was no fanatic who hallucinated spontaneously (73, 77). John's human mind is already saturated with biblical prophecy and symbolism. While Osuský allows that John experienced a divine ecstasy (73), it was not an ecstasy that displaced his human mind, but one that exalted it to the synthesis of his well-planned book, producing a clear, intelligible and present message of hope that endures. A regular refrain running through Osuský's commentary thus bemoans the speculative excesses and allegorical flights of eisegesis through the ages (120, 126, 143, 162, 213, although Osuský allows for allegory when the text explicitly announces a sign or itself offers an allegory, 151). Calculation and speculation that would decode contemporary events with the Revelation as if it meant to offer a time-table is not the right way to relate the message of Revelation to contemporary events. It is wrong not least because such speculation evades a central message of the book for believers in times of extraordinary suffering. This message is addressed to one and all, including would-be speculators and calculators so self-sure that they, unlike others, will not be 'left behind': repent now, while God yet delays, giving time for repentance.

Instead of speculation and allegory based upon a naïve reading of Revelation as a coded time-table for the end time events, Osuský insists that we find the key to interpretation instead in the historical circumstances to which the book itself points as providing the occasion for its composition. It seems clear that John writes during the reign of the Emperor Domitian (18, 46, 164, 166, 167); from this circumstance it is also evident why John must employ code-language to veil his meaning from hostile outsiders (21). Domitian's enforcement of the cult of Caesar (19, 82–3, 99, 122) is represented in Revelation as Rome's blasphemous act of self-divinization (165) which would force Christians to commit idolatrous acts (30). This is the way of a tyrant (33–4), who accuses the Christians of disloyalty (174) because they decline to participate in the civic sacrifices, in favour of their own Eucharistic meal (52, 82). As a result, the Christians are victims of imperial terrorism ranging from death threats to economic deprivation (175).

In light of the methodical procedure that has Revelation interpreting all preceding Scripture in the light of the now revealed goal of God's history with humanity in Christ, and that sees the historical occasion in the particular circumstances of the collision of the gospel of the Lamb who was slain with the self-proclaimed Son of God who sits on Caesar's throne, Osuský registers a number of important literary observations that provide clues to the book's theological interpretation. It is well-planned (113). In the genre of apocalyptic literature, it represents John peering as through a window into heaven where God's plan for the creation has been prepared and is now unveiled before him (73), so that the sufferings about to befall the saints on earth will not come upon them unprepared (91). The book purports to record the revelation of Jesus Christ (17) that comes from above (19); accordingly it is addressed to all believers of every time and place (18, 22, 25, 31, 47, 83). Here, Jesus Christ appears as the exalted Victor (88), who discloses the mystery of His Parousia, which paradoxically God delays for the sake of repentance even as believers must continue to expect it soon (27, 29, 92, 121, 145, 147).

Thus the motifs of divine delay and human eager-longing intertwine, ever giving time for repentance (114, 136–7, 140–1). While the New Jerusalem descends from heaven in the end of ends, the reign of God also grows gradually on earth (152). The future is already inaugurated (283), yet the beast, too, can gain temporary victories (170), so the struggling Christian must be born anew every day in order to progress forward (264). The embattled church fights a double battle against heresy from within (Osuský names Gnosticism and docetism, 49, 57, 63), and persecution from without. Just as it must know the *reality* of Christ's sufferings as the Lamb slain (against docetism), and the *unity* of God's creation with His redemption and fulfilment (against Gnosticism), it must learn from Jesus the paradoxical way of triumph in suffering. This way of triumph comes by confession of Caesar's crucified victim as Lord of Lords, defying the terrorism of the worldly powers. Non-violent (186) witness (88, 137, 145, 157, 236) is the paradigm of faith that Revelation, as a literary construct, models for believers. Their history of suffering witness on the earth, then, makes for the harvest of God; God permits their suffering (109, 258), indeed delays the Parousia for the sake of their persecutors' repentance, no less. When at last the harvest will be gathered in, its vast scope will have been purchased at the human cost of the suffering of the saints (134).

On the basis of this literary analysis, Osuský makes a number of theological points that are worthy of note. Whether in wartime or peacetime, life is a battle (44), although not one of violence met by violence, as humans ordinarily think. The hidden truth now revealed in the apocalypse is that war between the devil and Christ (154–5) transpires behind the scenes of human history, yet works out in human beings as a contest of these contending lordships over them (175). The apocalyptic battle is not a Platonic or Gnostic ontological or anthropological dualism (25, 82, 172, 190) between mind and matter or spirit and body, but the apocalyptic dualism of the ages, God asserting His proper sovereignty over the creation against usurping powers of darkness. These rebellious powers are the unholy trinity of the devil who fights God, the antichrist who battles Jesus Christ, and the false prophet who contends against the Holy Spirit (122, 171, 177, 186, 202).

We are already familiar with Osuský's typically tripartite schematization, derived from the doctrine of the Trinity, for example, of religion, Christianity and Protestantism. This scheme thus appears here again, although it arises inductively from exegesis of the text of Revelation, and by the negative antitype of devil, antichrist and false prophet. While the figures of the One who sits upon the throne and the Lamb who was slain are familiar enough, Osuský also finds the Holy Spirit in Revelation as the One who enlightens (75), and speaks with and through the faithful church to test the spirits (40, 86), just as the church's fidelity is itself tested under persecution (138). The 'works' of the saints of which the Revelation speaks are for Osuský the fruits of the Spirit-transformed heart, not deeds of merit (41, 56, 258). For *fides ex corde*, as the Reformation taught, transforms human desire (269, 273, 294) by redirecting it from enslaving idols to the one true God who liberates. Such saints are clothed by the Spirit in the righteousness of Christ (235), and are purified in this way by Christ (279), in union with Christ, (236) through sore testing so that 'in place of self-righteousness they are justified out of their faith in Christ' (68) – where faith itself is the Spirit's work and gift in His embattled saints.

It is noteworthy that Osuský finds occasion to polemicize here against antinomian versions of the doctrine of justification by faith as anti-Judaism, that is, as discounting the cost to God of free grace in Christ that has been purchased and obtained by the merit of the Lamb suffering innocently for sins as Isaiah's Servant of the Lord (42–3). 'John richly employs the Old Testament prophets. Revelation as a whole and its ideology testifies to the fact that its author, John, grew up more on the soil of the Jewish Old Testament, of the Bible, than of the philosophy and cultural opinion of the contemporary, educated Hellenistic world' (285). Osuský especially notes the Jewish association of idolatry with adultery (51, 61) as the background of the prohibition of the church, wed to Christ (53, 56), from bowing down to other gods. Such prostration would be prostitution. In keeping with the book of Revelation, Osuský can also, however, speak of Judaism as superseded (64) by the new, spiritual Israel (137, 153). As we shall see in the Conclusion to this book, a peculiar form of supersessionism is an important component of Osuský's very vision of the new polity and politics of the gospel, even as this creates its own set a problem for contemporary post-Holocaust theology.

As mentioned, the apocalyptic battle has a subtle and indirect, not obvious, relation to historical events; this relation dramatically symbolizes for Osuský the relation of the eternal God to time. On one level, Osuský's eschatological expectation is realistic. The revelation of God's goal for humanity by the exalted Christ gives direction to believers who otherwise would lose their way in the fog and friction of warfare (16). Without eschatology, Osuský declares, that is, without this real hope in God's victory, there can be neither faith nor love (255). So the Parousia of Christ which brings about this victory is embraced as the true content of Christian hope on which everything else depends, just as it is the subject matter revealed in the book. Yet God delays – again and again. Thus it is a great mistake to understand Revelation as providing clues applicable one-on-one to historical events as if it were, as a whole, an allegory of historical events providing a time table, rather than a revelation from above of God's goal for His creation, guiding believers in embattled history still filled with surprising twists and turns. As seen in Chapter 21, God's revealed goal, Osuský says, is something similar to what Augustine envisaged with his *civitas Dei* (247), a beloved community of all peoples (267, 283) that, as such, comes in time fragmentarily but in its fullness only comes down 'from above' at the end of ends, that is, in eternity.

This coming in eternity reflects the eternity of the biblical God, who is alpha and omega (23, 28), at rest but always working all (74), the One who was, who is and who comes (81). The temporality of the created world, by contrast, entails the fleetingness of things (162). That is why death (93, 97) is the riddle of riddles for humans oriented by nature to the eternal God, as Osuský thinks with Augustine, and why the enmity of death plumbs to the depths of the human plight (86–7). The proud creature would be God, but the humble God became human and triumphed for humanity in humanity, as the martyrs of Christ partake in Christ's own divine-human suffering of love for others. The Augustinian paradox continues: when humans turn from that eternal God who intends time and participates in time in order to redeem and fulfil time, in eternity, they do not actually succeed in storming heaven but plunge themselves into nothingness. 'Fallen, fallen is Babylon the great!' (Revelation 18.2). For us, turning away from this God in order to affirm this fleeting world against an uncertain transcendence paradoxically condemns the human creature to fleetingness without remainder.

Osuský is quite taken with the exegetical discovery that Sheol, or Hades, in the Bible, is not the medieval idea of a fiery hell of punishment (34, 97–8, 262) but the shadowy abode of the dead to which the exalted Christ now claims the key, preaching the gospel of eternal life even there to all its ephemeral denizens. What does resemble the medieval hell, however, is Revelation's abyss (123), the abode of the demonic enemies of God, to which they are in the end forever returned, shut up, never again to be released. Because God delays the Parousia to give time for repentance, we may hope for a humanly unpopulated abyss, Osuský suggests, but we may not assert it as if it were a human, even a believing human's, judgment to make. We cannot, in any case, assert an *apokatastasis* that reconciles even the devil and his servants (261). These true and ancient enemies can only be defeated finally and forever. Whereas the wrath of God is not vindictive, it is real (222), and so no pretext for Christian *Schadenfreude* (228) over the punishment of others; it remains a summons also to believers to their own life-long repentance (158), lest they likewise perish.

Eternal life is not the continuation of time (253), as is naively thought in the natural line of thought that moves from below to above. Rather, time becomes eternal, the mortal puts on immortality (254), when the eternal incorporates, so to speak, time upon the Last Judgment, when the dwelling of God has come to be with His redeemed humanity. The eschaton of judgment is the eschaton of meaning, in which the moral ambiguities of historical life are clarified and purified. Because this relation comes from above to below, eternity relates itself to time in a variety of such judgments up to the Last Judgment:

> Beside the 'Last Judgment,' Holy Scripture distinguishes many judgments. The judgment of God also echoes in the human conscience after the commission of sin, as also in God's justification of man through faith in Christ (Jn 3.18; 9.39; 12.31), as also in the death of every individual. Besides this there is also the collective judgment of God in human history. Every age, every individual is the last, but in the end all individuals also, indeed every age will have an end and the Last Judgment will come… The last, at the end in eternity, is the true judgment. This one decides, proclaims, make public all these other judgments (2 Cor. 5.10, Matt. 25.31-46) (259–60).

The moralistic connotations of 'judgment', and terroristic associations stemming from the medieval hell, can be misleading here. Osuský is in fact working, in accordance with his interpretation of the Revelation, to confine the devil to the abyss in order to give time to his foolish and unwitting minions to repent – as to slaves who have internalized their oppression.

The eschaton of judgment is the price paid for affirming meaningfulness in history – also the history, to anticipate Osuský's commentary on Job, that appears to us to be meaningless because of the prosperity of the wicked and the sufferings of the righteous. The eschaton of judgment is not about divine retaliation, but rather it comes as the divine vindication of righteousness and those who have suffered for its sake. Judgment also marks the passageway to the Augustinian vision of God, which secures the righteous forever in the rapture of love, so that never again can they fall away. In His 'glorious speech in the Sermon on the Mount, Jesus promised that those of pure hearts are blessed, because they will see God. They will look upon God's face' (284). Looking on God, the redeemed 'will serve God and reign over eternity. God created man to rule over nature, over paradise, but on account of sin man became a slave of nature. In eternity the original plan of God returns, man becomes the king of heaven and earth, though he does not rule over it brutally as the [figurative] beast [of the book of Revelation] did, but he rules with God in love' (284).

The resurrection to eternal life, then, is not the resuscitation of the corpse in a continuation of time, but the reception of a new and spiritual body in an eternal and spiritual fellowship (256–7, 260, 265, 266). The resurrection, like the apocalypse, comes from above; it is a 'miraculous' divine act (71–2, 120) in the sense that it is an utterly generous and purely creative action. Its miraculous nature, beyond all human power, imagination or comprehension, then, is the very point (252); the 'miracle' designates God, and God alone in a final act of majesty. The final miracle of resurrection in turn provides the reason why we must finally speak of the God enthroned, who shouts in victory, 'Behold, I make all things new'. This beloved community coming miraculously from above *cannot* be realized or achieved from below by human power, wisdom or merit. It is the culminating work of *grace alone* (270), the mystery of the eternal God who *gives* time freely in creation, gives at great cost Himself to time in the Incarnation, eternity to time in the Spirit's fulfilment victoriously. To be this God *is* to give – a fitting theological conclusion to the Genesis-to-Revelation narrative of Holy Scripture.

The Mystery of the Cross (1943)

Although this second wartime book appeared in 1943, Osuský dated his Introduction in 1942, hence, at a time, as he puts in the very first sentence, when 'they say that today's Europe is a great fortress, over which the twisted cross [of the swastika] waves' in triumph. There are in this book, published in a nation militarily allied with Germany, coded but unmistakable allusions to Nazism scattered throughout. For example, on Job 12.23, 'He makes nations great and then destroys them; he enlarges nations and then leads them away', Osuský glosses: 'by "making great" is understood nowadays what is called by the fancy expression, "living space"', the Nazi *Lebensraum*. The verse could be taken to mean that Nazi expansionist war is simply to be accepted as God's sovereign decree. But such a reading of the verse belongs to theologians who see in God only arbitrary power or unintelligible wisdom. Yet, it was in vain, according to Osuský, that Job's friends in 5.13-14 pointed to God's arbitrary power and unintelligible wisdom in this fashion. Job, too, acknowledges God's power and wisdom. The difference that divides such theologians emerges, Osuský explains, as Job calls directly on God's judgment with the protest: 'Why do the wicked live on, reach old age and grow mighty in their power?' (Job 20.7). That is to say: Make intelligible to me this sovereign decree! Show me the righteousness of this permission of evil!

The formulation is transparent. Just this is the – literally – burning question in 1942. Posing it honestly and relentlessly threatens the entire worldview of Job's friends. The question cuts against their education, indeed, as they think, against justice and God's commandments, if it is actually so that the wicked prosper. The Fourth Commandment promises the good life to those who not only honour parents but also reverence God, and so honour those who fulfil His holy will. 'But of what does life convince us?' Osuský asks. 'Precisely the godless do not perish but live long … How is that to be reconciled with God's righteousness or with God's law …? Ah, how sad experience is. Nor is it possible to deny this sad truth by some kind of fancy but empty talk or pious evasion' (142–3).

Transparent as this reflection is to the situation in 1942, in his insistence on the actuality of evil existing in defiance of God's will, Osuský is drawing on his theological tradition from Luther's explanation of the commandments. In the *Large Catechism*, Luther had acknowledged, indeed insisted upon, the same evident contradiction of human experience of evil to the commandments with their promised blessing; indeed, Luther made the same bitter observation, that the righteous suffer and the wicked prosper.[3] Faith, having God, having the one true God as one's only eternal good as commanded is often enough, Luther observed, marginalized and oppressed in this world where the innocent suffer and the wicked prosper. So faith in the one, true God that obeys His commandments, for Luther, for Osuský, for the book of Revelation and also, if Osuský's reading is right, for Job necessarily points forward to a promised future. This promised future is still invisible in the present groaning under structures of malice and injustice. It is present only by faith. As Jürgen Moltmann has maintained in contemporary theology, faith in the one, true God lives in hope of the coming of this God's reign *against* present experience, structured as it is by malice and injustice. Just this tension between experience and hope focuses attention on the cross and makes it all the more mysterious.

Osuský's reading of Job virtually verbatim recalls Luther's eschatological resolution of the question of theodicy[4] posed by the mystery of the cross: 'God is great in power, He is almighty, but also in His omnipotence He is not arbitrary but remains just, and never wrongs anyone. Weak human reason never grasps Him in these properties, in His essence, and therefore it has to trust that His action and counsel are just' (249). The alternative to trust based on God's promise of Himself to the suffering by His self-revelation is to be driven by the experience of actual evil to believe that God is a tyrant (86, 209) who sanctions the present order; theologically this is to hand the victory to Nazism. For such 'good does not go to the good, but to the violent. They have their god in the

[3] *The Book of Concord: The Confessions of the Evangelical Lutheran Church* ed. Robert Kolb and Timothy J. Wengert (Minneapolis: Fortress, 2000), 391.

[4] Martin Luther, *The Bondage of the Will* trans. J. I. Packer and O. R. Johnston (Fleming H. Revel, 2000), 314–8. See further, Thomas Reinhuber, *Kämpfender Glaube: Studien zu Luthers Bekenntnis am Ende von* De servo arbitrio (Berlin & NY: Walter de Gruyter, 2000); Paul R. Hinlicky, 'A Leibnizian Transformation? Reclaiming the Theodicy of Faith' in *Transformations in Luther's Reformation Theology: Historical and Contemporary Reflections,* Vol. 32, Arbeiten zur Kirchen- und Theologiegeschichte. ed. C. Helmer and B. K. Holm (Leibzig: Evangelische Verlagsanstalt, 2011), 85–103.

fist, in force, they deify their power and might…' (83). But to believe just this theological construction of God as tyrant, in accord with apparent experience, constitutes Job's peculiar temptation to resignation, according to Osuský.

Are victims thus to give Nazism the theological victory, that 'God is capricious, even selfish, or distributes happiness and grief for other, unknown reasons'? (151) Because of the discord of power and righteousness in present experience, God seems arbitrary (69). Not that Job is tempted to act as a Nazi, but that rather in his resignation he would acquiesce to their reign of terror, 'as if Job himself were an Epicurean deist, according to whom God is so transcendent that he neither sees nor cares about the fate of earthlings' (153), abandoning the creation to the will to power. This resignation corresponds to the Epicurean desire Job expresses at times in his terrible sorrows to die and so be freed from suffering (56): 'the living know that they have to die, the dead know nothing, nor do they have any reward, for their memory fades away' (99). In the end, to the extent that Job has succumbed to this peculiar temptation of the innocent victim to passive resignation, his sin is judged by God. 'His fault was that in the crush of pain he naturally and humanly wanted to penetrate into the mystery of innocent suffering… He spoke sincerely but also incorrectly. For God was not the reason for his suffering, but another', that is, the Satan (281). It is the undeniable fact in 1942, Osuský is saying, that the swastika flies triumphant over Fortress Europe. This, not God's will, is the cause of innocent suffering. That bad fact has been the occasion and starting point of his commentary.

So it seems, Osuský continues, that the people of Europe today are like the population of biblical Jerusalem on which another cross [than the swastika], the cross of suffering is laid:

> There are many Jobs among us: one who lost property, another children, a third suffers terrible disease. Why? For what? Behind this Jerusalem of suffering hovers Golgotha; there three other crosses protrude: the crosses of redemption, of the penitent sinner, and of eternal loss. Which one triumphs? Which one is yours? And which will be that of all Europe and of humanity…? I believe with Job in the God of love, and so in the victory of the first of these crosses. So that others also so believe, I exposit Job not as an academic endeavour, but out of practical needs that are spiritual and philosophical: suffering and a deepening faith in the midst of it (9).

While theodicy is a perennial question for all thinking people (18), and the book of Job has always been beloved 'especially by suffering Jews and Christians'

(12, note the inclusion of the Jews in this 1942–3 text), the specific occasion of this exposition is the present experience of war and Nazism's evident victory.

There is basis for such contemporary application in the text itself. Commenting on Job 24.12, Osuský notes that 'Job has in mind the sad relations in the city during times of disquiet and war, when citizens die of hunger and the wounded cry for revenge' (164). Job 27.14 speaks of three chief afflictions: war, hunger and death (177); these are not only a living memory from the First World War, Osuský remarks, but re-occur today as lived experience. Terrible as such things are, however, the spiritual suffering they bring is even more terrible. As we see in the case of Job, the suffering was not only the loss of property, the loss of loved ones, the loss of health, but in all this the loss of God who had been the meaning of Job's life (158). Job's greatest and most prolonged suffering, which actually fills the pages of the biblical book, is spiritual (130). The 'lament', for example in 23.1-17, 'ought not to be understood as spiting God, but rather as the desire for a perspective in terrible suffering that is more spiritual than physical. It is more a matter of spiritual suffering because Job does not know how to understand why God suddenly became his enemy' (157). Wanting God to explain, so that he could understand this enmity, Osuský says, expresses the 'entire problematic of the suffering person, Job' (158). Long before the outburst in Chapter 23, this lament about God's enmity has grown in intensity through the course of the dialogues, as Job repeatedly summons God to the dock to account for His hostile turn (58–9, 88–93, 131, 158, 213, 248). When Job saw how his wife and friends abandoned him in his grief and pain, he finally 'opened his mouth', but no longer in humble submission to God's will. Now, he speaks, Osuský supposes, not from the pain of human loss but from the dreadful feeling of abandonment by God, to curse the day he was born (51). The suspicion of his friends that some secret sin has brought down all this punishing loss on Job (30) is more than he can bear. It is intolerable, and Job protests.

Job had responded to his losses initially with exemplary piety, submitting to God's will (22–3) just because he regarded all the riches he previously enjoyed not as his merited reward now unjustly taken away but as gift. So he could declare: 'The Lord gives and the Lord takes away; blessed be the name of the Lord' (28). But what gnaws away at Job is his ignorance of God the Giver who so suddenly and without apparent cause turned into God the Taker. The reader, by contrast, knows that behind Job's perplexity is ignorance of the heavenly session, where the Satan has tempted God to put Job to the test (21, 74). The veil of ignorance over Job, though not the reader, makes for a double perspective on all that is said in the debates of Job with his friends about the hidden meaning of his suffering.

This literary device is meant to teach the reader that God's will, revealed to them in the glimpse of heaven's session given at the outset, is hidden in our experience (159), that the God of human experience on the earth is a *deus absconditus*. To come to just such knowledge, that God is hidden in our experience, however, is to learn a great deal indeed about God. That is the kind of learning that takes place within the narrative of Job's debates with his friends. To know this hiddenness on this level, moreover, is not a scepticism that professes to know nothing at all of God, but rather professes to know painfully that by hiding His will in a veil of adversity God has become one's enemy (36, 58, 157, 186, 196). Just this unprovoked but all too evident enmity is what Job knows about God in his ignorance of God's will (that the narrator has revealed to the reader). It is the truth about God that Job knows and dares to tell and from which he will not waver until God makes intelligible to him his innocent suffering and His own divine hostility.

So, unlike Job, the reader has been ushered from the outset of the narrative into the counsels of heaven where human destiny is determined (16, 74). Thus the reader understands the ultimate nature of Job's trial, namely, the Satan's accusation that Job loves and fears God for his own sake, not for God's sake (15, 17). God and narrator in fact agree about Job's genuine righteousness (17). But put righteous Job into my hands, the sinister Satan demands, and see if he remains godly. The Satan, Osuský comments, is a cynic, like Judas (17), who puts God to the test (18) in demanding that Job be put to the test, even though his power is only parasitical (18): he can only destroy what God has created, and even that he can do only by divine permission. He himself can do nothing creative. And he cannot harm God (151) no matter how much he harms the creature.

Thus the figure of the Satan is indispensable to understanding the nature of Job's trial; but neither Osuský nor the narrator of Job in his reading are content with this figure. Slowly, in the course of the book's debates, the Satan disappears, and its place is taken by that of the Leviathan, the great water monsters of the mythical hippopotamus and crocodile, which figure the forces of chaos against which the Creator God continually battles to sustain the creation (33, 172) as a 'system of blessing' (Brueggemann), until, in the final theophany, the Lord puts Job's trials into the context of this cosmic conflict (271) that God ever wages behind the scenes of human history.

In this cosmic context, the sufferings of the righteous appear differently from how they appear in the narrowly individualistic and pietistic perspective in which the question of theodicy is usually posed: in an unwittingly egotistical and anthropocentric way, as if the universe were arranged for anyone's personal comfort apart from the needs of others. In this cosmic context of the struggle of God against chaos, the suffering individual can at least be relieved of that spiritual suffering under the hiddenness of God by fleeing to the revealed God in faith. Under the mask of nature (174), the hidden God sovereignly and indifferently works all things (167, 170), whether by intention or permission. But for the human sufferer it is all one as it seems. God works all things, the good and the evil, the weal and the woe, the light and the darkness (173), indifferently so far as the sufferer is concerned. This mask of nature indifferent to human value is one aspect of the mystery of the cross, according to Osuský.

But the revealed God is the One who battles for the righteous sufferer, as for all and together with all, against the cosmic powers of chaos, as represented by the great Leviathan, to secure each together with all others for eternal life, that is rescued from eternal death as anticipated in the experience of resignation and spiritual despair. This 'severe mercy' (to use Augustine's phrase for holy deliverance from addiction to the false gods of self, 234) is to know the Creator as Redeemer and the Redeemer as Creator (215), with no escapist flights in Gnostic heavens far away, but coming instead to the patiency of faith (229, 238, 278) on this earth on which stands the cross of Christ. Just so, such perseverance in suffering requires a mediator (71), the Christ, the One who effects and thus makes known the saving God, and revealing the hope, not only for the forgiveness of the penitent, but also for the vindication of innocent victims (115, 130–1), which war so abundantly supplies (277–8), in the gift of eternal life (97):

> It grieves him why God hides from him, why He has withdrawn or rather turned an angry face to him, when he does not feel guilty. That riddle is the darkness in which he moves. That is one side of the mystery. But the other side troubles him no less, why it goes well for the godless. See! His own suffering and on the other hand the experience that more often than not things go well for the wicked, deepens him more and more and draws him to God [for an answer]. Job wants to understand the mystery of the cross by mere human reason and does not master it. The Czech theologian Čapek[5] puts it beautifully: 'This is the end of any natural religion. The order of the world, conscience, moral life and so on all provide some kind of vague notion of God. But this is the unknown God. The known God becomes possible only through revelation.' So far as God does not declare Himself, does not reveal Himself, we can have a notion that He exists, but we do not know what kind of God He is and why He acts as He does (160).

[5] Osuský provides the reference as Stanislav Čapek, *Jób* (1940), 187.

In exhausting the resources of ratiocination, in demanding an answer from above and thus finally coming to seek God's revelation, Job innovates. He pioneers, Osuský claims, a new path, by exploding the platitudes of theological moralism, and proclaims a new doctrine (77). Commenting on 14.15, Osuský avers that, over against his present experience, 'Job believes that God's wrath is only temporary, because the essence of God cannot be other than goodness and love, which holds creation dear, as parents hold dear their children. The German scholar Delitzsch,[6] with justice,' Osuský adds, 'calls the book of Job gospel, because in the crisis Job passes from faith in the God of mere justice to the God of surpassing goodness and love' (98).

That bald statement may seem a little too easy, and it reflects Osuský's continuing reliance on the notion of liberal theology that religious experience is mediated in human consciousness by the progressive development of representations of God, the Christian one superseding the Jewish one. Osuský's insight is actually deeper than that. Human reason wants answers for the riddle of innocent suffering, but, finally, reason at its best is left with conundrums that resolve only in heartless legalism, brutal tyranny or sheer despair. The friends of Job who came to mourn with him turn against him; they question Job's righteousness on the legalistic ground of the doctrine of the Two Ways of blessing and curse (Deuteronomy 27–28) that seems to teach that all suffering comes as punishment from God (30). Commenting on the first speech of Eliphaz in Job 5, Osuský writes:

> it contains truth but also untruth. Truth, that God both punishes and rewards; untruth, that in Job's case it was a matter of punishment. His speech is certainly serious and dignified, but for such an afflicted person as Job there is little feeling of compassion and comfort in it, and it offends because it does not acknowledge Job's piety nor truly perceive his pain… It betrays a wise, but also dry learnedness, which coldly asserts, 'See, we have searched this out; it is so. Listen and take it to heart!' (Job 5.27). Indeed all three friends have searched this out, but they have not thereby penetrated the mystery of the cross (47–8).

Rather, the friends make themselves judges over God (147) in presuming to know the cause of Job's suffering in some secret sin.

In the process they fall sinfully short of true friendship by forgetting compassion. The 'friends came to sorrow with Job, but their compassion, even though it showed in the beginning, disappears… and with it the fear of God also disappears in them' (51). The sinful arrogance of the self-proclaimed 'orthodox'

[6] Osuský provides the reference as Franz Delitzsch, *Biblischer Commentar* II. Band (1876), 615.

shows itself especially, Osuský thinks, in Zophar's heartless pride. He points at the wisdom, the omniscience of God, but, in reality, behind that seeming defence of God, lies concealed only his own self-conceit (81). Such attempts to defend God by blaming the innocent victim for its victimization are shameful (90). In the end, however, Job turns the table on his 'unfriendly friends' when he exposes as wicked those who profess to be righteous, just as they in their conceit have made out Job, who truly is innocent, to be wicked (175). In the end, God confirms this reversal of judgment by Job on the friends when He judges their witness as false, but confirms Job's as true (279).

Faith, in contrast to unaided reason, answers the question of human suffering in a complex way. God does punish. Suffering can befall for sins known as the just recompense for evil deeds, but also for sins unknown, especially social sins to which individuals blind themselves. We should not imagine that God like a *deus ex machina* intervenes to punish, any more than He does to rescue, especially in the situation of a collective judgment on social sin. We should rather understand divine punishment as the Pauline 'abandonment' of the wicked to their own evil desires; this sinfulness inevitably becomes its own punishment (60), just as blessing, likewise, naturally accrues to those who love God above all and all God's creatures in and under God (283). But any such concrete judgment in history is undertaken in faith, hence by the penitent who confesses sin and justifies God in His judgment. Such judgement cannot be made outside the situation of faith and it is risky to presume the capacity to make it in a case other than one's own. What can be discussed, on the model of the prophets of Israel, beyond one's own risky judgment in faith about oneself in the confession of sins, Osuský thinks, is social sin. God permits 'innocent' suffering, as it may seem to the pious individual, for one's share in the unrecognized sins of one's society. War is just such a collective catastrophe, which sweeps in its path the righteous and the wicked alike, who perish not for personal transgressions but as active or passive members of structures of malice and injustice whose allotted time has passed. Such social suffering collapses simplistic theories of reward and punishment on an individualistic basis (179).

Faith, in Christian perspective, Osuský reminds us, begins with this: God spared not his own Son but gave Him up for us all (19, 25, 85, 218). In the light of this supreme fact of God revealed, the Christian further understands that the trinity of divine power, wisdom and love may in its heavenly counsels require us to suffer, not as punishment for sin, personal or social, but also redemptively out of love for others. There is no greater love than to lay down one's life for one's friends. There are still other divine purposes: as with Job, one purpose is to test whether faith is true and patient or false and greedy. Another, as revealed to the reader in the heavenly session, is to defeat the Accuser, playing at its own game. Yet again, as Osuský suggests is urged by the whole book of Job, one learns suffering for the sake of a theodicy of faith, not theoretical but practical. Such a theodicy justifies God, who cares for the creature as member of His creation and so teaches the creature by suffering to recognize solidarity with nature and human society, divesting the religious illusion of a special exemption for the pious who have isolated themselves from others by self-righteous religiosity. God may have even more divine purposes, above all teaching sufferers to learn compassion by learning of God beyond justice as love, long-suffering love that is patient (218–19). Suffering may thus teach the true wisdom of trusting God also in severe adversity, in this way also fearing God and not lashing out against foes real or imagined, desiring retribution in blood.

So the mystery of the cross, for faith, does not cease to be mysterious (39, 45, 150). Any one of these divine purposes may grant such understanding to the sufferer who by its aid perseveres in risky faith. Appropriating any one of them is a personal decision and risk of faith. The overriding conviction, however, is in God; this is what faith believes and so knows: evil must also serve God (85), as the cross of God's own Son served as ransom for our sins and then gave way to His glorious resurrection for the pardon, life and peace of all and of all together.

The reader will have noticed again the conceptual affinity of Osuský's interpretation of Job with the Lutheran philosopher of the early Enlightenment, Gottfried Leibniz, or, more broadly, Augustine's theodicy from the opening books of *The City of God*. The conceptual debt is to Leibniz, but the gravamen is closer to Augustine. Like Augustine in his defence against the accusation that the weakness of God commended in the proclamation of Christ crucified had undermined the empire and brought about the barbarian sacking of eternal Rome, Osuský, too, seeks to reverse the Nazi indictment of Christian weakness. Pursuing theodicy in this way as faith's prophetic understanding of its struggle in the world where God's will is contradicted by actual evil,[7] the purpose is to execute the right kind of critique of anthropocentrism (265).

[7] Theodicy of faith provides the backdrop to Paul's teaching of the justification of the ungodly, as N. T. Wright has rightly seen: 'Paul, like all first-century Jews, had a "plight," though it is not to be identified with that of the puzzled existentialist, or for that matter that of the conscience-stricken Protestant. The "plight" consisted of the sorry state of Israel, interpreted as a problem about the covenant faithfulness and justice of the creator God who had called her to be his chosen people. To the extent that this sorry state included the present sinfulness of Jews as individuals, the normal 'Lutheran' reading can be contained within this analysis'. N. T. Wright, *The Climax of the Covenant: Christ and the Law in Pauline Theology* (Minneapolis: Fortress, 1992), 261.

The wrong kind of critique reduces human beings to the beast, as in Nazism, in the name of restoring the innocence of nature. The right kind of critique makes human beings those animals responsible to God for the world, even, if not especially, in their innocent suffering. This critique of anthropocentrism executes Augustine's *severe* mercy. Apart from Christ, that is, God revealed in the manger and on the cross as God who cares eternally for his temporal and vulnerable creatures *as such*, that responsibility seems unbearable. Indeed, Job found it unbearable until the theophany of God made it bearable by putting Job's sufferings into the context of God's cosmic battle against the great Leviathan, the Satan who threatens creation as a system of blessing by demanding that love be put to the test.

It is at this juncture that Osuský finds a conceptual resource in Leibniz. Like Leibniz, Osuský is not content with a mere theology of lament (54), for this is only animal pain, a kind of shrieking reaction that, if it does not surpass pure pain, only reinforces passivity and resignation (233), instead of empowering the perseverance that can stand up not only to brutes but also to pious torturers who fault victims for their victimization. But human beings remain human even in their suffering, and human dignity here consists in insisting on one's innocence, asking and expecting an account from one's Creator for one's sufferings and His hostility (278).

Osuský's account, drawing on Leibniz, makes the sharp and helpful distinction between natural, moral and metaphysical evil (19): natural evil is bodily and psychological pain; metaphysical evil is the vulnerability to harm of any conceivable creature, to wit, the doctrine that metaphysically only God is and can be invulnerable (232). Moral evil presupposes both natural pain and metaphysical vulnerability to harm. Only creatures, and indeed intelligent creatures that ask about the meaning of their sufferings and experience anxiety about their vulnerability, can sin. They sin when they seek to make themselves invulnerable, rather than trusting in their Creator's promise of protection by obedience to His commands; such faith affirms vulnerability, patiency, then, and does not seek to disown it. The false desire at the heart of moral evil is thus the Promethean fantasy of invulnerability, the serpent's *sicut Deus eritis*. The remedy of *false* desire is, accordingly, that *severe* mercy by which the sufferings that God sends remake human affections by returning them to the knowingly vulnerable stance of faith that loves God above all and all things in and under God and perseveres in it.

Can God be loved in this way? Osuský, true to his nineteenth century education, holds that medium of God's revelation is the representations of God in the human mind as these pass by in the parade of history. Some think of God as the Intelligent Designer, but the Nazi war machine is intelligently designed. Others think of God voluntaristically as sheer arbitrary Power; but what else is fascism but the deification of caprice and war power? Humanists in the train of Plato's Socrates think of God as only good, but such good is merely an idea, helpless to stop the actual evil of the idol of militarism, or the false faith of fascism that science and technology will save us, when they rather multiply the capabilities of actual evil. Power, wisdom and love are indeed divine properties; the idols of fascism have power over human beings just because each in some way exploits a facet of the divine reality. But for Christian faith reflecting the Trinity, the *power* of God the Father almighty Creator of all that is not God, revealed in the strange *wisdom* of the Cross of His Incarnate Son providing that severe mercy that is folly to the world perishing from its own lust for domination, to create actual goodness as the costly *love* of God shed abroad in believers' hearts by Spirit's infusion – these three are one together, the living being of the one, true God.

This harmony is what Osuský has learned from Leibniz: the divine trinity of attributes –power, wisdom and love (259, 276, 277) – must be imagined and thought as harmonized in the one, true God, so that God never actualizes any of His divine properties unqualified by the others (76, 83, 88, 184). Indeed, we are to see just such an actualization of God's power, wisdom and love in Job's gracious prayer for his 'unfriendly friends' following the theophany at the end of the book.[8] In this petition for the forgiveness of his enemies, Job is thus a type of Christ: a 'beautiful, truly Christian, indeed Christological moment. The friends came near to him, spoke ill of him, accused him, were suspicious of him and so they turned into enemies. But Job? He prayed for them. We have here come to the climax, a great reversal' (281). In such surprising ways, the living God harmonizes His properties in actions that make Him lovable to His enemies, even His pious enemies.

We would misunderstand the theodicy of Christian faith that Osuský extrapolates from the book of Job, if we expect it to fulfil a philosophical function. It is not a theoretical justification of God, but a proclamation of the God who spared not His own Son so that those in the state of innocent suffering neither deify

[8] Much the same as in another work in the Wisdom genre: when Joseph at the end of his saga with his brothers, who had sold him into slavery, offered reconciliation on account of the supervening work of God: 'You meant it for evil, but God meant it for God' (Gen. 50.20). In commenting on this text, Luther, too, employs the trinity of power, wisdom and love to parse the story. See Paul R. Hinlicky, 'Law, Gospel and Beloved Community', In *Preaching and Teaching the Law and Gospel of God* ed. Carl E. Braaten (Delhi, NY: ALPB Books, 2013), 91–113.

their victimizers in their brutal power and cruel intelligence nor internalize their theological representations or rationalizations to reinforce resignation and despair. As a proclamation of the God who in the end brings Job to pray for his enemies, since by speaking to Job from the whirlwind God has overcome his enmity, it works to make sufferers agents of God's own ongoing work of redemption. These agents are those who rise up to pray for their persecutors even as they walk through the valley of the shadow of death not fearing their evils. As a proclamation of God, it gives the representation of God not as a block of cold ice frozen to human sorrows but as the holy trinity of power, wisdom and love, that works saving reversals in a lived history with human creatures.

Defence of the Truth *(1946): Discerning True Christianity*

We conclude this chapter by resuming our investigation of Osuský's apologetic, *Defence of the Truth*, a work in which Osuský's profile as a biblical theologian becomes unmistakably clear, even as it yet coexists in some tension with Osuský the philosophical apologist. Although it appeared in 1946, Osuský went to work on it following the completion of *The Mystery of the Cross*. Thus it was composed in the course of the dramatic year, 1944, that concluded with Osuský's two months in the Gestapo prison for his support of the uprising in August against the Slovak fascist regime.

As Karl Barth had pointed out just a decade or so earlier, the doctrine of the Trinity is the specifically Christian thing theology has to say about God.[9] We have noted throughout the Trinitarian structure of Osuský's thought, with Religion reflecting the human orientation to God, Christianity bringing the Incarnate Son to free those addicted to idols or enslaved to demons, and Protestantism representing the Spirit's work that purifies the Great Tradition so that the gospel of free justification is told publicly, clearly and purely. We have just noted, as well, how the trinity of divine attributes, power, wisdom and love corresponds to the Trinity of persons, each at work in its distinctive way yet each mutually qualifying the other in God's history with humanity. This powerful wisdom of divine love works Christological reversals that expose the religion business and create in its place beloved community. In this chapter we have seen how Osuský develops this structure of theological thought from what we might

[9] Karl Barth, *Church Dogmatics: I/1, The Doctrine of the Word of God* trans. G. W. Bromiley (Edinburgh: T&T Clark, 1975), 301.

call today a 'post-critical' reading of Scripture that avoids naïve literalism but just as forcefully asserts the Trinitarian claim to truth, Christologically focused.

Thus the middle part of *Defence of the Truth* begins: 'The source of Christian faith and the rule of life is the Bible'. Indeed, the Bible is the 'source not only of faith, but of knowledge of Christian faith'. Osuský immediately concedes in critical mode that 'it is true that we say that the Word of God is in the Bible and not that the Bible is the Word of God'. The Word of God, for Osuský, is Jesus Christ, the living Person to whom the Scriptures bear a normative witness. But critics of Christianity are hardly satisfied with that important distinction. 'There is not a book in the world which has been as criticized, shamed, persecuted, destroyed, burned as the Bible... by natural scientists here, historians there, elsewhere philosophers and literati, indeed more than once also by theologians'. Faced with this attack on the Bible, Osuský draws near even to his sometime nemesis, Juraj Struhárik. He borrows from him a classification of critics of the Bible. First are those who are against the Bible because the Bible is against them as sinful people who, naturally enough, do not hearken gladly to the Bible's criticism of them (61). Another class are the indifferent who rely on popular opinion to cast scorn on the Bible, and neither read nor study the Bible for themselves. With these two kinds of critic, little can be done theologically because the problems are not intellectual but spiritual. But in a third category we find serious objections to the Bible, on which theology must shine some light:

> They base their criticism of the Bible on the following objections. It is, they say, impossible to trust the Bible because already the very titles of individual books are incorrect. Uneducated people wrote them. There are many mystifications in them and they contain a worldview that has been overcome [by science]. There are many conflicts between individual events, many vulgarities and unbelievable wonders, so, on the whole, the Bible is antiquated (62).

We are familiar already with this kind of criticism, and Osuský's reaction to it, from the Linhart-Struhárik controversy discussed in Chapter 1. Although Osuský does not mention by name Rudolph Bultmann's famous essay from just several years before on demythologizing Scripture, it is evident that Osuský is now concerned to address the same set of concerns as did Bultmann. How is the modern person who listens to radio broadcasts and flips the electric light switch on and off to believe in a world populated with invisible spirits affecting events and human destiny? What kind of false obstacle to Christian faith is posed by the mythological worldview which the Bible with its gospel message concerning Christ reflects?

On one level, Osuský's answer to this set of concerns is assuredly not Bultmann's program of *demythologization*,[10] for that would amount to a denarrativization that evacuates the knowledge of sinful humanity and the saving God which Scripture gives to faith. The Greek word, *mythos*, is after all simply a word for story or narrative. Biblical narrative is indispensable to Christian faith and its knowledge of God, its very matrix. Rather, as we have seen, Osuský gropes for an appropriate *deliteralization* of Scriptural narrative that avoids false conflicts with scientific knowledge of the creation and makes it clear that theology's narrative is about God, not the creation which God Himself gives to science to know.

On another level, however, Osuský's answers are of mixed value, and remain so, as we shall see, even in the *Gallery of New Testament Figures*, his magnum opus that will occupy us in the next and final chapter. Osuský never wholly frees himself from the spell of the nineteenth century historicism that thinks that such modern questions about the believability of Scripture as an historical record can be met with more than trivial proofs of the Bible's supposed historical credibility. I will not much consider these naïve arguments for the historical credibility of the Bible, because Osuský himself sees in his clearer moments that the credibility of Scripture is to be assessed on the entirely different plane of its own claim to truth. Indeed, Osuský repeatedly acknowledges in principle what he says here at the beginning of Part Two of *Defence of the Truth*: 'the Bible is not about worldly knowledge, because the Bible does not want to be a textbook for some science, but it is about religious knowledge, an education and inspiration by the true Spirit of God'. In this perspective, 'the Bible withstands every enemy', because the true and underlying conflict has to do with the human will, or rather unwillingness to believe in the God who comes to us in Jesus Christ for the cause of the beloved community. The exposition of Osuský that I offer here follows this better line of thought.

This line of thought, indeed, leads Osuský to a version of epistemic perspectivalism, which he may have drawn from the Leibniz whom he otherwise draws on. In perspectivalism, the question of critical thinking is posed otherwise than by Plato's classic differentiation of the shadowy appearance of the copy in the flux of becoming that is the sensual world from the clarity of its form or idea beyond time and space in the realm of self-identical being. Perspectivalism does not distinguish appearance and reality in this dualistic way. Rather, in

[10] Rudolph Bultmann & Five Critics, *Kerygma and Myth*, ed. H. W. Bartsch (New York: Harper & Row, 1961).

Leibniz-like fashion, it holds that anyone's view of things is from some location in space-time. Human interest causes a knower to attend to something in the blooming, buzzing confusion of pure experience. Here, any perceived particular is attended or focused from such and such an interested and particular perspective, producing a finite intuition of something attended to. This intuition of something in the literally incomprehensible whole is an appearance of reality. One focuses attention. One attends to something. Only in this way is anything in particular visible and as such knowable. But this focusing of attention is also – and this is a critical distinction – one among an infinitude of such perspectival takes on reality. In its inescapable finitude, no particular perception, true as it is in context, can claim comprehensive and as such timeless and universal knowledge. It can only claim to be a true grasp of a reality by a particular knower for a particular purpose and audience from some particular location in space and time. The latter accent on audience reflects the social location of human knowledge in perspectivalism. A subject knows an object in interpreting it to an audience, such that this interpreted object itself becomes an object of further interpretation, and so on to infinity. The human world within the natural world is thus a great web of belief and a process of critical communication.

Thus, when Osuský addresses the question of the credibility of biblical history, he points out that we would not be able to believe *any* historian in the world, if in principle we doubted their human interest in the subject they are describing. Historians, too, focus from somewhere on something for some one. 'Why, every historian selects from the material that has been researched and combines it according to his own view. Historiography is not photography, it is never a snapshot of reality; it is always more or less coloured by the subjective views of its writers'. Thus, even among secular historians treating the same subject, we see how each describes things differently, even if consciously avoiding deception or tendentiousness. The real question is, rather, whom to believe when everyone gives testimony from their own standpoint and from there sees something that is so. For we cannot dispense with judgment, even though in principle we lack the comprehensiveness requisite to certain knowledge. We must come to judgments about testimony, whether willingly and carefully or not. So it is, then, with the Bible: even when we find the same things described from different perspectives, the differences are only in insignificant details, according to the varying perspectives and interests of authors. But they are looking at the same thing, which provides unity in the essential matters of saving significance (63).

The same goes for vulgarities reported in Scripture. Since the Bible is a book of religious and moral life, and in life there are sins, the Bible cannot ignore them; but in recording them it does not idealize them. The Bible is a realistic book. It depicts people as they are and as they ought to be in light of God's will. This is what the Bible is really concerned about, God's will with regard to the human condition: sin, salvation and eternal life. The fact that it contains the mistaken scientific ideas of the age in which it was written is not a genuine problem, unless one falsely seeks in the Bible a scientific textbook (64). What is old is not necessarily antiquated. To be sure, especially in the Old Testament there are antiquated things concerning ceremonies, sacrifices and purifications, and so on. But who is looking for that? We are interested readers, looking for medicine for the sinful soul before the holy face of God. We read the Bible from this particular perspective of faith: what must one do to be saved, so that one becomes a child of God? For this the Bible will be a guide that is not 'overcome' by science nor able to be overcome, but rather a reliable guide that leads to Christ, who is the way, the truth and the life. In Christ God is revealed and to this gift the entire Bible points.

The nineteenth century radically questioned the person of Jesus Christ, and thus attacks focused on Jesus and all that coheres with His life and teaching. David Friedrich Strauss portrayed most of the biblical beliefs about Jesus as myths, and later this led to doubt that Jesus even lived at all. But we know that Jesus was folly to Greeks and a stumbling block to Jews. How do you mythologize that? Peter denied, Thomas doubted, Judas betrayed, the disciples argued about primacy, Jesus rebuked their little faith and in the end they all deserted Him. How do you make that up? (66) Josephus, the Talmud, Tacitus and Suetonius all attest the existence of Jesus in history. And if one complains that there are very few sources outside the Bible attesting this, the hostility of the world to Jesus not only explains the lack of outside sources but also raises the counter-question of why so much energy had to be expended on attacking a figure who was alleged to be only a fiction.

If opponents do concede that Jesus, who elicited so much opposition, actually lived they may yet object that Jesus was insane. They point to hallucinations at His baptism and then in the wilderness, or the belief that He will come in glory as the Son of Man. But such attacks are just unscientific ad hominem (68). Whoever wants to prove a lot proves nothing. Jesus was a genuine human being in whom there is a beautiful harmony of mental properties and abilities. If we take to heart modern psychology's discovery of the unconscious, we can understand how Jesus's extraordinary states of consciousness are possible rather than diseased. In any case, Jesus was not only an ordinary man but also God's Son. As we dig deeper, we see that the real opposition of modern tendencies of thought is to the Bible's presentation of Jesus Christ as the God-Man who mediates between God and humanity. The tendency of modern thought is towards monism, rejecting any kind of ontological duality between creature and Creator, between sinful humanity and the holy God. Thus it denies a priori the need for a mediator. Of course, the Bible has the heavenly voice of God attesting Jesus to us: 'This is my beloved Son, in whom I am well pleased' (70). If we prefer in our modern monism to disregard heaven's testimony and affirm only that Jesus was a good person, even a perfect person (yet not God's Son), we are caught in an impossible contradiction. Can an ordinary man be perfect or righteous in the sense of sinlessness? How do we explain the teaching and works of Jesus, even as they appear to natural human reason, without the explanation that this person is the Son of God? How do we explain that His teaching spread in spite of the great opposition and contrary opinion of the world? (71)

What is significant here is less such unconvincing apologetics, replete with rhetorical questions that beg serious critical questions about receiving the Biblical witness at face value, than Osuský's dogmatic acknowledgment that he now agrees with contemporary Russian Orthodox theologians – N. Lossky and D. Merežkovskij are frequently invoked – who affirm that Jesus was not only truly human but also truly God, hence the God-Man. This is yet another advance toward classical Christian orthodoxy beyond his earlier theological liberalism. Just so, this affirmation raises the further dogmatic question about the reason that God became human (72), as the early medieval Western theologian Anselm posed it in his rational querying of the doctrine of atonement. And, in further agreement with Anselm, Osuský continues, if we ask *how* that incarnation happened, the doctrine of the conception of Jesus by the Holy Spirit from Mary the virgin provides an answer. Perhaps recalling his earlier doubts about this in the conflict with Struhárik, Osuský now writes: 'The only one who can receive this mystery of the conception – the most difficult mystery in Christianity – is the one who believes in the power of God and thus accepts the possibility of a wonder'.

To affirm a possibility is not, of course, to warrant any particular claim to historical actuality. Affirming this possibility, which is the God to whom all things are possible, manifest in wonders, Osuský nevertheless deliteralizes. We could take Luke's testimony to the overshadowing power of God, he writes, not as substituting for a male who gives his seed to the female, but as the creative power of the Creator making a new creative initiative within the old and fallen world. In that case, belief in Jesus as the new and true human being appearing within the world of old and fallen human beings expresses an article of faith in the picture language of a virginal conception. The article of faith, or dogma, does not depend on a literal reading of the picture language. It is and remains Christian doctrine that Jesus from his conception is destined by God to be the New Adam appearing in the midst of, and under the conditions of the Old Adam (73).

We can take the same approach of deliteralization to the article of faith concerning Jesus's descent into hell, which at first sight seems very odd and has thus been the subject of many attacks. But much depends on how we understand the word, 'hell'. Do we take it eschatologically as the place of lost and sinful souls at the end of the world, or historically as the underworld, Hades, a place of temporary dwelling for the souls of the departed until the resurrection? Osuský says the first understanding of the Creed's formulation is not correct. Rather the soul of Christ, like that of all others, descended upon death to the shadowy realm of the dead and by this descent at once completed the state of Christ's humiliation and at the same time began the transition to His state of exaltation. The dogmatic point in this picture language is that Jesus is not only the saviour of those who come after Him in history but also of those who were before Him. He goes to the dead, then, to show them His salvation, the victory over death gained by His glorious resurrection. This is the correct sense of this peculiar article of faith (74), which can only be gained by a deliteralization.

Thus we see again for Osuský that in his more 'post-liberal' moods he consistently holds to the ecumenical doctrine of the ancient church, but by way of a hermeneutical process of deliteralization. The descent into hell is and remains Christian doctrine, because it tells us about the saving God in relation to the lost and dying creature, and indeed assures that this saving work continues the work begun by Jesus in His earthly life, and extends it universally. Doctrine may be, but it does not have to be, bound to historical claims or traditional understandings.

The same procedure applies in consideration of the resurrection. Osuský acknowledges that the risen One appears only to believers, but he also sees that believers were compelled by the reality of the resurrection to be changed (75). The 'resurrection' thus had historical effects that hallucination cannot account for. Yet again, however, Osuský makes a deliteralizing move: 'We should consider whether our present, crude, fleshly body, which decomposes in the grave, has to be what rises from the dead. No. Jesus arose in a glorified body, which is the guarantee that we too shall also rise. To change this earthly, fleshly body in glory – that is truly the creative power of God' (77). It is necessary, he continues in discussing the ascension, constantly to bear in mind this glorified body of the risen Christ when faith in Him as the Risen One faces the tribunal of reason. As Paul himself teaches, what is crude, fleshly, material, earthly cannot enter the kingdom of heaven. Even though human reason cannot otherwise represent the matter (just as it cannot but picture the realm of the dead as the 'underworld'), theological understanding sees differently and so does not fall victim to the accusations of the critics.

Treatment of the 'great mystery' of the Trinity follows, on which, Osuský notes, not a few have cracked their brains (78). He is concerned, like all Western theologians, emphatically to deny that the doctrine is or entails tritheism, 'because, just as the soul, more than the body, is the essential part of the human being, so God's oneness and unity is more essential than the revelation in the state of the three persons' (79). This formulation, again traditionally Western in inclination, sounds modalist, as if God in eternity is one, but in historical manifestation appears as three. Osuský does not perceive the problem.

He continues that if anyone objects that in the representation of the three persons there is temporal progression, the reply is that there is also progression in the Trinity: 'God the Father is from eternity, God the Son is begotten from eternity but born in time, God the Spirit is from eternity, but from the Father and the Son proceeding'. This does not sound modalist at all, in that (even at the unnoticed cost of projecting motion into the eternal being of God) it ascribes the Trinitarian processions to the immanent life of God. Indeed, only so, Osuský continues, can it be true that, in the Incarnation, God became human and not a human being God. We do not wish in the latter, pagan way to divinize our heroes. Recalling the Arian controversy, Osuský comments that Arius was right if divinizing a creature is what we want to do in Christology, that is, to divinize Jesus as our hero. But Athanasius was in fact right when he affirmed that the Logos was first God and then became human out of love for humanity in its perishing state. This becoming of God is a great mystery, which human reason cannot fathom, so it is a great stone of stumbling (79).

Nevertheless, it deeply coheres with the hierarchy of value Jesus proclaimed in the Sermon on the Mount: always and everywhere in the first place we have to value the treasure of heaven. 'The soul is the treasure above all treasures, as the French philosopher Malebranche (1638–1715) beautifully deliberated. We also have to value all other treasures, but in lesser degree, according to their value. Whatever prevents such counting the cost has to be removed. Jesus acknowledges no compromise' (80). But there is a hierarchy of value also in the Triune God: above God's omnipotence stand wisdom and justice, and thus above justice stands love; love is the highest virtue in God. So God loves, and also Jesus Christ loves, and so he teaches also His children that 'they have to love their enemies – this is the truth and the very height of the manifestation of love, which is the central idea of the entire teaching of Jesus'.

Does this divine love lead, as Darwinism seems to indicate when it teaches that life is battle, or as Nietzsche in fact claims, to a slave morality? Some have understood Nietzsche's thought well and taken it spiritually. But many others have taken it as licence for violence. Yet this entire worldview rests on a great error that is refuted by more than one epoch of history. Its most fatal error is that it regards love and its expressions as weakness (81). 'Just send an army to war in which the soldiers have no love for the things for which they fight, and you will see the error' (81) – an allusion perhaps to the recent performance of the Slovak army allied with Nazi Germany on the Russian front. History refutes this error. 'Let us grant', for the sake of the argument:

> that it would be necessary according to the opponents of love to strike the word from the dictionary and replace it with hatred, which is the opposite of love and also a great power. How would life be, where would that lead humanity? We have illustrative examples in the last two world wars. Life would be hell, and it would be worse for us than for animals. We would flee from it. And what overcomes hatred, battles, wars, what tames bestiality? Only love and so love cannot be weakness… If you object that love for others is only covert self-love, how do you explain self-sacrifice? What power is it that it actually does conduct us to service to others? Love! (82).

With regard to the imminent challenge of Marxism-Leninism in this respect, Jesus, Osuský tells us, was neither a revolutionary nor a reformer, as we understand these words today. Rather, He leavened the world with a constant, spiritual revolution in social relationships in the interest of the kingdom of God. From his teaching as from leaven great social reforms have followed and still follow. For example, He valued labour:

> Physical labour was devalued in antiquity to such an extent that such an idealist thinker like Plato scorned it as something for slaves to do. We know that also Aristotle justified slavery because he regarded physical labour as a punishment. Even some Christians understand labour as God's punishment and grounded that view in the curses spoken in Genesis 3. But Jesus is not like that. We can see how highly he valued labour from his doctrine that the worker is worthy of food and pay (Matt. 10.10), from the parables about the workers in the vineyard (Matthew 20) and about the talents (Lk. 19.11-27). Jesus gave lived expression to the value of labour when He washed the feet of the disciples (Jn 13.1-20).

> All this witnesses to the great love He has for labour, the great value He places on service... The objection, then, that Jesus and His apostles undermined the power of the working people does not stand up to scrutiny. Labour is a physical and spiritual-moral blessing. It is the property only of humanity; it forms humanity and society and it creates culture. There is nothing worse than unemployment (84).

The only possible objection to Jesus from the angle of workers, then, is to the previously mentioned hierarchy of value: 'for there are higher values than property. It is necessary to remember that we do not live by bread alone (Matt. 4.4), that we should not gather treasures on earth (Matt. 6.19), that we cannot serve both God and mammon. Woe to the rich one, who is a slave to his property!' (84). But also woe to the poor who merely want to be rich and thus risk becoming likewise enslaved. Surveying all such evidence, Osuský asks 'who can deny that the teaching of Jesus and His apostles is socially oriented and that on this foundations it is possible and worthwhile to build a social program and social praxis?' (86).

Osuský affirms this possibility, but with the following proviso:

> In this work Christianity must be directed by Holy Scripture because it is the source of faith and the rule of life generally, so also it has to be the rule for social labour and the guide for resolving the social needs of the times. As such it must avoid two extremes. We are not free to forget that when Jesus Christ represented the chief task as seeking first the kingdom of God and its righteousness, he also taught that the kingdom is not of this world even though it has to be in this world... That means that it must act according to the principle of Jesus not to mix the spiritual with the worldly, not to identify with any form of the state, political party, condition or class, in a word not to politicize the gospel. On the other hand, however ... it is not possible to take no interest in the destiny of people in the nation, state or other social forms of common life in community, nor to be satisfied with the level of social practice to date. Since God takes interest in the weak, it is not possible to stay blind and deaf to them and not to help wherever there is woe and Scripture demands help. Christianity must teach Christians not only to see but also to feel woe, to awaken and cultivate conscience, to help where help is needed, and not only by charity but by planned, organized social-welfare work. The Swiss thinker Ragaz rightly wrote that when Christianity becomes more social, socialism will be more Christian ... Christianity must work out its social ethics in greater detail and more relevantly, at least as much as in its individual ethics... Holy Scripture is certainly not a practical sociological textbook, but that does not mean that it

> does not have perspectives on social forms and their lives: on marriage, family, nation, race, state and the relation of employer and employee, on work, on property, on various defects, on the difference between the poor and the rich, on the relation of the individual and the whole and finally on voluntary help not only in charity and good deeds, but in the obligatory service of support (88).

Osuský goes on to discuss briefly some Scriptural perspectives on various social forms.

Marriage is instituted by God for our good and should be preserved accordingly for one man and one woman. We are to love our nation after the example of Christ, who felt Himself called and sent to its lost sheep and wept over its unhappy fate, or according to the example of Paul who was ready to die for the salvation of his own people, yet testified that in Christ there is neither Jew nor Greek. In matters of race there is equality before God and in history, as also among the nations. We are bound to give to Caesar what is Caesar's, under the condition that it is also necessary to give to God what is God's; and if these obligations conflict we are to serve God rather than people. The churches cannot regard it as shameful if legal and secular organizations take over charitable work, but on the other hand it would be an error if these attempts to solve the social question disabled Christian love and voluntary charitable work. Rather ecclesial and secular institutions should complement one another:

> What would be ideal is that earthly social forms were happy and life joyful, so that no one exploits another, everyone has sufficient employment, so that social differences gradually moderated, and no one had to fear over their life, about the future in the event of unemployment, infirmity, disability, abandonment, sickness, old age, but instead the individual and the whole society cooperated in harmony, so that property and material things served wellbeing and the higher spiritual interests of all (89).

The only question that remains – so it seems to Osuský as he draws to a conclusion – is whether it is possible to accomplish this without the church.

We often hear from individualists that it is possible to have religion without the church, that is, without visiting the worship assemblies in the church building or elsewhere. The individualists say that you can worship God also at home, through a broadcast on the radio or through other forms of media. But this is one-sided and to a certain extent dangerous and selfish. The chief fault is that it thinks that religion is only about the good of the individual and not also about all the others. The church as a religious community is necessary to salvation, not in the sense of being a mediator between God and humanity, but as the nursemaid of religious values and education; in this way both the individual and the human collective draw near to achieving their divinely destined realization of the Kingdom of God on earth. The individualistic misunderstanding of religion is not a manifestation of true freedom but only of caprice (90). Why, it would do no harm to today's rationalized and anarchized Europe to reflect on the idea of all-unity, emphasized and cultivated by the oriental religions, especially by the Indians!

Precisely in these times troubled by different currents and inflamed by various ideas we can reduce matters to two basic ideas: the individual and society. One side grounds society on the individual, proceeding from the stance that society is composed of individuals. The other side fights for society, because, according to this side, the individual is only an atom of the whole, society, to which he owes his existence. In the church, this question appears as follows: must one care only for self, and the church proclaim salvation only for the individual? Or from the perspective of the salvation of the whole must the church not also work for the salvation of the individual? Does the individual, or the fellowship of the church, stand in the forefront?

We know that according to Christianity selfishness is wrong, but do we realize that there can also be spiritual selfishness? Isn't this question a rebuke not only from the enemies of Protestantism but also from the careful and objective listeners in our pews, who also observe how we live? In saying this, Osuský carefully notes, he is not saying that the Roman Catholic Church is thereby justified for standing on the other side of this polarity between individual and society, as when the collective of the church swallows up the individual, just as on the political and economic fields communism swallows up the individual (91). But the truth is that the individual is referred to the society and society is referred to the individual. The one cannot be without the other, and there must rather be mutuality and cooperation between them. The individual is responsible for the salvation of his own soul, but also for the salvation of his church and humanity. And the same applies for the church as a religious society, which must care for each and every individual. Whoever thinks about himself, about his own soul, must also think about the church! And these demands only intensify when we do not forget that the church is not only a human community but also God's community and as such an absolute value.

We cannot prove that Christianity is the absolute religion, for that is a matter for the future to decide. We can only decide by faith and on the basis of the evidence so far. From the conditions thus far known and from the values which true, pure, biblical Christianity brings, Osuský draws his conclusion: 'I am convinced that Christianity is the absolute religion. Theoretically nothing better is possible. Progress can only consist in correcting errors and inadequacies in certain churches and applying more in practical life in order to do what it ought to do' (92). A more perfect representation of the one God is not possible than as revealed by God's Son, Christ, that He is a just but also loving Father of all people and the whole world. As the famous German theologian and philosopher, Ernst Troeltsch (1865–1924), wrote, Osuský continues, the Christian ideal regarding the kingdom of God transcends the world of space and time so that it is eternal, for all peoples for all times. It does not preach flight from the world, but changing the world so that humanity has to become perfect like God. God empowers us for this task by the redemptive work of Jesus Christ and the sanctifying work of the Holy Spirit. It does not suffice only to erect a beautiful ideal; but rather what is needed is provision of both the will and the strength to realize the ideal of the kingdom of God, and, when we fail, to raise us up again in faith.

Christianity has not realized this ideal, but it is realizing it. For God wants to change human beings, and thus change the world into the kingdom of God. Contemporary people themselves also now judge that it is necessary to change the world and that human beings should be changed. God's way through Christianity is slower but surer than these contemporaries imagine. For when we examine the reasons why Christianity has thus far not realized the ideal, we discover ourselves: weak, fragile, sinful people. For this we do not need less but more Christianity! But only true, pure, biblical Christianity helps (93).

So Osuský concludes his defence of Christianity against the anticipated attack by Marxism-Leninism, by preparing the way for his own attack on Catholicism to follow in Part Three of *Defence of the Truth*, as we considered previously in Chapter 2. On reflection, this middle part on Christianity is, and can be, no more than a transitional reflection on Osuský's part, where he is still trying to reconcile the heterogeneous elements in his thought, stemming from his education on the one side and his life experience, also as a believer, on the other. The odd appeal to Troeltsch, above – who famously debunked the alleged absoluteness of Christianity in history, the very claim Osuský is making – along with the retention of the liberal, Kantian frame of reference of ethical idealism, as well as the root assumption that God works through the progression in the history of thought to provide purified representations of God effecting a corresponding change in human consciousness – all these are all evidence of Osuský's enduring debt to the theological liberalism of his education.

Clearly, his immediate purpose in this defence of Christianity was to secure a place for the Protestant church in the work of cultural reconstruction following the catastrophe of the Second World War. But this defence failed. The shop-worn platitudes of Osuský's too traditional theism and insufficient, tacit Trinitarianism[11] cannot, despite his best efforts, stand up to the radical demands for human transformation that the times demand. Such platitudes can neither muster the church to the work Osuský's calls for, nor can they satisfy the Marxist suspicion that utopian socialism and ethical idealism are every bit as much an opiate of the people as the individualistic, otherworldly, spiritually selfish and escapist religiosity that Osuský has otherwise so trenchantly exposed and criticized. Only the final disillusionment that his fate under Marxism-Leninism brings will lead him to a better understanding of his own best insights. As we have seen in the commentaries on Revelation and Job, those best insights are into a new path for Christian theology in a post-Christendom world. On this path, Christian theology without patronage must learn to stand again on its own two feet, the gospel and the Bible, to speak to a world *ever* at war. For this task, not demythologization but deliteralization is necessary, that is, not deconstruction of biblical narrative which tells the saving story of the warring world's pacification in Christ, but interpretation of this very biblical narrative as knowledge of the one God who is freely determined to redeem and fulfil the creation by the missions of His Son and Spirit.

[11] Osuský 'does not fall into the line of theological liberalism even though he was temporarily influenced by it. Yes, his religious thought is saturated by philosophical theism, but it is not a theism without Christology and soteriology. Osuský's interpretation of Jesus is not only religious-ethical or humanistic, but above all theological and Christological'. Gažik, 83.

4

Biblical Theology in Samizdat

Problems in Interpreting the *Gallery*

In this chapter the task is to interpret Osuský's posthumously published magnum opus, *A Gallery of New Testament Figures*. This is a daunting challenge, for to begin with it is impossible in the scope of a chapter to convey the vast range and scholarly erudition on display in Osuský's work of three parts sketching the figures of Jesus, of His disciples and opponents, and of Paul and figures associated with him. Suffice it to say that he is engaged with the broad spectrum of New Testament scholarship of his time. He knows the major contemporary figures like Schlatter, Cullmann, Kümmel and Aland; the giants of the earlier liberal period like Schweitzer, Zahn, Deismann; and pioneer critics of the Enlightenment like Renan. He engages in a running conversation with the contemporary Jewish scholar, Joseph Klausner, and a host of lesser-known figures writing in German, Czech or Hungarian. Notably missing is only the thought of contemporary Rudolph Bultmann, the absence of which, as we shall see in the Conclusion, makes Osuský's wrestling with the problem of New Testament mythology inconsistent and not equal to his better lights and higher purposes.

Let me acknowledge from the outset, then, certain ambivalences to be found in the *Gallery*, which might be thought to speak against my interpretive thesis that Osuský is abandoning apologetics for catechesis. On the one hand, Osuský requires historical understanding of the biblical text (79, 81, 132, 372, 447, 641, 682) in order to extract the kernel of knowledge of God and humanity from the historically conditioned husk (152). He insists on facing up to the historical development of doctrine (447, 533), errors (238, 240, 324) and more serious contradictions in thought within the Bible (351, 443, 589, 669, 671, 694). He expresses incredulity, therefore, in relation to 'conservative theologians' who hold to a doctrine of the Bible's 'verbal inspiration' (601). He is very critical of the pious legends found in the apocrypha (e.g. 105, 201) and extends a demythologizing critique (369) from there especially to the representation of mental illness as demonic possession (e.g. 204, 219, 241, 348–9, 360, 373).

On the other hand, he affirms the category of miracle (90, 93, 96) as a lens through which to see God active in human affairs (30, 199, 202, 211, 215), and spends a great deal of effort to interpret the resurrection miracle not as the resuscitation of the corpse but as the gift of a spiritual body (261, 273, 314–7, 403). In the same way, he takes the canon of Scripture as normative (604) as well as trustworthy (37, 84), not because it was miraculously dictated by God but because it reflects the guidance of the Spirit in creating, in preserving by selection from alternative writings (323), and then in integrating the human words of the biblical authors (in spite of errors, 81) into the canonical whole. As a result of this divine procedure of the Spirit, a fitting theological method of harmonizing (105, 126, 135, 140, 413, 457, 621) can show, he thinks, how the biblical writings complement and fulfil one another (264) in constructing the great panorama of the Genesis to Revelation Bible.

Yet this canonical critical procedure can easily stretch beyond a post-critical hermeneutical procedure in theology to an apologetic affirmation of supernaturally guaranteed and rationally demonstrable historicity (60, 147). This stretch goes so far at times that Osuský confidently dates to the month certain events in the life of Jesus (e.g. 174, 176, 185). From this kind of overly confident historical reconstruction, the eminently predictable Christian 'worldview' emerges, with God as loving father (112–13, 126), not the Old Testament tribal God of strict retribution, Yahweh (158), at the climax of progressive revelation. Such remnants of nineteenth century historical criticism in the awkward form of conservative apologetics appear throughout the *Gallery*, unintegrated with the more interesting moves towards a post-modern hermeneutic.

As argued at the close of the preceding chapter, the latter would require a method that takes New Testament apocalyptic seriously, but not literally. The notion of deliteralization (cf. 2 Cor. 3.6) that I am deploying in this analysis requires that the special form of New Testament speech should be respected and appreciated. This is centrally the catachrestic metaphor of the 'Christ crucified', the paradox that is not the nonsense of a contradiction but an innovation in language that makes ordinary language serve new and divine purposes.[1] This paradox, moreover, is the basis for Osuský's decisive rejection of political Messianism, as we shall see. Not only, then, can we repeatedly see instances of deliteralization in Osuský's biblical interpretation, but the procedure can claim to be methodologically central, if Osuský is to be consistent with his own better insights.

In any event, the *abstractions* that must be made from this rich and wide-ranging work to make a chapter-length interpretation manageable cannot but do violence to Osuský's style. His is a style that lovingly luxuriates in portraying the personae of the New Testament and then relating the portraits to one another, in the process generating theology that speaks sometimes quite directly to his current situation, as we shall shortly see. He calls the literary portraits of biblical figures that he draws 'profiles', and repeatedly reminds us that these profiles, especially in the first part concerning Jesus, are not 'biography' (137, 235, 269, 274–5, 324, 290, 405, 431). He calls upon Emil Brunner, here, to parse the modern Christological problem of the relation of the Jesus of history to the Christ of faith. 'The name of Jesus is for those who know Him from history (Peter, James), while the name Christ is for believers who know Him from the resurrection (Paul), from eternity, from God (John)' (322) – evidence again of Osuský's tacit perspectivalism.

Thus to try to know Jesus from history, as the genre of biography would do, fails fundamentally because it cannot know Jesus as the Christ, the Son of God. Concretely, it cannot unify the multitude of contradictions presented in the New Testament portraits of Jesus: 'He helps others – but in life He did not help himself; He was poor – and gave the world the greatest gifts. He drew close to no one – and died as a criminal. He forgave – and nothing was forgiven Him; He is most praised – and also most shamed … He preached against retaliation – and His life was a battle against evil. He was truth – and truth murdered Him. He died – and lives …' (321). Biography cannot follow or fathom this strange movement nor explain Jesus immanently as the unfolding of a unified personality. 'Consider, dear reader! Who can understand Him in these paradoxes? Who sufficiently, faithfully and artistically pictures Him or exhausts Him? All pictures, statues, etc., do not know how to grasp the richness of His mystery. All biographies are only attempts. We are too weak to capture everything about Him, because He is not only a human being as we are only human beings' (321).

[1] I have discussed this in detail in a number of places but see especially Paul R. Hinlicky, 'Luther's Anti-Docetism in the Disputatio de divinitate et humanitate Christi (1540)' in *Creator est creatura: Luthers Christologie als Lehre von der Idiomenkommunikation* ed. O. Bayer and Benjamin Gleede (Berlin and NY: Walter De Gruyter, 2007), 139–85.

The persona that is profiled hereby is a profile of paradoxes that describes but does not define the mystery of the person, Jesus Christ the Son of God.

Thus Osuský thinks of the New Testament narratives as a kind of gallery, displaying portraits and scenes that, rightly understood as profiles, complement one another, and, at the end of academic study, provide a panorama of types (365) in which followers but also opponents emerge as mirrors of Jesus (212, 439, 442). We could say, then, that he is retrieving the premodern notion of the subject or agent as the manifestation in the public world of a patient-agent, a *persona* in Latin, or in Greek, a *prosopon*. In the New Testament, we meet the figures of Jesus, His Father and their Spirit, and we discover through their interactions their interrelations. And in discovering their interrelations, we discover their mysterious unity.

Such retrieval in fact captures the New Testament's presentation of Jesus as a man on a single-minded mission, whose character is disclosed not by divulging or probing the contents of His self-consciousness but by interactions with others in actualizing a divinely determined destiny. This persona yields to a descriptive, a posteriori ontology (474), not a speculative, a priori one that comprehends. A descriptive ontology thus preserves the mystery of Jesus's person and does not even try to comprehend it theoretically. It provides a pragmatic knowledge of Jesus in the interest of the faith that receives Him as a gift and rises up to follow Him as a task given with this gift. It is pragmatic knowledge of faith in and for the contested, conflicted world of apocalyptic. 'If you do not believe in God, you believe in the devil; if not in Christ, then in the Antichrist; if not in spirit, then in matter … You must believe in something, whether you want to or not. There is no absolute unbelief. There is only the question of what is better, which belief overcomes evil and death. Any old faith does not save' (562).

Because this is the nature of New Testament faith in correlation with its mysterious object, Jesus Christ, Osuský continues, trying to answer theoretical or philosophical questions in theology is a category mistake. For this reason as well, anthropomorphism in the biblical depiction of God given through faith in Jesus Christ is both natural and inevitable and unproblematic, provided that it is qualified by the reminder that God, as Creator of all that is not God, is a singularity, so to speak, an incomparability beyond all that finite creatures can know or even imagine (563). For Osuský, what is rather more urgent, however, is to deliver the new picture of God as loving father beyond justice and beyond being which comes from the gospel's portrait of Christ Jesus, the Risen One who was crucified, the Son who makes the Father known in the Spirit who gives faith.

This, I dare say, is an innovative style of theologizing for Osuský's time, even though it has a precedent[2] in Martin Luther's theologizing in his own late-in-life magnum opus, the so-called *Commentary on Genesis*. I say, 'so-called', because the Latin title of Luther's work, *Enarrationes in Genesin*, should be translated *Re-narrations*[3] *in [the book of] Genesis*. The nuance is that Luther draws out meaning from Scripture by retelling the biblical stories to his tacit, that is, contemporary, audience. He does this by expanding on the sparse sketches of the persona presented in the biblical narratives, to explicate, often psychologically, the situation of faith for the reader. One might, critically, dismiss this as 'hagiography',[4] but, if so, it is not meant, either by Luther or by Osuský, uncritically. In the same way, and for the same motives as Luther, Osuský profiles the figures in his gallery to make their predicament before God, and God's work to sustain them in trial, intelligible for contemporaries. Just as Luther celebrated the human, all-too-human 'saints' in the Bible to make their struggles transparent to contemporary believers, Osuský notes the programmatic approach he has taken:

> The words of Peter to Cornelius when the latter bowed down to him, "Stand! For I am also only a man" (Acts 10.26) are beautiful words. I acknowledge that just these words caused me to write in this gallery about people and not about some unnatural beings, which by their own holiness do not touch the earth, who are not even human beings. That makes for a chasm that cannot be bridged between us and them, even if nevertheless we are commanded to follow their example. Peter was certainly a great man and yet he did not permit Cornelius to address him as holy, and so he made Cornelius stand up … so that in a friendly conversation they went together into his house … (611).

Re-narration, or profiling, is thus an 'existential' way of making the story imaginable and thus appropriable to contemporary readers (e.g. 132, 191, 221, 408, 423, 482). It risks, of course, a kind of reductionism over against the 'objectivity'

2 I am not claiming that Osuský draws explicitly on Luther in this connection or even knows Luther's Genesis commentary. Rather, this manner of 'enarration' would be a possibility latent in his Lutheran tradition that could have been mediated to him in a variety of ways. The parallel is striking and cannot be merely coincidental.

3 See Kenneth Hagen, *Luther's Approach to Scripture as seen in his "Commentaries" on Galatians 1519–1538* (Tübingen: J. C. B. Mohr [Paul Siebeck] 1993). 'The term that Luther used through his work and throughout his life to describe his publications on Galatians was "enarrare" or "enerratio…" To "ennarate" Pauline theology means to set forth in detail Paul's theology in the public arena. "Narrate" (narratio) means to tell the story. "Ennarate" (enarratio), not an English word – at least not yet –, means to take the message out and to apply it, that is, to tell the story in public' (50-1).

4 Dennis Bielfeldt, Mickey Mattox, and Paul R. Hinlicky, *The Substance of Faith: Luther on Doctrinal Theology* (Minneapolis, MN: Fortress Press, 2008), 37–8.

of the biblical story to states of human consciousness, although neither Luther nor Osuský succumb to that error. For them, the specific situation of faith cannot be reduced to whatever states of consciousness the reader imputes to self or story, because faith has an object to which it clings. Faith stands and falls with the putative revelation of God conveyed through biblical narrative. For Osuský, as for Luther before him, theology sourced from biblical narrative is about lost humanity and the saving God. Interpretation that tells some other story is not methodologically sound.

Thus Kenneth Hagan 'pleas' for an 'approach which is consistent with and appropriate to the item under consideration… Actually, theology is at stake. The Bible is all about God; it talks about God, to God, and for God … To interpret Scripture with methods and techniques that are not only extraneous to Scripture but also contrary to its message is not consistent methodology. It takes Scripture out of its own environment and forces it into a different "think system", thought structure, or a different grammar'.[5]

> There are obvious inconsistencies in the modern approach. Scripture is linked and limited to its historical settings, or historicized. Historicists historicize everything but historicism, or, more commonly put, philosophical relativists relativize everything but relativism … Scripture is not primarily a historical document; it is theology in service of God. Just as theology should not dictate the conditions and limits of other disciplines be they philosophy or history, neither should other disciplines dictate the conditions and limits of theology.[6]

This correlation of biblical narrative with theology as re-narration is what Osuský has also understood, even if it at times he continues to confuse it with conservative apologetics.

With the proviso in mind about the necessary abstractions to follow, let me note further that I am selecting for discussion what I see as Osuský's leading themes, and interpreting their significance for Christian theology after modernity and after Christendom. This selection, obviously enough, is the work of this author, not Osuský. Chiefly my selection is governed by the shift that had taken place with the ascendancy of Marxism-Leninism, which has officially silenced Osuský and makes his work in the *Gallery* a subversive and defiant act of hope. This shift, moreover, moved Osuský from the previously predominant postures of humanist philosophy, ethical idealism and theological liberalism by

[5] Hagen, 38–9.
[6] Ibid., 61–2.

way of an ever firmer grasp on his heritage from the Reformation to the apocalyptic theology of the New Testament.

Osusky's traditional 'confessional Lutheranism', stemming from the Augsburg Confession (446, and thus through Melanchthon to Luther), is presupposed throughout the *Gallery* and often surfaces. He can virtually equate the biblical canon with the sixteenth century confession of justification by faith (449). Commenting on Luke's penitent thief, Osuský writes: 'Thus when Jesus promises him paradise, He comforts him for his repentance and faith, and without works of the law justifies him out of grace' (432). But for those justified by faith who have still to live, works necessarily follow. He explains this just like the sixteenth century reformer: 'the thought [of James] that faith without works is dead must be delimited by the word that also works are dead without faith. Faith is the root and works are the fruit. It is not necessary to set them against each other, but rather alongside each other in the right order' (621, cf. also 393, 619). Thus the Christian proclamation is the gospel in the gospels (145), the treasure in the earthen vessels. God's Word is both law and gospel (73, 144), where the proclamation of law serves as a mirror to show the self how God sees it (151). Correspondingly, the Christian ethic requires a parsing of the experienced world by the doctrine of the Two Kingdoms (425, 427, 453). At the centre of this dialectic (652, not then a theology of progressive revelation) is Christ as mediator (650) according to the theology of the cross (444). The paradox of Christ crucified is to be sustained (192, 197, 290), so that Christ can only be received in trust, *fiducia*, (144, 201, 373), that is, *fides ex corde* that reorganizes human affects (404). Such faith comes about in the believer as a spiritual resurrection (387). The consequent patiency of faith (186, 190), like Job's (375, 378), is emphasized in this way as the abiding root of faith active in love. Faith lives before God (149) conscientiously in union with Christ (658), who is the victor (306–7). Thus Osuský retrieves the classical Lutheran Christological emphasis on the divine movement of Incarnation as an act of humble love for the unworthy, as opposed to the proud, 'pagan' deification of the creature as a hero (258). He lays the accent Christologically not on the duality of natures but on the unity of person (469–70, 489, 659). All this is classically Lutheran.

The shift from humanist philosophy, ethical idealism and theological liberalism to apocalyptic theology by way of Reformation theology should not, however, be understood so much as a repudiation as a reorientation. It should not be understood as a repudiation of the critical legacy from liberalism, or the social orientation from humanist or idealist philosophy, but rather as a 'post-liberal', or 'post-critical', or 'post-modern', or 'post-Christendom' move, which is decidedly not a return to the past but groping for a new future. It represents a search for a way forward after the door has been slammed shut and sealed on the former theological project of nation-building within the framework of Christendom. To appreciate more fully Osuský's struggle for a new style of theology from the Bible in the situation of post-Christendom, we have to set the historical stage for our interpretation of the *Gallery* by rehearsing the sad story of Osuský's removal from office for his 'reactionary tendencies'.

Persona non grata and the Failure of Apologetics

In October of 1949, Osuský published one of his last essays, commemorating the 30th anniversary of the founding of his beloved Slovak Protestant Theological Faculty in Bratislava. It is a very interesting piece for all the personally experienced history that he reports in it, beginning with the observation that, five years earlier, in October of 1944, it was impossible to celebrate the school's 25th anniversary:

> The time was not propitious. It was the moment of cruel retaliation during the temporary suppression of the second [Osusky counts the 1848 uprising as the first] Slovak national uprising. There was then neither taste for nor thought of reminiscences. The academic year of 1944–5 was so extraordinary that there were not even regular exams at the school. I myself in those days was detained by the German *Sicherheitsdienst*, and locked up in isolation for 63 days. I was investigated in three two-hour interrogations with questions like this: How do you theological professors educate the young pastors, if they are all in the uprising? Do you lecture on the philosophy of German National Socialism? Italian fascism? Or, do you regard Nazism as antichristian or antireligious? Why did you as a bishop not work hand in hand with the government of the Slovak State? Why did you not send out a pastoral letter of warning that Protestants should not participate in the uprising? And so on… [7]

Five years after those events things have changed dramatically. His hope in the 1946 *Defence of the Truth* that ascendant Marxist-Leninists would at least see and acknowledge positively the difference between progressive Lutherans and reactionary Catholics, as we shall now describe, was profoundly crushed. The hope in apologetics has manifestly failed to persuade determined opponents,

[7] *CL* LXI (1949), 403–4.

because at its depths the conflict is not merely a rational one. At is depths, it is a conflict of faiths, of theologies – an *apocalyptic* struggle.

Yet, as Osuský proceeded in 1949 to give his account of the efforts of the past thirty years to establish a quality theological education for Slovak Protestants, he did not signal any premonition that within months he would be removed from his professorial position and forced into premature retirement, forbidden to preach, teach or publish. On the contrary, he recounts with justifiable pride not only his own academic achievements, along with those of his colleagues, but also their success in educating 567 students and sending 421 of them into the ministry of the church. Osuský applauded what he calls 'the ecclesiastically positive direction of the faculty which consists in the modernization of the old orthodoxy and of the national spirit in the Christian sense'.[8] He also notes, although without comment, the recent (that is, after the February 1948 seizure of power in Czechoslovakia by the Marxist-Leninists) introduction into the theological curriculum of a course on the 'foundations of scientific socialism'. As he draws the memorial essay to an end, he permits himself to breathe a brief prayer for graduates, 'that God would help the living to withstand the most difficult of exams, that of life'.[9] That brief prayer is the only hint in the 30th anniversary essay in 1949 of trouble approaching.

In the first published report from the theological faculty after the war, in 1946 Dean Beblavý corroborated Osuský's account of the events at the end of the war. He reported that 'a sizeable part of our students participated in the Slovak National Uprising. In this semester [Fall, 1944] tenured Professor Dr Samuel Štefan Osuský could not lecture because he was imprisoned for two months by the German police and after his release into freedom he required three months of medical recuperation'.[10] But very much *unlike* Osuský in his 1949 note on the newly introduced course in 'scientific socialism', Beblavý went on to note that, with the resumption of normal life following the war in 1946, the faculty had introduced a 'new discipline, apologetics, which in these times is very important and up until now was not in the curriculum of theological study on our faculty'.[11] This new course was undertaken by the recuperated Osuský; no doubt it included study of, or study based on, his simultaneously published *Defence of the Truth*. Indeed, we might call this brief post-war interregnum between the end of fascism and the beginning of the Marxist-Leninist

[8] Ibid., 407.
[9] Ibid., 408.
[10] *CL* LIX (1947), 49–50.
[11] Ibid., 52.

regime the 'period of apologetics', or rather, 'the period of the rise and fall of apologetics'.

Anxiety about the ascent of the Marxists visibly pervaded the Lutheran church in the years following the war. The highly esteemed General Bishop Čobrda published a talk he had given to the church's general assembly in 1946 in which he first noted some positive developments upon the end of the war. For example, based on its experience of the participation of Christians and especially Lutherans in the anti-fascist resistance during the war, the hitherto secular gymnastic movement, the *Sokol*, had recently, Čobrda reported, 'entered upon the correct path, knowing and explaining religion as a positive source of spiritual and moral power, inevitable for attaining and securing the freedom of nation and state', even if the *Sokol* still had a way to go in reassessing its relation to the community of the church.

Having thus reminded his audience of the progressivity of the Lutherans, and given an example of a hitherto indifferent, if not hostile, secular movement reassessing its relation to the Christian religion, Čobrda next turned his attention to a recent article on the relations of the Communist Party in the Soviet Union to religion. Recounting it, Čobrda offers the following ominous assessment:

> The magazine, *Young Bolshevik*, instigated a discussion of the relations of the Party to religion. It recommended that tolerance be shown to believing party members and that it be patiently explained to them how harmful religious faith is. The newspaper, *Pravda*, proclaimed that it is impossible and unacceptable that members of the party believe in God and observe religious ceremonies, for that indicates an abandonment of Marxism. In the same way also Stalin proclaimed: "The party cannot be neutral over against religion and it conducts antireligious propaganda against all religious prejudices. Because religious prejudices oppose science, every way of religion is equally against science." That at least is clear and sincere speech. And the church is right to be curious whether the Czechoslovak Communist Party shares this absolutely negative stance toward God, religion and church. For if they stand on a materialism that denies spirit and everything that coheres with spirit, the believing person, especially the believing Protestant, would have no place in the Party.[12]

Čobrda's conclusion, too, is clear and sincere speech. Since 'every way of religion is equally against science', the party will not be able to recognize any real difference between progressive Lutherans and reactionary Catholics. Some

[12] *CL* LX (1948), 8.

voices appearing in the church's theological journal during this uncertain time of transition and would-be apologetics saw as clearly as Stalin and sounded out even more sharply. For them, the best defence was to go on the offensive.

Pastor Ján Hano (1920–89), who had earned a doctorate in theology in Bratislava, destroyed his academic career prospects by publishing the following 'sincere words to our Protestants who are also Communists':

> If Marxism, or communism were only a political party, as many would understand that, it would not be necessary for us to concern ourselves more closely with it. But communism has become a new religion, which wants to establish heaven on earth, which inflames the hearts of thousands and millions by faith in the earthly paradise of the proletariat. This faith has its saviours, gods, saints and also its tortured and its martyrs! It is all about a new view of the world and humanity! It is about so much more than the interests of one class, party, or caste. It is about God, eternal life, the salvation of the soul and the meaning of our lives.[13]

Sharp as such aggressive critiques of 'political religion' were, the more typical apologetics sought to find common ground, as we saw Osuský himself seeking, for example, stressing the social nature of 'pure, biblical Christianity' in his apologetic at the end of the last chapter. According to Gažik, however, Osuský consistently rejected the Marxist-Leninist claim of being 'scientific' socialism; he charged that this claim 'violently appropriates the results of the natural sciences and derives atheism from them. In the past on this account Marxism called its hypotheses and theories philosophical materialism and not a scientific worldview, or even scientific atheism. These new terms are a *contradictio in adiecto*'.[14] In a study written in 1948, 'Masaryk's "Social Question" in regard to the stance of Marxism toward Religion', Gažik finds Osuský retrieving Masaryk's 'thorough and consequent critique of the philosophical and sociological foundations of Marxism' from fifty years before. Osuský, for his part in the study, concentrated on the one-sided and hostile approaches of Marx and Engels to the phenomenon of religion... The reductionism of the origin of religion to social-economic roots is precisely the greatest misunderstanding and indeed distortion of religion from the side of Marx'.[15] For all his effort at

[13] *CL* LIX (1947), 203.
[14] Gažik, 36–7.
[15] Ibid., 39.

mediation, Osuský's reasoned critique of Marxism was unmistakable and a matter of public record.

When the Communist Party ascended to power in February 1948, the Lutheran church's governing council, the General Presbyterium, expressed its position along these lines of seeking common ground by recalling its own 'mission to build the Kingdom of God in the hearts, families, congregations and in the entire nation and state, a kingdom of good and beauty, truth and justice, peace and love'. For the sake of this mission, the statement continued, the church 'gives to Caesar what is Caesar's', and reminds one and all in its ranks 'to be subject to the governing authorities' – awkward counsel from a church just recently boasting of its resistance to governing authorities. The statement then went on to spell out the common ground between Christianity and communism:

> As the Protestant church has proclaimed from the beginning … that all power in the church derives from the congregation, and thus from the believing people in the consciousness that we are all equal, it does not and cannot acknowledge any class differences and it cannot authorize any economic or social injustices. Thus it works in the spirit of Christ's teaching, and, in the new political arrangements, it will work according to its powers and possibilities for the advancement of living standards and for the moral and spiritual perfection of humanity. By its moral and spiritual authority it wants to help and will help also the new government of the Czechoslovak Republic in its tasks of reconstruction… by the grace of God it wants to cultivate godly, believing Protestant Christians of pure character founded on morality for the nation and state … [Thus it] prays and in trust expects the understanding and comprehensive support of the Republic and its new government … [16]

There is a clever watchword that is appropriate as commentary on this statement: 'Beware what you pray for!' One could argue, of course, that the minority Lutheran church in the relatively backward part of the reunited Czechoslovak Republic had little choice other than to accommodate to the new reality. There is accommodation, however, and there is accommodation. The salient observation, rather, is how the habit of nation-building thus shows itself as so deeply engrained in the tradition of European Christendom. This habit is in fact the deep motive for theology as apologetics. In this way modern Christianity, especially, has hitched its wagon to the nation-state with pretentious and highly questionable claims to be the soul or conscience of the people, when in fact it

[16] *CL* LX (1948) 94–6.

pleads obsequiously for political establishment and financial support. Ironically enough, with new legislation this is just what came about under communism, and it became the legal instrument by which the state subordinated the churches to its own agenda of radical 'reconstruction'.

Later in 1948 a Lutheran church delegation under the leadership of Bishop Čobrda travelled to Prague to meet with the new regime. The meeting was reported in the church's journal. In his greeting, the bishop – well known, like Osuský, for his criticisms of Bolshevism, as we observed above – emphasized that 'the mission of our church is not to do politics but to penetrate the lives of individuals and society with the leaven of Christ's gospel so that the building of the Kingdom of God on earth would be helped by that... The Slovak Protestant Church wants to work for these ideals loyally and with understanding also in the new political arrangements ...'. In his response, Klement Gottwald, head of the Communist party and the new Czechoslovak president, acknowledged the 'progressive reputation of the Slovak Protestant church', and, according to the report in the church's journal, 'expressed the hope that the church would further preserve this good, progressive tradition'.[17] Because the new constitution guaranteed the freedom of religion, Gottwald continued, it also required religious tolerance and the legal equality of all confessions and churches – music to the ears of longsuffering minority Protestants, still hoping in their public vindication as progressive over against the fascism of political Catholicism. Gottwald then added, according to the report: 'The socialist goals which the state pursues demand the firm unity of all people, which is founded on the community of national and social interests'.[18] This need for 'firm unity' in building socialism would shortly take its toll with passage of new legislation on church-state relations, not only on the politically incorrect Catholic Church but also on the politically correct Protestants.

With the predominant Catholic Church in mind, one historian describes the beginning of the communist purges of church leadership this way: 'In the middle of 1950, the seminaries were brought under state control and their number was drastically reduced; few students were able to complete their

[17] What Gottwald actually meant was somewhat different from the journal's rosy report, which in hindsight was clutching at straws. It contained a veiled threat: 'You Lutherans in Slovakia have a good tradition. In your church there were always progressive and democratic elements. But it is not possible to rest on old laurels. What was positive yesterday can become negative today, if it does not go with the spirit of the times. I hope that you will preserve your progressive reputation'. Cited by Pešek in *Sláva Šľachetnýn II: Evanjelická cirkev a.v. a politika v 20. storočí* [Glory to the Noble Ones II: The Lutheran Church and Politics in the 20th Century] ed. Ján Juráš et al. (Mikuláš: Spolok Martina Rázusa, 2012), 28fn8.

[18] *CL* LX (1948), 240.

studies. According to the law, basic military service lasted two years, but for monks and priests it was extended to three years or more'.[19] Given the more 'progressive' reputation of the Lutherans, in another study the same historian tells how from the Protestants Osuský was singled out for removal from the theological faculty in this 1950 action – even though his purge turned out to be only the beginning of what was finished two years later:

> The membership of the former theological faculty was preserved in the reorganization of 1950. The one exception was the rejection of Samuel Štefan Osuský, the former bishop of the Western district. The leadership [of the Party] however gradually matured to the view that instruction was conducted in a "conservative and reactionary spirit." Therefore especially in the middle of 1952 an essential change of personnel was realized in "the interest of improving the political situation." In the official report about the activity of the Slovak Protestant Theological Faculty from the end of 1952, it was directly asserted that instruction was "conducted in an orthodox way up until the 1951–52 school year and that persons lectured there who can be regarded as typical ideologues of reaction." [So Beblavý and most of his remaining colleagues were removed from office in the summer of 1952.] In place of the 'reactionary' professors new 'progressive' professors came, while workers for the Slovak Office for Church Affairs directly taught the [new mandatory course] on Social Doctrine. These instructors were supposed to suppress theological views, corresponding to the interests of state power. [20]

Yet another historian calls these 'progressives' the 'patriotic pastors' for their loyalty to the new regime, and describes how they conspired with the Communist Party to engineer a similar purge of the ecclesiastical leadership that was also completed in 1952.[21]

The reason for, in 1950, singling out Osuský for dismissal from the theological faculty was unintentionally but unmistakably revealed in a report to the

[19] Pešek, *Slovakia in History*, 296. Pešek's chapter contribution in this volume gives an up-to- date English language summary of 'the establishment of totalitarianism in Slovakia'.

[20] Jan Pešek and Michal Barnovský, *Štátna moc a cirkvi na Slovensku 1948–1953* [State Power and the Churches in Slovakia 1948–1953] (Bratislava: VEDA, 1997), 189.

[21] Norbert Kmeť, *Postavenie cirkví na Slovensku 1948–1951* [The Stances of the Churches in Slovakia 1948–1951] (Bratislava, VEDA, 2000), 279–97. Perhaps the loyalty to the communist regime by 'patriotic pastors' stands behind Osuský's apparently coded remark in the *Gallery* that we should endorse 'neither a celebration nor a superficial stoning of the traitor, Judas', for 'who knows how many of us are as weak as Judas was…? It does not seem right to think that he joined Jesus already with the intention of betrayal. Things are not so simple' (579). A merciful judgment on Osuský's part that stings all the more for exposing the opportunism lurking in Judas-like disillusionment with the patiency of faith and the way of the cross. See, further, Pešek, *Odvrátena tvár totality*, 147–8. For an English language account of the Catholic experience, see Jan Chryzostom Cardinal Korec, S.J., *The Night of the Barbarians: Memoirs of the Communist Persecution of the Slovak Cardinal* trans. Peter-Paul Siska et al. (Bolchazy-Carducci, 2002). John Palka tells a parallel story about the disillusionment suffered by his parents during Stalinization in *My Slovakia*, 88–94.

arriving students at the beginning of the new school year, following Osuský's summertime dismissal. The new Dean Štefan Kátlovsky (1906–68) explained the reorganization of the faculty underway.

> Nowadays the materialistic worldview holds sway in the greater part of humanity, a worldview that does not acknowledge faith in God. It does not make sense for us to plunge into a contest of ideas and waste energy on this. Why, there are now urgent tasks of life, which need to be fulfilled. It is well known how many strive to preserve peace, how the whole world is interested in that. We have to ask the question then whether despite differences in ideas cooperation is possible, for example, in the work for peace, peace also for the homeland in the solution of social questions? Is it not self-evident that the good Protestant Christian must work for peace and be against war, which destroys not only material but also spiritual values? Does not the good Protestant Christian have to work for the blossoming and wellbeing of the homeland? Were not Protestant ministers always good patriots ...? We do not fear such cooperation.[22]

Daniel Veselý, the theological student mentioned in the Introduction, who along with eleven others was expelled in 1952, reported that Dean Kátlovsky was in fact overwhelmed with fear just a year and a half after assuring students in 1950 that there was nothing to fear.[23] In 1950, however, Osuský's apologetic theology had become for Kátlovsky a 'waste of energy'.

Kátlovsky went even further, however, on that occasion in the fall of 1950, to positively embrace the changes. He admonished the students to celebrate the new legislation which had the state taking over financial control of the churches and their institutions: 'You now have the conditions and possibility that theological students have never before had. Your social, medical and cultural conditions are guaranteed by the state'. So he encouraged them to keep current with the new world aborning. 'The world is in labour pains, a new generation, a new society is being born ... We know that today's socialist society coming to birth needs ministers, who know how to pay attention to real life and see its needs. To the building of a new society we want to contribute, also with our spiritual talents'.[24]

Several months later, Kátlovsky published for the church public another report concerning the 'reorganization of theological studies'[25] that had taken

[22] *CL* LXII (1950), 333.
[23] Pešek, *Odvrátena tvár,* 145.
[24] *CL* LXII (1950), 334.
[25] Ibid., 384–6.

place over the previous summer. He explained that the changes had taken place throughout Czechoslovakia according to the new law passed in May, so that higher education would serve 'the building of socialism in our land' and guarantee access 'for the sons and daughters of working people' to university education. Making no mention of Osuský's removal, he stressed not only the continuity of the new staff with the previous faculty but pointed again to the many advantages in the new arrangements.

First, he wrote, because all the seminaries and theological faculties in the nation were removed from the university system, the equality for which the Slovak Protestant Faculty had long agitated had now been achieved. 'By this law our faculty was actually made the legal equal of all the other faculties of theology', that is, all equal in being equally demoted from university-level status. Second, the abolition of the small, rival theological schools concentrated all Protestant theological education in 'our faculty', boosting the number of students. Third, the law's stipulation that theological students would be educated in 'the spirit of the people's democracy' meant that the state, through its Office for Church Matters, would now oversee the welfare of the theological faculty. This brings about, Kátlovsky continued, the great advantage that the 'state now cares for the social, medical, cultural and moral needs of students… so that even a student who is penniless will be able to study in peace'. The same advantage applies to the teachers. 'While in the past there were always difficulties, insufficient lecturers and thus professors who were heavily burdened, now we begin the school year with sixteen members of the faculty, more than we could ever wish. So the state here at the outset offers proof that it truly wants to take care of our faculty. We have expressed to the government our heartfelt thanks for this…' (385–6). In short, the new arrangements were nothing less than an answer to prayer. Such was the new world in which the internally exiled Osuský researched and composed his final work.

A Reading of the *Gallery of New Testament Figures*

Because Osuský became persona non grata after 1950, next to nothing is available in public records to inform us of his reactions to his unhappy fate or how he filled the remaining quarter of a century that remained to him until his death in obscurity. We can only make a few inferences about this from the *Gallery*. A first and preliminary observation is that for the most part the apologetic approach has been abandoned. In its place a catechetical approach to theology predominates, by way of the literary device Osuský employs of staging the entire book as a conversation between a knowledgeable father and a curious, sometimes sceptical, son. Supposedly they are discussing biblical scenes, for example, the Christmas crèche. While this literary device cannot but strike a contemporary reader as 'corny', it actually reveals much about the situation and audience of theology as Osuský envisaged them in his writing between 1950 and 1959.

The public space of theology has been constricted to private conversation within the family. The elder is teaching in a dialogical, not dictatorial fashion; the younger is playing a role of the at times curious and at other times sceptical seeker (e.g. 92, 314, 464, 467), who has internalized a great deal of the Marxist-atheistic critique of religion, Christianity and Protestantism, from public schooling. Osuský is thus still willing to undertake what Lindbeck called an 'ad hoc' (as opposed to a 'systematic') apologetics, that is, setting the record straight in cases of false or demonstrably tendentious criticism in order to get to the truth. But these occasional defences are subordinate to the father's predominately positive approach of lifting up and explaining for the son's consideration the figures that appear in the various scenes of the New Testament. The post-Christendom theologian learns to stand on his own two feet, namely, the gospel of Christ and the Bible from which that gospel sounds. Such standing is vulnerable. Difficulties cannot be swept under the rug. The son's critical, even sceptical questions must be honestly answered.

Second, we can infer from the massiveness of the project and the research that went into it that Osuský personally did not despair of a Christian future after the collapse of his life-long labour in nation-building for a renewed Christendom led by 'pure, biblical Christian' religion. The end of Christendom is not the end of Christianity but a new beginning for it. As Gazik describes the matter following Osuský's deposition from the theological faculty: 'He had to cease publically to work and to publish. In fact then he was done with his educational and academic work on the faculty and in the church. He was only sixty-two years old, still then in an active and creative phase of life. Disillusioned he withdrew to seclusion… In spite of this he was not resigned, because precisely in these unfavourable times and relations he plunged into writing the far-reaching work, *Gallery*…'[26] So he continued on the trajectory already begun in his turn to the Bible during the catastrophe of world war as the only foundation on which

[26] Gažik, 8.

a future Christianity could stand. In his Author's Introduction, Osuský tells us how he had once written in his diary:

> Often I read the Bible. But probably the Bible was never so close to me as during the sixty three days of political imprisonment in isolation in 1944, when dignities and name were taken away and I became a mere number. When many friends abandoned me, the best friend – the Bible – did not abandon me. She so conversed with this imprisoned, weak and declining person and so deepened my feeling for people that I forgave them, and she so strengthened my faith that I easily overcome the suffering. Holy, dear Bible! What can you do when people do not read you or consider you? But how powerfully you speak and work, when someone opens your old, but not antiquated pages, reads, and reads and meditates. Only why do many people not take joy in you? (9)

This poignant reflection brings us the first topic now to be discussed in presenting and analysing the *Gallery*.

The Theological Subject

Who is the person who knows in theology, if theology is knowledge of God? Who knows God? Under what epistemic conditions does this subject arise? The question in Christian theology cannot be gainsaid. The putative word of God that Christianity purports to tell the world comes to the human self from outside the self to transform the self. How does this happen?[27]

Osuský reflects on the doubt expressed by the imprisoned John the Baptizer, when he sent his disciples to inquire of Jesus whether He was the expected One to come (Lk. 7.18-23). He wonders about this question of the imprisoned Baptizer and what stands behind it. 'What moved John to ask something like that?' The classic historical critic would see here an indication that John has never known Jesus nor believed Him to be the coming One to whom he had pointed. But Osuský, taking the canonical text in its final form, sees the question instead to reveal John's subjectivity. Why does miracle-working Jesus not rescue him from Herod's prison, as he might well have expected? 'Why is Jesus silent? Why does He conceal himself? Such questions and many similar ones spun around in John's head. And to the theologian a deep psychological problem is put on the table by them: what has happened and taken place in John's soul?' (70) The Baptist, Osuský at length answers, was displeased by the report of

[27] See further on this topic, Paul R. Hinlicky, *Beloved Community: Critical Dogmatics after Christendom* (Grand Rapids, MI: Eerdmans, 2015), 193–293.

Jesus's ministry of mercy. 'John was trained in the representation of God as the strict Lord; he did not recall that the God of Jesus is the God of love as well as righteousness' (72). As the theological subject changes its representation of the theological object and audience, then, the subject changes as well.

The intertwining of fear and doubt with coming to faith in New Testament stories fascinates Osuský. Speaking to the question in Christian doctrine that has long troubled him, the conception of Jesus by Mary the Virgin, Osuský's father tells his son that the 'conception belongs to the world of wonders. The same applies here as we said about other wonders: many such and similar questions that connect with them bubble up not infrequently from a correct, seriously intended curiosity and desire for knowledge of truth, which we have to honour. But questions can also arise from malice, cynicism and idle curiosity'. In such forms of apparently honest curiosity, attacks take place. 'And if it happens that you hear such a question, always distinguish whether it is a good question, well intentioned. But if it is malicious, you may reject it with the strict words of Jesus, "Do not give what is holy to the dogs or throw pearls to swine" (Mt. 7.6)' (96). The *disciplina arcana* of theology is *not* a universal discourse; that has become clear now. The question of theological subjectivity – *who* wants to know and why? – stands as the cherubim guarding the gates of Eden against unauthorized trespassing.

The central New Testament figures that allow Osuský to explore theological subjectivity are Peter and Paul. The renaming of Simon son of Jonah as Cephas, Petros, 'the Rock', designates the transformation of the self that has come upon this self from outside of itself at the word of Jesus. Peter 'always steps forth as the representative; he has therefore much responsibility and must constantly remember not to be weak, shaky Simon but the solid rock, Peter!' (456–7). To this end of the new theological subjectivity, however: 'the blood of the cross does not cleanse mechanically. The cleansing and sanctification is the outcome of a long line of cleansings, the climax of which is the cross. Already the fact that God the Father sent His Son indicates in advance the long chain in reality, in which one link connects to another… Not Simon, but Peter…! How difficult for him to leave the old and how difficult to accustom himself to the new' (459). He so often appears as 'the weak, wavering Simon and not the solid rock' (460). He sleeps on watch, while his Lord is in agony. 'Truly Simon, not Peter! A moment ago he asserted that he was prepared to go wherever, to prison, even to death and now he does not know how to watch even for an hour. A strange sleep. How could they sleep?' (462)

Commenting on the Easter story of the encounter of Peter and the Risen Lord at the Sea of Tiberius in John 21, Osuský writes:

> 'Simon, son of Jonah, do you love me more than these?' Notice, my son, the address. He does not address Peter but returns to the beginning, when he was still only the son of Jonah, Simon. He addressed him twice that way before. The earliest was at their first meeting (Jn 1.42), then after his confession (Matt. 16.18). Now comes the third time. The three most significant moments in Simon's life. Notice the question whether he loves him more than the rest. Not for nothing does Jesus use the words, "do you love," and again the comparative word "more." Both inform Peter that he is not yet Peter; he has to examine himself, since not even a year earlier he acknowledged that on his faith Jesus promised to build the church. But now he has denied this faith. Jesus wants to test whether he still regards himself as first, as higher over the others (470).

By contrast to the Simon who boasts of his piety and commitment, the apostolic Peter who heals the lame man in Acts 3 does not have silver or gold, but what he does have, in new-found trust in God, he gives to the cripple. 'We discern here that in Peter there is no longer the previous superiority and conceit, but humility before God… What a great difference there is between the Simon who followed Jesus in His lifetime and the present Peter! No longer does he waver, or deny, but confesses and powerfully witnesses. By word and deed. And he will witness also by martyrdom' (477).

The conversion of Saul the Pharisee to Paul, apostle to the nations, gives Osuský another, corresponding account of the new birth to theological subjectivity, with an accent on the framework of apocalyptic theology that undergirds it. The word of the Risen Lord already indicated to Saul how the former man, who strove to separate Israel from the nations by strict zeal for the holy traditions of Israel, would now bring the gospel to ungodly Gentiles:

> A new and difficult problem for Paul. As Saul he expected a terrible punishment for the nations, and behold! God has had mercy… The Lord who chose and called him like one of the former prophets of the Old Testament had revealed Himself to him in Jesus His Son. The righteous and strict Lord has become for Him the Father and the risen Jesus has revealed Himself to him as to one prematurely born (1 Cor. 15.8) and received him into His service… The Christophany (Christ's self-revelation) ceased, but the spiritual apocalypse, repentance and new birth do not end (649).

Corresponding to this experience of new birth to theological subjectivity are all Paul's characteristic apocalyptic antinomies: 'Moses-Christ, works-faith, sin-cleansing, circumcision of the flesh-circumcision of the heart, slavery-freedom, flesh-spirit' (661).

Apocalyptic conflict is triggered by the coming of the Messiah, according to Osuský. 'Chasms open up, yes, the kingdom of the Messiah breaks through with difficult battles, through the cross to glory' (46). Precisely the inauguration of a new epoch breaking in with Jesus's ministry of mercy offends Jesus's fellow Jews:

> The Jews expected the Messiah to come at the end of this eon and the new age then to come about. They did not acknowledge Jesus as Messiah, because they still expected one. We acknowledge and receive Him because by His coming the new age has already come, which proceeds in linear parallel to the old, sinful time. For us then the word, age, does not indicate only a temporal but also a saving boundary. The Christian is already here and now in the eternal age (164).

The confession of Jesus as Messiah can thus divide members of even the most intimate forms of life in the old age, such as the family, for He 'has not come to bring peace on earth, but a sword', a battle against evil, against the devil (189). 'Behold how the old world contests the new world in the souls of people!' (222).

But in accenting the apocalyptic, Osuský has not forgotten nor disregarded the deliteralizing insights gained in his study of the book of Revelation. Commenting on the apocalyptic discourses in the Synoptic Gospels, and their reinterpretation in the Farewell Discourse of the Johannine Jesus, he writes that Jesus:

> stands on the soil of the Old Testament theophanic prophets Isaiah, Zachariah, Daniel and other apocalyptic literature. He sets out also from the notions of his own day, from the Apocalypse of Enoch during the government of the Hasmoneans… Most of all this relates to the apocalyptic images of the Orient, behind which we must seek the kernel of Jesus' teaching, because also in this question it is a matter of the fulfilment of the Law… The kernel is fulfilled in the perspective indicated at the very end of Jesus' apocalyptic discourse in the word, Watch! If that is the point, then the discourse is not any systematic-dogmatic instruction about the last things (278).

For Osuský, in other words, apocalyptic is not about the literal end of time but about the time of the end, the eternity of God, breaking into a strong man's house to bind him and plunder his goods (Mk 3.27).

That little parable of Jesus, expressed on the occasion of the opponents' charge that Jesus casts out devils by the prince of devils, indicates that 'when Jesus Christ came to the earth, the empire of Satan was already here but now the empire of God begins. From then on battles between them play out on the earth. God's kingdom grows in battle, the building of the church is erected and completed, because it is the empire of eternal life' (448). Osuský finds the figure of the devil indispensable for telling the apocalyptic gospel. The doubting son gives voice to the objection: 'But Father, there is no devil. That is a remnant of old, primitive, demonic superstition, which says that originally there was a light bearing star which fell from heaven and therefore is called Lucifer, Bearer of light.' Osuský's father character replies, 'My son, precisely those people who deny the devil prove by their lives that he exists.' It is the representation of the devil as some fearsome monster that is superstitious. If it were so that such a monster existed, people would indeed flee from him. But if, as Luther said, 'he is handsome and bright and a flatterer, people would run to him like Eve ran to the apple' (129).

Note again the deliteralizing move. It is the devil in the guise of an angel of light that we must truly fear. We wage war against this disguised devil not by multiplying superstitions but by loving God. As God is truth, the devil is exposed as the cunning lie that masquerades as truth, who deceives and so leads into sin. The truth of all truths is that God is the Creator of all that is not God, so that salvation consists in the fulfilment of the double love commandment; the lie is that we can be as God, knowing good and evil other than the double love commandment, thus wreaking havoc on the ecology of created life and rendering it unfit for beloved community. This bright and cheery lie murders (255). One does not indulge in superstition, rather one overcomes superstition to see *this* battle of good and evil, of God and devil, waging over humanity and after human souls, seeking their allegiance. 'The historical truth is that Christianity was born from eschatological hope. Eschatology was the driving force in the first century of Christianity'. But today eschatology is handed over to the sects and we are the weaker for it (543). Apocalyptic, in Ernst Käsemann's famous and contemporaneous words, is the 'mother of Christian theology'. We must learn to access this again, but we cannot access it without the right kind of hermeneutic that takes apocalyptic seriously as knowledge of God, not literally as a cosmological schedule given over to curious speculation but leaving – leaving behind! – the world to the devil.

In fact, we cannot know Jesus Christ at all apart from this apocalyptic turn of the ages. The important Pauline statement in 2 Cor. 5.16 about not wanting to know Christ 'according to the flesh', Osuský maintains, means that Paul 'does not want to know the historical Jesus but the glorified Christ, who revealed Himself to him on the road to Damascus, for the old, the temporal and the historical has now passed away and what remains is what is eternal and glorified. Do not ask after the prophet Jesus, about His teaching, but about the High Priest Christ and His sacrifice'. Of course that apocalyptic epistemology of the theological subject does not mean an elevation of Paul over Jesus, reducing the human being Jesus to an empty cipher to be filled with Paul's mythical content, but rather understanding with Paul that our access to the man Jesus is through the apocalyptic turn of the ages that reveals Him as the Christ, the Son of God who by His cross 'loved us and gave Himself for us' (Gal. 2.20). The apocalypse gives birth to the new theological subject in knowledge of *the theological object*, the crucified and risen Lord Jesus Christ (661–2).

The Theological Object

The 'prophetic office must be connected with the High Priestly office, the historical with the eternal and gloried' (661). This connection, Osuský maintains, gives the *anti-docetism* in Christology, according to the understanding that the divine Logos truly *became flesh and dwelt among us*, full of grace and truth. In just this true, tangible humanity, Jesus Christ, is knowable and must be known theologically as the Son of God. This specification of theological objectivity is also a special contribution of the apostle Paul. Christology is the chief pillar of Paul's theology in the broad sense. The love of Christ took hold of him on the road to Damascus and so gained him that he became His slave, as he says in the greetings to his letters. The subjectivity of Paul the apostle is thus bound to the Christ who loved him and gave Himself for him. The love of Christ is the object of Paul's faith, which unifies him with Christ. Osuský repeats for emphasis: 'Christ!', meaning that Paul looks upon Jesus from the perspective of the revealed Christ and not from the opposite direction. He does not discover a humanly inspiring personality in the historical Jesus which bubbles up to faith in Him, but with new apocalyptic eyes looks upon the crucified one who died accursed as now the Lamb of God bearing away the sin of the world. Consequently, as in Philippians 2, Paul traces the course, or way, of the Christ, from His pre-existence in equality with God to His earthly existence in humility and obedience to His post-existence at the right hand of God to live and reign forever.

The saving work of the Christ is elaborated along the same objective lines: 'Christ redeems, liberates and saves us from our three greatest enemies, from the devil, sin and death, in that death is from sin and sin is from the devil' (659–60). That is why justification by faith in this Christ Jesus signifies the saving union of subject and object in this theology, that is, in this knowledge of God. Osuský express the thought sharply: 'His blood is the payment for our sins. It certainly does not make the unjust man just, but rather justifies him…

The prophet, the historical Jesus did not even help the apostles but only the sacrificed High Priest and risen Christ helps. The witness of Jesus to Himself does not help, but only the witness about the cross of Christ' that is spoken on Easter morn. From this perspective the theological subject sees Jesus, the Lamb of God (64) whose death atones (449, 450, 454). Osuský knows that this sharp differentiation from Paul the Apostle concerning the Christ Jesus known only to apocalyptic faith corresponds to Luther. 'It helped him to understand the difference between the law and the gospel. The law is the summary of that which is demanded of us and the gospel of that which is given to us'. What is given to us, the love of Christ as object of trust for the unworthy and perishing sinner, is the objectivity of the faith which justifies. For, 'by faith we receive His Spirit into our heart, which according to Jewish ideas is the seat of life' (659–60). The helpless self in bondage to the lie comes into the truth by the coming to it of the One who truly helps – precisely – the helpless. As such, faith clings to its object as to its only help.

Presupposing from the outset, however, such a Pauline perspective on the unification of the theological subject and theological object, Osuský does examine the earthly life of Jesus from the gospels. He thinks this 'profile' important to justifying faith in Christ Jesus. The denotation of the name, Jesus, makes a material difference to the object of faith, Jesus Christ. This content from history is important, not least because it disillusions political Messianism (46, 72, 120–1, 130, 318, 213, 221, 236, 455, 458) and forces faith in Jesus to be only faith in Christ Jesus, that is, only in the Crucified One, defeated in the world yet vindicated by God to reign in the world to come. In his profile of Jesus from the gospels, Osuský accordingly sketches a man of sorrows and acquainted with grief (275, 277, 417), not a figure of beauty to attract us but a man who knew poverty (103–4, 239). His patriotism (267) was love for His people in their lost and broken condition; it was neither violent zealotry (463–4, 576) nor chauvinistic nationalism (210). His way was service not domination (473). Osuský even speaks of a 'love of wisdom', that is, of Jesus's '*philosophy* of love' (155, 179), which consisted in the double love commandment (400). He probes along these lines into the 'personality' of Jesus (120–1, 124, 133, 224, 237, 304), which he imagines as soft and almost feminine, the personality of a listener not a talker. He tries to decipher Jesus's human motives (366, 391, 397), and finds them in His baptismal calling (112, 124), which made His messianic mission an 'internal necessity' (111).

Historically, the baptism by John in the Jordan was Jesus's 'inauguration' into the Messianic office (126); and the Transfiguration, anticipating His resurrection, divinely confirmed that office to the disciples (218). The inauguration of eschatology begins already, then, in the life of the earthly Jesus, so that from that time onwards, until now, two societies, as Augustine said, interpenetrate (280) on the way until they are divided in the Last Judgment. While admittedly, then, 'the concept of the kingdom of God, which is so central in Jesus, stands in the background for Paul because in him the salvation of the person and humanity dominates in place of it' (660), the sense of salvation for Osuský retains from Jesus's proclamation of the Kingdom (145–6, 159, 168, 194) the social sense of a cosmic redemption (698). Disillusionment from instituting the reign of God by politics as usual does not mean dispensing with the social nature of salvation, but rather with establishing this hope in the gracious activity that God alone performs for humanity.

The dangerously individualistic heresy of Gnosticism otherwise haunts readings of Paul when believers forget Jesus's earthly way (113–14, 123, 126, 137). But God is not concerned to rescue a handful of pious individuals for an otherworldly heaven. God is working to bring about on the earth His beloved community. When we pray, 'Thy kingdom come!', the meaning is that we desire it for us all. 'We do not pray in Jesus' spirit in a selfish way, that it come only to us, but rather to the whole world, the universe. "Thy kingdom come" – not my kingdom, not where I will be, not where we will be, not to demand it at all but rather to be there when and where God is pleased to send it… Thus we desire and have to desire that the empire of our heavenly Father comes, the empire of love' (159).

When we think of the kingdom of God, accordingly, we cannot think as the Jews did at that time of some earthly region, Osuský continues, but of: 'a universal state between God and humanity both in the individual and in the collective sense of all humanity. We have to have in mind God's reign both in the spirit and heart of the individual and in the mutual relations of the entire human society' (169). Because the concept of the kingdom of God is bound up with the law of love, according to Osuský's Jesus, 'the sense of human life does not relate only to the individual and his salvation, as that is one-sidedly understood and not infrequently especially among some so-called "decided evangelicals," [i.e. those who have personally 'decided' for Jesus] but to the human race and its destiny' (193). The objectivity of Christian salvation, thus, is not reducible to such human 'decisions', even though the gift of theological subjectivity consists in the division of the new self from the old. But the newness of this new self is being for others. It cannot even conceive of its own salvation apart from that of others, no more deserving than itself. Every new person in Christ, *pars pro toto*, indicates the claim of the saving God on the entire creation; every new person in Christ is new as member of the dawning beloved community of God, which is represented by the visible church in history but not reducible to it. The kingdom of God that begins in Jesus Christ and Spirit-wrought faith in Him aims at the redemption and fulfilment of the creation.

Significantly, Osuský makes this crucially important point about the social and indeed cosmic nature of Christian salvation in a muted but unmistakeable polemic against the 'mechanical and materialistic understanding of history according to which matter is the driving force, economic interest'. We will explore this muted polemic, which saturates the *Gallery*, momentarily. But for the moment, the point here to is see how the affirmation of Christian salvation parallels that of Marxism, taken as a rival, as a political religion: 'the sense of humanity is not only in the salvation of the individual, but of the entire humanity, and that in mutual relations to God as the Father and to humanity as a whole, also mutually in relation to God and members of humanity' (194). Immediately following this passage, Osuský cites from Anders Nygren's celebrated study of Christian love, in order to specify the divine love of the beloved community as creative self-giving, thus poised 'against the so-called natural human love, which is no more than "liking" someone out of selfish desire' (194) – a surgical strike aimed at the pretension of the proletariat to be the universal class.

How has Osuský been able thus to integrate a Pauline theological epistemology with the material content of the Synoptic gospels? How has he been able to unite the glorified Christ with the man of sorrows whose entire life was suffering struggle for the Kingdom of God? The answer at first glance will be off-putting to contemporary readers. Osuský cannot 'agree with the opinion that John's records have no historical worth' (139; Osuský regards Matthew, along with John, as an eyewitness, 390, 458). Indeed, Osuský regards the Gospel of John as historically *more* credible than the Synoptics. 'Happily, the evangelist John as an eyewitness immediately and from the beginning, when he discovered the inadequacies of the reports of his predecessors in the Synoptic gospels, filled in the facts' (135). Yet things turn out to be a little more complex than these seemingly bald and for us today unlikely assertions. It is in fact the case that Osuský rightly sees that the Fourth Gospel is the theologically indispensable 'bridge' between the earliest Christian narratives of Jesus and the later ecclesiastical doctrine of Trinity and the Person of Christ. But his historical account of this bridge is not convincing.

His theory of the composition of the Gospel John holds that three levels can be detected in it. The first and oldest concerns the conflicts which befell Jesus during his stays in Jerusalem; the second level of material is the story which the eyewitness, John, wrote at the end of a long life at the request of his disciples and friends in Ephesus; while the third level reflects additions that John's pupils composed to fill in gaps and smooth out the materials in the first two levels, thus producing the canonical Gospel of John (522–3). What is of enduring significance in this historical reconstruction is that Osuský detects the background of the Gospel in Judaism. In this way, he avoids the error of scholars who regard John as a 'pagan coloured tradition about Jesus, merely an historical novel' that was accommodated to Gnosticizing tendencies. Osuský praises the Czech scholar Souček's 'better way' of describing the events in the Gospel of John as written with a 'double signification', denoting both what Jesus once said, and what John wants to say about Jesus to his own day and age. 'How much easier it is to understand everything in this way. In this case there is also enough space for John's theology. Only so is it possible to defend the historical value of the gospel and turn back various objections' (523).

It is not necessary to follow Osuský in the details of his unlikely historical reconstruction in order to redeem his basic theological point. Osuský himself sees what the Gospel of John has done, for example, in fusing together the distinct Synoptic stories of the Transfiguration and the Agony in the Garden of Gethsemane (223) to avoid having Jesus hesitate to do the will of the Father who sent Him and to represent the glory of Jesus as His willingness to suffer and die for His friends (223). In adopting Souček's 'double signification', he anticipates J. Louis Martyn's pioneering analysis of the story of the man born blind in John 9 as a 'drama on two levels',[28] telling on one level of the contemporaneous expulsion of Jewish Christians from the synagogue following the Roman defeat of the Jewish revolt and on the other level a healing story from Jesus' life time (377–8). Osuský even understands that the doctrine of Trinitarian perichoresis articulated in the High Priestly prayer of John 17 marks a significant step in the historical development of the early Christian doctrine of the Trinity (258). To preserve these insights, and to let them function to effect the union of the theological subject and the theological object, as Osuský manifestly wishes, one must let John do what manifestly John does: deliteralize the inherited gospel narrative by interpreting it as knowledge of God.

All that is necessary historically, then, is to locate the Johannine community, which stands behind the canonical gospel, in the mainstream of early Christian

[28] J. Louis Martyn, *History and Theology in the Fourth Gospel* 3rd Edition (Louisville, KY: Westminster-John Knox, 2003).

development.[29] It is not necessary to save the historical value of the gospel as an eyewitness account; indeed, the defensive effort of conservative apologetics to do so may obscure the far more important theological value that John contains. That theological value is found by seeing the Gospel as a crucial, but necessarily later, integration of various apostolic trajectories. So John is not, as Osuský rightly contends, a pagan or Gnostic development on the margins of early Christianity. John knows the Synoptic traditions, and as artfully as deliberately reworks their materials in order to deliteralize, but not renounce, early Christian apocalyptic theology. As a result, the 'crisis' Jesus still brings to the human world, whenever the gospel of Christ is proclaimed according to the Gospel of John, is not the commencement of the end of time; but it is the in-breaking of the time of the End. In that light, one would not apologize for Christian faith by seeking to show common ground with 'this present evil age'; instead, one presents Jesus, and lets the division of the ages occur as it will.

Contesting Marxism and the Theological Audience

We conclude this chapter and prepare for the conclusion to this book with a survey of *Gallery*'s treatment of Marxism. More precisely put, our purpose here is to see that the chief 'critic' of Christianity to whom Osuský is responding is Marxism-Leninism, or 'Bolshevism', as already in the 1937 lecture Osuský had analysed Soviet Marxism under that name. In that 1937 lecture, Osuský had reduced Marxism in the Soviet Union to a doctrine of dynamic materialism, secreting dehumanizing implications for anyone with eyes open to see: 'As in metaphysics matter is the first element, so in history the basic motor force is matter, i.e. economic interest. The human being is the product of economic relations. The idea does not form relations, but relations form the idea. Everything ideological – politics, laws, morality, philosophy, religion –everything is only a reflection, reflex, superstructure of the economic. History is the contest of economic classes, which develop in time'. He went on to spell out the dehumanization implied in this debased worldview, which writes violence into the very script of reality this way: 'Morality is what serves the proletariat. Good is what is profitable to the proletariat. Evil is what is not profitable to the proletariat... Before Bolshevism... good was whatever served the employer class. Behold the dialectic! There are no absolute moral norms, as there is no absolute

[29] See further Paul R. Hinlicky, *Divine Complexity: The Rise of Creedal Christianity* (Minneapolis: Fortress, 2011), 69–95.

truth'. Osuský was already then raising the question with this critique whether Marxism was a new and rival faith, a political religion. Just so, he offered an immanent critique in 1937:

> We will not overcome Communism by boasting of our own superiority. It is necessary to deal with it seriously and thus to overcome it philosophically ... I point to a contradiction already in its foundations. It denies the absolute, the eternal, and yet begins with matter as its own absolute and eternal. This is the most basic contradiction. No dialectic overcomes this. Also in the very title there is a contradiction: either dialectic or materialism, not both. If dialectic is valid, why begin precisely with matter? Just so I am equally justified in beginning with mind. Why begin under the influence of economic relations and not with mind, i.e., the ideational side of life? The very reality of their ideology in advance of the realization of their own ideal proves best the error of their perspective. Why begin with work and not with theory like they do? Why with the whole and not the individual? Why with necessity and not freedom? Why with the inconstant rather than the constant? Why with the temporal and not the eternal? Why with the relative and not the absolute? Why with the less and not with the greater? And so on. Dialectical materialism has to fall to pieces on these contradictions.

But the ensuring attempt to overcome communism by apologetic theology and countervailing idealistic philosophy has failed, as we have seen. By the time he is composing the *Gallery*, Osuský's response to Marxism has ceased to be an argument in favour of philosophical idealism. Following the catechetical approach he has now undertaken, the response to Marxism takes the new form of a critical dogmatic clarification of true and false Christianity.

The refrain from Ragaz sounds again and again: if Christianity were more social (as we have learned above from the *Gallery* that it ought to be), then socialism would be more Christian (e.g. 176). Not by accident, Osuský's Jesus in the *Gallery*'s profile is a poor man (103–4, 239), a worker who honours labour (120, 'Honour to labour!' was a current communist slogan). Thus the Christianity that the Marxists attack is exposed as a badly understood, and hence badly practiced, Christianity. Christians themselves need first of all to see this. Perhaps they themselves are the first to misunderstand Christianity! As in 1937, Osuský continues to hold that Jesus's teaching about the primacy of the Kingdom of God cannot be harmonized with the mechanical-materialistic understanding of history, according to which the driving motor of history is material force, economic interest (194). But now it is the apocalyptic reign of God manifest in the proclamation of the Messiah's cross, not philosophical idealism, that is incompatible, not with matter to which the kingdom comes redemptively, but with revolutionary violence.

Thus the significant Marxist theorist, Karl Kautsky (1854–1938) – no friend, by the way, of the Soviet Bolsheviks – is faulted by name for badly understanding the words of Jesus in the Sermon on the Mount about having no anxiety about food, drink and clothing, when he draws the conclusion that Jesus teaches people neither to care nor to work (168). The point of Jesus is just the opposite: it is those who do not trust in God who are filled with anxiety, no matter how much they work. Marxists are inconsistent, on the other hand, when they also try to claim Jesus for violent revolution. Kautsky 'badly understands Jesus' word that he has come to bring a sword and fire on the earth (Mt. 10.34 and Lk. 12.49), when he judges Jesus to have been a revolutionary. Jesus revolutionized the soul …' (208). Osuský thus repeatedly reverts to this Augustinian hierarchy of value (148, 193, 197, 355, 391, 393–4, 438, 453–4, as to the First Commandment, 132, 254, or to the Kingdom of God, 145–6, 159, 168, 194), just as the right understanding of Jesus's Sermon on the Mount requires. This hierarchy of value is not the mind-matter dualism that Marxists imagine, along with none too few Christians. The two tables of the Decalogue form a unity that is expressed in Jesus's word to the rich young man, 'Go sell all that you have and give it to the poor; and come, follow me'. This invitation points to Jesus's *koinonia*-ism that the first Christians wanted to actualize (the 'fraternity' of the French Revolution, Osuský claims, 479), not communism. Osuský's insistence on the hierarchy of value to seek first the kingdom of God by not seeking treasure on earth, where thief can break in or moth consume, exposes the sinful root of revolutionary violence. 'But I have pointed you to the first table, to the First Commandment, to the good God, so that you do not proceed only from self to the neighbour but also to God. For in love to humanity, selfish love of self can be concealed, but not in love to God. If false love hides there, it is not true love, for we learn true love from God' (394). Jesus's and the New Testament's vision of beloved community is not Platonic dualism, then, but the apocalyptic conflict of the ages, which prophetically exposes the sinful unbelief not only of the powers that be but also of the powers that would be.

Not understanding this distinction rightly, Marxists inconsistently claim that Jesus looked only to eternity and lost time from view, that Jesus looked upon God and forgot about humanity, that He thought about the heavenly home and lost consciousness of the earthly one beneath his feet. But in reality Jesus's teaching is about the coming of God's kingdom to the earth where God's will is to be done as it is in heaven. Jesus accordingly teaches us to pray here for daily bread. Critics similarly attack the parable of the useless slave in Lk. 17.7-10 as if it were authorizing slavery, when the parable rather binds one and all, boss and worker, equally to God (179). The story of Mary and Martha is unfortunately explained in an erroneous, Gnostic way (Osuský regularly blames heretical Gnosticism and docetism for the ontological dualism that Marxists are in fact attacking as if it were orthodox Christianity, for example, 384, 491, 533, 535, 662). It is Gnosticism, not Christianity, to teach that it is only necessary to care for the spiritual side of life, not the physical. But Jesus's entire activity in words and deeds contradicts this otherworldly interpretation (384).

What Marxists do not grasp is that apocalyptic theology, with its Augustinian hierarchy of value defined by the double love commandment, is in fact *both* the source of the salutary secularization of human life *and* also the defence against the unholy profanation of life that Marxism portends. Osuský demonstrates this claim by his discussion of the Sabbath day controversies of Jesus (240), quoting the Johannine Jesus, 'My Father works till now and I also work' (Jn 5.17). Osuský glosses: 'God works constantly, not even the Sabbath prevents Him. He governs the world, does the work of redemption, giving life, helping' (245). Jesus in proclaiming such a God whose kingdom comes wants to block the escapist notion that those dedicated to God are released from human obligations (248–9). God does not want to turn lay-people into priests, but rather priests into lay-people, that is, into those who sanctify the profane world by bringing it back under the loving dominion of humanity made in the image of God for likeness to God. Jesus was opposed to divorce because the image of God is social: it is not the pious soul, nor the exalted individual, nor the rational element in humanity, but the human couple forming the basic unit of society to whom the command and blessing of dominion is jointly assigned: 'Look how Jesus levels the exalted male! And exalts the woman!' (260). The command and blessing of Gen. 1.26-28 for human dominion in covenant partnership with the Lord of the universe gives us a biblical theology of holy secularity as Jesus enunciates in Mk 10.10 even as it draws a boundary of sanctity around human life on the earth (cf. Gen. 9.6).

Commenting on the promise of Jesus to Peter and the disciples in Mk 10.30 about receiving beloved community both 'in this age … and in the age to come eternal life', Osuský exclaims, 'Striking and beautiful words!'. And he explains why:

> Remember them, my son, and never forget them, for they solve a difficult contemporary problem! And when I analyse them you will see that Jesus makes

> a differentiation between time and eternity, earthly and heaven, physical and spiritual; he does not neglect one or the other, as the unbeliever does, when they criticize Christianity for turning attention only to eternal, heavenly, otherworldly, spiritual things and in reaction against this misconstruction do not believe in what is eternal and beyond the grave. To the question of what we will have of the spiritual and the eternal, Jesus speaks of a reward for time and eternity (454).

Recalling then how Mark's Jesus added to this promise of an inaugurated eschatology also the accompanying warning about persecution, Osuský darkly acknowledges that 'it is true that spiritual workers, leaders, philosophers, artists, theologians and so on are often exposed to misunderstanding, persecution, depriving themselves of life or being deprived of life by others'. But, he asks, 'what is decisive: long life or the value of life? What is better, an imperfect temporal life or a perfect eternal life?'. He is *not* thinking apologetically in terms of Pascal's wager, for he continues, 'Suffering is a test, a sacrifice, but sacrifices redeem the world! The motto contains much: live temporal life under the perspective of the eternal!' (454) Christianity thus offers to such disciplined lives of its disciples a genuine, holy secularity that aims at, and is capable of, self-giving, the freedom to love wisely and well.

This is holy life in the sense that it is life lived *coram Deo*, before God, who is the true audience of theology – Osuský's heavenly Father who sees in secret and knows in secret. The profanation of this world that Osuský discerned in ascendant Marxism for making an idol of it is only the reverse side of his Christian freedom, lord of all and subject to none on earth because subject, or rather beloved child, of the heavenly Father; bound, a servant to all on the earth, freed to love others as a true child of that same heavenly Father. A salient sample of such holy secularity, emerging in the course of the *Gallery*, is Osuský's contention for *feminism*. He lifts up Elizabeth, Mary's kinswoman, as the first to praise Mary and the fruit of her womb:

> The first word of praise, from a woman. How remarkable, since women in that time were regarded as lower creatures, a creature which had its own special section in the Temple. Yet here... a woman is the first human witness to the Messiah! Someone correctly noted that the woman Eve was first to sin and the woman Elizabeth was the first to bless and, as a herald, to welcome the Messiah, redeemer of sinners (33).

Anna, the prophetess in the Temple from the same second chapter of Luke, indicates how 'the Son of God will be the saviour of widows and also of fallen women but above all will be the one who magnanimously elevates women to equality with men' (49, see also 262). Jesus the teacher rejects the sexual double standard: 'Not only women, but also men' may not commit adultery. 'We have to emphasize this because in that time women were inferior and men were superior, and the fault of adultery was more ascribed to women than to men. But when Jesus focused on the root of adultery and fornication in the desires and wandering eyes of human beings, he spoke not about women but about men' who look with lust (153). According to Jesus, 'God is our Father and we are His children, so we value women and children', in distinction 'from the pagan opinions of those times, which esteemed only adults and elders, while women and children were regarded as lower or as equal to worthless forms of life and lumped with them, but not with human beings' (225). In those days, they regarded the words of women as nonsense, but women were the first witnesses of the resurrection. 'It is noteworthy that in spite of everything the disciples still did not believe the women and were critics of them ... [although the risen Jesus] rewarded them for their faithfulness and love in accompanying Him from under the cross to the grave' (310, see also on the Samaritan woman, 341). In sum:

> women were then regarded as lower forms of life, like children and slaves who had no rights. They had no feeling for themselves and the court did not regard them as worthy witnesses, and so on. When women were convinced, then, of how Jesus elevated them as equals to men, how he helped anxious mothers and widows, how he loved, blessed and healed their children, they could not but be inflamed with trust and love towards Him (344).

At a moment in history, when the ordination of women to the ministry was beginning to be discussed in his church,[30] Osuský pointed at 1 Thess. 5.19 as proof that the first Christians did not quench the Spirit – who spoke also in women (605).

Such 'holy secularity' sees holiness or sanctification not in flight from the world or transcendence of it but in the coming of God to dwell with people in a renewed creation. It continues to renew creation, for example, in now exalting women to equality. Such is the positive fruit of Christianity in Western history. In their caricature of the Christian religion, the rival Marxists do not understand this holy secularity. But the deeper question posed throughout the *Gallery* is whether the Christians do.

[30] See *Ordinácia Žien za farárky v cirkvi*, [The Ordination of Women as Pastors in the Church] Zborník ed. Sidonia Horňanová and Igor Kišš (Bratislava: Evanjelická bohoslovecká fakulta, Univerzity Komenského, 2007), 121–60. Ironically, the 'full employment' policy of the communist regime, together with the pressure imposed by the regime to discourage careers in the ministry, facilitated the Lutheran church's decision in the 1950s to begin ordaining women to meet its shortage of clergy.

An Equally Personal Conclusion

How do you write the conclusion of the story of one who was in his life-time denied a conclusion? How do you evaluate the ideas and contribution of one who was denied the opportunity to finish what he had started? Through the previous chapters we can detect and trace out the trajectory Osuský's theological thinking was taking. In the process, we can appreciate his sensitivity to the spiritual situation of his times and we can probe the subtle self-critique in which he was involved. But if we stopped there on the grounds that taking up and continuing one of the loose threads of his life and thought would be a speculative exercise that transcended the unhappy fact of the violent and premature termination of his activity, we would be giving a posthumous victory to his persecutors. 'Objective' historiography cannot say more about this than to describe the bitter fact with cold, disinterested clarity and leave us there, with a monument to his memory.

But in deepest continuity with Osuský's own stance, I would urge and will now act on the conviction that theology writes from faith for faith. In the unlikely case that the reader has not noticed it, let me say for the record that this book is theologically *interested*. It cannot settle with the description of a past event and leave the matter there. It must, having described the past with all the critical tools available, receive from it the witness of faith and continue it into the present. So this 'conclusion' takes the form of continuing Osuský's turn to the Bible today, that is, after Auschwitz.

Osuský began his intellectual journey with ethical idealism's faith in the progressive teleology of history and ended in dismay and disillusionment at the revolutionary pretensions of Marxism-Leninism, which collapsed into the long night of Stalinism, snuffing out his light – at least for his own lifetime. For a brief moment, he could celebrate the victory over fascism and be celebrated for his courage and integrity and clarity of mind under apocalyptic conditions. But the apocalypse was not finished. And we would be foolish to think that it is finished now. No new world order emerged from the collapse of Bolshevism in 1989. The current path is neither economically nor ecologically sustainable. Science and technology could help us but they may also destroy us.

We have traced in the preceding chapters the gradual, but finally dramatic, turn to the Bible and the recovery of the apocalyptic narrative of the 'Christ crucified' that, in Ernst Käsemann's famous and almost simultaneous words, is 'the mother of Christian theology'. We have seen how Osuský gropes for an alternative to Bultmann's project of demythologization, which saves the narrative, not, as Bultmann, by vacating it, but rather by deliteralizing it, as I am proposing; this procedure, I have argued, issues in a new kind of theologizing from the Bible, to speak the dark realities of post-Christendom.

There remain, as we have seen and taken note, remnants in the *Gallery* of the nineteenth century project of building the Kingdom of God on earth by the spread of Christian civilization. With a surgeon's scalpel, Gažik goes to the heart of the matter: Osuský does not despair *enough* of the possibility of retrieving the old metaphysics. 'Osuský does not sufficiently master the fact that many people of the modern period have become in principle nonreligious, that war has either weakened or wholly destroyed their faith. Opinions about the transcendent, the problems of God and immortality, metaphysics, the doctrines of theology and church have ceased to interest modern people'.[1] But Osuský in places did recognize, according to Gažik, the need to seek a revision of the old metaphysics, and found some inspiration in Henri Bergson's vitalism. Gažik sees possibilities here for a new metaphysics 'beyond the boundaries of positivistic science and the materialistic explanation of the world'.[2]

In our book,[3] Adkins and I have similarly argued that 'materialism' is no longer the (bogeyman) materialism when it is not philosophically conceived in qualitative antithesis to the Idea, but rather on a plane of continuity with the latter, as poles within a dynamic chaos, the manifold of experience, the flux of becoming. Deleuze's metaphysics explicitly invoked the precedent of Bergson. Theology arises here on this plane of immanence, just as Gažik's Osuský clearly saw and expressly held, from putative 'revelation' – that is, in theology as the learned preaching of the figure of Christ Crucified from the Scriptures. Osuský's

1 Gažik, 52.
2 Ibid., 53–4.
3 Adkins, Brent and Paul R. Hinlicky, *Rethinking Philosophy and Theology with Deleuze: A New Cartography* (London and New York: Bloomsbury Academic, 2013).

final work may be seen as charting this new orientation in post-Christendom theology. At the same time, however, Osuský's new orientation remains mired in the anti-Judaism to which today post-Holocaust theology has rightly become very sensitive. Of course, the same criticism could be made of theology's following Bultmann into neo-docetism.

Independently, and coming from the different history and social location of North America, I have named this new orientation of theology 'critical dogmatics'. In the past years, as I have intensively studied Osuský and prepared to write this book, I have often noted to my conversation partner in all things (who is also my wife of more than forty years), that, had I not been born some twenty years before Osuský died, I should be convinced that I was somehow his reincarnation – so striking are the parallels that I have discovered between us in philosophy and theology. I have been, accordingly, assiduous in guarding against the temptation simply to recast Osuský in my own image in the writing of this book. But, given the inaccessibility of the sources to the English-speaking world, I can only give the reader my word for that. I can hardly deny, on the other hand, what will seem obvious to the reader who now knows something of Osuský but also of the author of this book from his other works: We are kindred spirits. The evidence for my reading of his legacy is before the reader. My interest in him as a theological subject, as an object of theological knowledge to be interpreted for the contemporary audience of post-Christendom in Europe and North America and beyond, is not hidden but on the table for critical examination. If I have succeeded in making Osuský known, both in his life's work and for the cautionary tale his life-story tells, I am grateful.

Critical dogmatics is a contemporary form of critical thinking about God and the world, which arises from a putative word of God, spoken in the resurrection of the Crucified Jesus, and which strictly, rigorously, descriptively and not speculatively makes the singular claim to truth: God is to be identified as the One who is freely determined to redeem and fulfil the creation through the missions of His Son and Spirit. That is the 'dogma' in critical dogmatics, which makes this form of human thinking not the free thinking of philosophy but the freed thinking of theology that knows Jesus as the merciful and saving Lord of all. It is critical, however, in its sober intellectual honesty that fully appreciates that its authorizing word of God is putative and thus undertaken only in a stance of risky faith, vulnerable not only to the indifference or hostility of this world, structured as it is by malice that corrupts the law written on human hearts into self-justifying injustice, but above all to its own falsification in the eschaton of judgment. It is just this vulnerability to falsification that I wish to explore now, in conclusion, with respect to the theological anti-Judaism which attends Osuský's final book of New Testament theology.

Just as there is Judaism and, then, there is Judaism (so also with Christianity!), there is also anti-Judaism and, then, there is anti-Judaism (consider, for example, the text of Amos 5.21-24, one of Martin Luther King, Jr's favourites). Indeed, the capacity for prophetic self-critique is one of the glories Judaism brings to the nations. First of all then, as we have seen, it should be noted that (certain) anti-Judaism(s) does(do) not lead of fatal necessity to modern anti-Semitism. The contrary occurs in the case of Osuský, who rejected the Slovak fascist state's racism, protested its legal intrusion into the self-understanding and discipline of church life with respect to the baptism of Jews as well as the inhumanity of its antisemitic civil policies, and in the terrible hour risked himself publicly to protest the deportation of Jews to Poland. It is not a failure in this regard if Osuský also identified perceived injustices committed by Jews against the Slovak poor, especially when the decisive factor in this acknowledgment was neither race nor religion but class conflict and imperialist loyalties.

In hindsight, we might well moralize that acknowledging this fact of social perception only aided and abetted the tacit support of the population for the policy of deportation. In fact, that is an imponderable. And in fact the protest, including this acknowledgment, did succeed in galvanizing opposition to fascism, rescue of Jews, and finally an armed uprising. The more salient truth is that genuine moral equality requires equal vulnerability to critique. The distinction between religious anti-Judaism and racial antisemitism, thus, is possible, even viable from the traditional Christian side. What Christians have not understood so well, however, is that this distinction is not as easy from the Jewish side, since Judaism is both a people and a religion.[4] In any case, post-Holocaust theology is rightly engaged in a thorough-going reconsideration of the varieties of its traditional anti-Judaism[5] which, unexamined and under the conditions of Christendom, undoubtedly created the cultural preconditions for the Nazi mass murder, and to that extent are liable for it.

4 See further on this, *Before Auschwitz*, 159–66.

5 In terms of the New Testament, Paul's theology of Judaism in Romans 9–11 denies the revocation of Israel's calling, but Matthew's diatribe in Chapter 23 prepares the way for the 'blood guilt' interpretation of the supersession of the Jewish people, and John's demonization of Jews in Chapter 8 prepares the way for the motif of Jewish obstinacy before the evident facts of Christian truth. What is historically striking is that Paul writes before the destruction of the Temple, while Matthew and John are writing after that catastrophe, when the organization of normative of Judaism by the descendants of the Pharisees required the expulsion of Jewish Christians from the synagogue. Critical historical insight into these vicissitudes demands a theological sifting of the various trajectories of anti-Judaism in Christian history.

Second, and in accordance with the above, we have to observe that Osuský is not *uniformly* anti-Judaic. In the *Gallery*, he is engaged in a running dialogue with the Jewish scholar, Joseph Klausner (1874–1958), and his important book, *Jesus of Nazareth* (197, 203, 211, 215, 218, 419, 429), from which Osuský learned a more nuanced understanding of Jewish sectarianism (118–19) during the Second Temple Period. In the process, Osuský also acquired a definite respect for the Pharisees of Jesus's time (331, 358, 377), among whom Paul the apostle had been trained (642).

Third, let us simply and quickly note that supersessionism is a game of one-upmanship that anyone can play. Nazis claimed to supersede Christianity's religious anti-Judaism with scientific-racial antisemitism. Bolsheviks claimed to supersede Christian utopian socialism with scientific socialism. In both cases, they were imitating Christian claims to have superseded Judaism, or Protestant claims to have superseded Catholicism. And Islam, let us not forget, claims to have superseded both Judaism and Christianity, just as ancient Israelites claimed to have superseded the Canaanite population of the promised land. Side by side with his early ethical idealism, as we saw in *War and Religion*, Osuský achieves the prophetic insight that at the root of all such chauvinism is the presumption that History is God. By the time of the *Gallery*, he has come to understand this debilitating exchange of triumphalisms even more deeply as an idolatry – how else does the suffering Job or the suffering Christ *resist* History than to refuse Its finality? – even if he is not yet in a position to think thoroughly and radically on this insight into the end of the project of Christendom. But it does move him to the stance of apocalyptic theology, namely, *denying* that History is God.

And yet, fourth, the poisonous trope of Judaism as the negative antitype of Christianity remains operative also in the *Gallery*, such that Judaism disappears as an actual historical phenomenon and becomes whatever the Christian apologist needs to supply an enemy image. Judaism is responsible *both* for imperialistic henotheism (146) *and* for cosmopolitan deism (256). Judaism aspires to theocracy (214, 403), but this is only a pretext for the domination of its own tribe over others (399). And so on. Discussing the song of Zechariah in Lk. 1.67-79, Osuský's father admonishes the son, 'Only beware and do not understand this hymn of praise as if it were already written purely in the spirit of Jesus! No, here is still the spirit of Jewish desires and ideas about the last things… It is necessary, my son, to take note that it constantly speaks about the LORD of Israel and about the people of Israel. That is not yet the pure spirit of Jesus. It is not God the Father of all humanity in the Christian spirit' (36). Jesus, the father character assures the son, sees that Jewish 'piety is formal, cultic, ceremonial and hypocritical' (118). Citation of such sentiments from the *Gallery* could be multiplied.

But the depth of the problem theologically is that matters central to Osuský's own late in life disillusionment with the fusion of power politics and Christianity are at stake in some such differentiation (witness the 'patriotic pastors', who, as we saw in Chapter 4, conspired with the new communist regime to replace him). His own groping after a post-Christendom mode of Christian theologizing is tangled up with this negative trope regarding the Jews. As hinted throughout the course of this book, however, increasingly crucial to Osuský's understanding of Christianity is the fact (the tangle is deeply rooted: according to the same Gospel of John which demonized Jews in 8.44) that 'when Jesus realized that they were about to come and take him by force to make him king, he withdrew again to the mountain by himself' (Jn 6.15).

Osuský's rejection of political Messianism and his embrace of a theology of the cross turns on some such differentiation. It is the theological basis of his equally prescient and powerful critiques of the twentieth century political religions, as also his reticence about contemporary Zionism. The modern Jewish scholar Joseph Klausner writes, as Osuský quotes: 'for Jews it is impossible to separate religion from the nation. He is right. We also are in a difficult situation, when we hear the name, Jew: what are we to understand by this name, religion or nation?' (148) Indeed, for Osuský, the disappointment of nationalistic Jews in the purely religious mission of Jesus stands behind the betrayal by Judas (430, 441). But the question can be turned back on Christians, who in Europe from the beginning have been making 'sisters' out of nationality and religion, fusing and confusing throne and altar. To respond to this dilemma of a Christian criticism of Jewish nationalism turned back on Christians themselves, Osuský resorted to the standard nineteenth century claim of liberal theology that Judaism represents an ethnocentric particularism, while Christianity brings about a universal vision of humanity (147, 379, 399–400).

Since we know today that Christianity does not escape the 'scandal of particularity', Osuský's solution here becomes something of a dead end for us. So, also, his repeated contrast of the representations of the angry Jewish Jehovah and the loving Christian Father of Jesus; this invidious contrast depends not only on a falsification of the witnesses of the two Testaments (there is mercy in the Hebrew Scriptures and there is wrath in the New Testament) but on the Cartesian-Kantian epistemological frame of reference of liberal theology. This frame of reference holds that God's relation to humanity is mediated by the history of ideas about God, and so occurs in the realm of consciousness, which in turn is held idealistically to determine natural and material forces in humanity. Osuský's repeated philosophical defence of spirit over matter is bound up with this frame of reference. As a result, the drama of God surpassing God in the cross of His Son to find the way into our world of violence and shame to justify the ungodly, as the New Testament's apocalyptic gospel has it, tends to be recast as the cultural evolution from particularistic Jewish justice to universalistic Christian love (145, 179).

The epistemological preoccupation of modern philosophy is, in any event, inadequate to theology that still wishes to tell apocalyptically of One who breaks into the strong man's house to bind him and plunder his goods (Mk 3.37). As Osuský himself knows in his better moments, theological ideas are servants not lords, articulations of a living and present Lord, not the vicar of an absent one. Osuský knows this from Reformation theology. It is precisely the gap between the sign and the thing signified, or the idea and its referent, that may be occupied by the authoritarian institution of salvation, claiming monopoly in the market of religious representations in the sordid business of religion. In this institution of salvation, Christianity is accidental, not essential. By the exigencies of history, it happens to be 'our' cultural tradition's way of representing God, which presumes as its own possession all of 'our' people in their religious 'needs'. But it is the living and present Lord who is the Mediator in the joyful exchange of human sin for the righteousness of One who came not to be served but to serve; not ideas about Him, even the right ideas about Him. Here the Spirit unifies the sign and the thing signified where and when it pleases God. Here the Scriptures are not a sourcebook of representations of God further to be selected and developed by theologians thinking along ethnic lines; but opened and exposited they form the place in the world from which the Christ of God speaks words of prophetic critique and apostolic reconciliation to those today who have ears to hear and eyes to see.

In this light, I now conclude theologically, we honour Osuský's legacy when contemporary Jews and Christians reason together scripturally, understanding about each other that the same divine message of critique and reconciliation sounds from both Testaments. The American Jewish religious philosopher Peter Ochs has argued for this in *Another Reformation: Postliberal Christianity and the Jews.*[6] Ochs' book investigates and warrants a 'reparative' hypothesis that enables

[6] Peter Ochs, *Another Reformation: Postliberal Christianity and the Jews* (Grand Rapids, MI: Baker Academic, 2011). The following paragraphs are adapted from my review of Och's book in the *Journal of Scriptural Reasoning*, vol. 13, no. 2 (November 2014), http://jsr.shanti.virginia.edu/back-issues/volume-13-number-2-november-2014-navigating-john-howard-yoders-the-jewish-christian-schism-revisited/ republished in *The Logic of Schism and Unity: On the Current State of*

nothing less than collaborative labour for healing schisms that betray the cause of the God of Abraham.[7] So far as he succeeds in this, Ochs does not so much settle things once and for all (that is exactly *not* his purpose!) but rather opens up for all concerned new paths of exploration for the repair of schism – *ad infinitum* to the eschaton of judgment, the Day of the LORD. Ochs argues that contemporary 'postliberal' Christian theology is *not* supersessionist with respect to Judaism, in the lamentable ways that both classical and revisionist ('liberal') Christianity have been; rather, it attends to the healing of debilitating schisms within Christianity that are thought to be rooted in the originating schism of primitive Christianity, that is, when normative Judaism and early catholic Christianity were born like the rival twins, Esau and Jacob. Presupposed, then, is not only theological liberalism's critique of classical theological triumphalism but also a contemporary neo-Reformation critique of liberalism's triumphalism in Protestant progressivism: hence Ochs' title, *Another Reform*ation.

Post-liberal commitments in Christian theology consist, for Ochs, 1) in undertaking reparative unity among the divided churches and beyond; 2) in reformation by return to the sources in Scripture-study and Scriptural reasoning; 3) in an ecclesial hermeneutic of Scripture as the ecumenical church's book; 4) in a narrative reading of the Gospels as themselves re-readings of the Old Testament in the light of the Spirit made known in Christ. Only the first of these commitments is lacking in Osuský as we have come to know him. To be sure, the first two commitments were lacking in the predominant Roman Catholic theology of his time.

Ochs' hypothesis that these methodological commitments correlate with, if not entail, the rejection of Christian supersessionism with respect to Judaism, then, has the following sense: because such theologians know the Israel of the Hebrew Scriptures and know Jesus Christ and His apostle Paul as Jews of this Israel, and because, accordingly, they also know for themselves the Jewish perplexity at the kerygma of Christ Crucified[8] (kindred, as Ochs lays out, to Jewish perplexity in the sufferings of Job; note the parallel to Osuský), they cannot but see in living Judaism separated sisters and brothers. The gifts and calling of the Jewish people must be believed to be as irrevocable as the

Jewish-Christian Engagements, (Eugene, OR: Pickwick Publications, 2016), Chapter 13, and appear here with the permission of the publisher.

7 Ochs includes Muslims in the project of Scriptural reasoning, as would I also. But I think there is sufficient difference in this relation to require another line of reasoning from the one I am pursuing here. So I will bracket the question.

8 As I have put the matter in my systematic theology: Jewish perplexity at the 'good news' proclaimed in 'Christ crucified' must become a principle internal to Christian theology itself (*Beloved Community*, 416–29).

Christian's, if Christians today are with integrity to sustain as well belief in their own calling. This advance back to risky and responsible faith in a world still awaiting its redemption, and so awash with political Messianisms, reflects a new formation of Christian theology in the postliberal mode, neither the old, all-too-confident dogmatism, nor its liberal clone, the secularizing faith in progress. Rather it is trust, alight in the darkness, from within the belly of the Leviathan.

Interestingly, such moves would come at the cost of overcoming the remnants of mere philosophical theism and modern idealism in Osuský. Ochs's call to Scriptural reasoning among the spiritual descendants of Abraham contains a sharp rejection of the Platonic ideal of knowledge as *theoria*, that is, as pure intellectual gazing that supposedly unites the finite mind to the divine in a timeless ontological union. If I may cite John Dewey, here, on behalf of Ochs's case: the 'classical theory of knowledge' in 'Greek thought regarded possession, contemplation, as the essence of science, and thought of the latter as such a complete possession of reality as incorporates it with mind'.[9] Dewey noted as well the assimilation of this ideal of *theoria* in 'the medieval Christian period… [which] carried out under new circumstances the old idea that the highest end and good of man is knowledge of true Being, and that such knowledge in the degree of its possession effects an assimilation of the mind to the reality known'.[10] If we follow this critique, Osuský's hierarchy of value, which he derives from Augustine, comes to a fork in the road. It may be grounded and oriented either by Plato or by the Sermon on the Mount, but not by both. In the latter case, the knowing subject of theology is located in the flesh, here on the earth, among the poor, responding to cries of distress, not in leisured contemplation inferiorizing labour as fit for slaves but not for free thinkers.

Ochs's rejection of Platonic *theoria* as the ideal of knowledge for theological purposes serves to retrieve and advance a Scriptural-Jewish critique of idolatry. This also makes clear that silence when one should speak in the name of the LORD is no less idolatrous than speaking of the LORD when one should reverence the divine Name in silent adoration. Here, the idol is not merely or chiefly a finite representation falsely claiming to capture the divine; such is the merely apophatic critique of images descending from Platonism that Ochs regularly criticizes for missing the kataphatic descent of the Scriptural LORD to deliver. Rather, by way of Scriptural reasoning, the idol is exposed as the

[9] John Dewey, *Experience and Nature* (New York, Dover, 1958), 134.
[10] Ibid., 153.

work of human hands or human minds, hence as the symbolization of human self-deliverance in place of reliance on the LORD, who first and freely delivered Israel from Egypt and, precisely in so-doing, descends (cf. Exod. 3.7-8) as the saviour who comes from beyond all human possibilities. Just this saving God is not reducible to His relation with creatures.

This is the LORD who faithfully works renewal from historical disasters, Ochs maintains, in the same pattern as the Exodus, by the remembrance of His Word in the Spirit's community: from the Babylonian exile, from the destruction of the Temple and loss of the Land, and now from the Shoah. This alternative critique of idolatry, more Jewish and Scriptural, as an reparative response to actual evil, comes in distinction from, and in place of, the philosophically dominant Platonic critique on the level of representations, which sees earthly copies made by human poets as twice removed from the aspired intellectual ascent to union with nameless deity. But union with deity, for Ochs, can be received only as a gift from God the Giver in the gift of the Spirit who is working *hic et nunc* for concrete repairs in human history that remove whatever may hinder the coming of the Beloved Community.

Dyadic thinking, Ochs holds, exacerbated by the foundationalism of Cartesian-Lockean modernism, correlates with religious triumphalism and Christian supersessionism. If repaired by the emergence of triadic thinking in pragmatism – the subject who knows the object in relation to some audience within the flux of becoming – a chastened post-modernism can imagine and act on new ways for living together peaceably. Under these conditions, 'Disagreement justifies disagreement in response, but it is no warrant for more than disagreement'.[11] Achieving disagreement among separated brothers and sisters is one 'peaceable' way to envision thinking about the persisting differences between communities of faith and their Scriptures.

Christian supersessionism, by contrast, injures not only Jews; in smearing Jews, it maims, also, Christians, as Ochs reads Lutheran theologian Robert Jenson, for it '*breaks* Israel's hermeneutic and thereby *obstructs* the hermeneutical claim of the New Testament in relation to the Old: replacing not only Israel with the church but also the church's scriptural *claim* on Israel with the pronouncements of some new religion "that knew not Jacob" and had no means of reasoning any longer with Jacob'.[12] The ongoing permutation of North American liberal Protestantism into Gnosticism (following, in

[11] Ochs, 70.
[12] Ibid.

inverse, American fundamentalism's antecedent 'left-behind' pre-millennialism, a Gnosticism wrapped in apocalyptic-literal packaging) is evidence enough for this claim. The sappy, sentimental good God of Jesus set off from the strict and wrathful God of the Jews is and remains, incredibly but factually, the vicious trope of liberal Protestantism's 'antisemitism of a higher order'.[13]

Contemporary Anglican theologian Ephraim Radner, however, has reminded us that political liberalism today is imposed upon 'us wicked Christians' (Luther) as a penitential discipline in response to the crimes of Christian violence which are also sins against the Christian claim to truth.[14] Contemporary American Jewish political philosopher Mark Lilla, in his stimulating book, *The Stillborn God*,[15] rightly chastises the fanaticism of those still lusting after the absolute in time, secular and religious alike, of which the recent century was filled. Salient, here, as Lilla might recognize (for his 'stillborn God' turns out to be the sappy, sentimental deity of liberal Protestantism that inspires no one but recovering fundamentalists), is the parable Jesus tells in Luke about a person who was delivered from a demon, but who did nothing to fill the resulting void; so the expelled demon sought out seven worse than itself, and returned to fill the vacancy in the person's soul. That is the cautionary tale to be told again and again in today's post-Christendom.

What can fill the vacancy of life between the times is not false claims to intuit and possess the End in political messianisms, but true faith that learns the patiency of life together, on the way to the End of Days, by hearing the Scriptural promises of God. For Christians, as all the post-liberal theologians whom Ochs discusses would affirm, that would surely be the Eucharistic assembly, insofar as it proclaims the Lord's death until He comes again. But for the categorical rage of his anti-Catholic polemic, we can well imagine that Osuský would concur with this. Jews and Christians know the dialectic of 'seeking the welfare of the city in which we dwell', precisely by delivering penetrating prophetic criticism that our liberal order cannot provide for itself, offering mercy and hope from beyond its immanent resources.

Jews and Christians might all the more powerfully do that work together as friends in prophecy that speaks truth to power. Such is the profoundly important work in hope for what Royce called, and Martin Luther King, Jr.

13 I note with pleasure in this connection Ochs's observation that North American 'Lutheran theologians are disproportionately represented among the strongest Christian critics of supersessionism and the strongest advocates of deep theological engagement with Judaism' (71).

14 See my discussion in *Beloved Community*, 382–6.

15 Mark Lilla, *The Stillborn God: Religion, Politics and the Modern West* (New York: Vintage Books, 2008).

proclaimed, the Beloved Community that is ventured by Ochs in his instructive book. In enforcing legal equality, the liberal political order – the multicultural Czechoslovak democracy to which Osuský was dedicated – makes this hope concretely possible, but it does not define it, let alone entail it. The hope for the Beloved Community of God is drawn instead from the deep wells of the Scriptures by those who reason prayerfully with them and thus also work reparatively with one another. The twentieth century sojourn of Samuel Štefan Osuský pioneered a path forward in this direction.

Works Cited

Works of Samuel Štefan Osuský

Osuský, Samuel Štefan, *Vojna a Náboženstvo* [War and Religion] (Mikuláš: Tranoscius, 1916).

Osuský, Samuel Štefan, *Dejiny Náboženstva* [The History of Religion], 2nd edn (Mikuláš: Tranoscius, 1922).

Osuský, Samuel Štefan, 'Smyseľ slovenských dejín' [The Meaning of Slovak History] (1939b) from the archives of the library of the Protestant Theological Faculty, Comenius University, Bratislava, accessed in 2014 with the aid of librarian Vlastislav Svoboda and Prof Dr Peter Gažik.

Osuský, Samuel Štefan, *Koniec Sveta z Jánovho Zjavenia Vyložil* [The End of the World Exposited from the Revelation of John] (Mikulaš: Tranoscius, 1941).

Osuský, Samuel Štefan, 'Pastoral Letter on the Jewish Question (1942) (with Pavol Čobrda) translated and introduced by Paul R. Hinlicky, *Lutheran Quarterly* XXIII/3 (Autumn, 2009), 332–42 from *SN II*, 227–32.

Osuský, Samuel Štefan, *Tajomstvo Kríža z Joba vyklade* [The Mystery of the Cross exposited from the book of Job] (Mikuláš: Tranoscius, 1943).

Osuský, Samuel Štefan, *Braň Pravdy* [Defence of the Truth] (Mikuláš: Tranoscius, 1946).

Osuský, Samuel Štefan, *Sluzba Narodu* II [Service to the Nations II] (Svaty Mikulas: Tranoscius, 1947).

Osuský, Samuel Štefan, *Galéria Postáv Novej Zmluvy: Historicko-psychologická trilógia* [Gallery of New Testament Figures] Mikuláš: Tranoscius, 2009).

Osuský, Samuel Štefan, 'The Philosophy of Fascism, Bolshevism and Hitlerism', translated and introduced by Paul R. Hinlicky in *Before Auschwitz: What Christian Theology Must Learn from the Rise of Nazism* (Eugene, OR: Cascade, 2014), 193–220.

Other Works Cited

Adkins, Brent and Paul R. Hinlicky, *Rethinking Philosophy and Theology with Deleuze: A New Cartography* (London and New York: Bloomsbury Academic, 2013).

Aschheim, Steven E., *The Nietzsche Legacy in Germany 1890–1990* (Berkeley, Los Angeles and London: University of California Press, 1994).

Baer, H. David., *The Struggle of Hungarian Lutherans under Communism* (College Station, Texas: A & M University Press, 2006).

Barclay, John M. G., *Pauline Churches and Diaspora Jews* (Mohr Siebeck).

Barth, Karl, *Epistle to the Romans*, trans. E. C. Hoskyns (London: Oxford University Press, 1972).

Barth, Karl, *Church Dogmatics: I/1, The Doctrine of the Word of God* trans. G. W. Bromiley (Edinburgh: T. & T. Clark, 1975).

Bartholemew, C., ed., *A Royal Priesthood: The Use of the Bible Ethically and Politically*, (Carlisle: Paternoster, 2002).

Bayer, Oswald, *Martin Luther's Theology: A Contemporary Interpretation* trans. Thomas H. Trapp (Grand Rapids, MI: Eerdmans, 2007).

Bergen, Doris L., *Twisted Cross: The German Christian Movement in the Third Reich* (Chapel Hill, NC: The University of North Carolina Press, 1996).

Bielfeldt, Dennis, Mickey Mattox and Paul R. Hinlicky, *The Substance of Faith: Luther on Doctrinal Theology* (Minneapolis, MN: Fortress Press, 2008).

Bonhoeffer, Dietrich, *Sanctorum Communio* (Minneapolis: Fortress, 1988).

Bonhoeffer, Dietrich, *Creation and Fall*, Dietrich Bonhoeffer Works, Vol. 3 trans. D. S. Bax (Minneapolis: Fortress, 1997).

Braaten, Carl E., ed., *Preaching and Teaching the Law and Gospel of God* (Delhi, NY: ALPB Books, 2013) 91–113.

Brown, Peter, *The Rise of Western Christendom: Triumph and Diversity A.D. 200–1000*, 2nd edition (Oxford: Blackwell, 2003).

Bultmann, Rudolph & Five Critics, *Kerygma and Myth*, ed. H. W. Bartsch (New York: Harper & Row, 1961).

Burgess, Joseph A., ed. *The Role of the Augsburg Confession: Catholic and Lutheran Views* (Philadelphia: Fortress, 1980).

Burleigh, Michael, *Earthly Powers: The Clash of Religion and Politics in Europe, from the French Revolution to the Great War* (New York: HarperCollins, 2005).

Čarnogurský, Pavol, *Svedok Čias* [A Witness to the Times] (Bratislava, 1997).

Childs, Brevard S., *Old Testament Theology in a Canonical Context* (Minneapolis: Fortress, 1986).

Dawidowicz, Lucy S., *The War against the Jews, 1933–1945* (New York: Penguin, 1987).

Dewey, John. *Experience and Nature* (New York, Dover, 1958).

Ericksen, Robert P., *Theologians under Hitler* (New Haven and London: Yale University Press, 1985).

Filo, Július st., *Spomienky a úvahy: Láska zraňovaná aj uzdravujúca* [Reminiscences and Essays: Love Wounded and Love Healing] (Prešov: Vydavatestvo Michala Vaška, 1998).

Filo, Július st., ed., *Christian World Community and the Cold War: International Research Conference in Bratislava on 5–8 Septermber 2011* (Bratislava: Evangelical Theological Faculty of the Comenius University, 2012).

Frank, Günther, *Die Vernunft des Gottesgedankens: Religionsphilosophische Studien zur fruehen Neuzeit* (Frommann-Holzboog, 2003).

Frank, Günther, *Die Theologische Philosophie Philipp Melanchthons (1497–1560)* Erfurter Theologische Studien Band 67 (Benno).

Gažik, Peter, *Samuel Štefan Osuský: Moderný filozof náboženstva* [Modern Philosopher of Religion], (Žilinská univerzita, 2012).

Gentile, Emilio, 'Fascism as Political Religion', *Journal of Contemporary History*, 25/2–3 (May-June, 1990) 229–51.

Gluchmann, Vasil, *Slovak Lutheran Social Ethics*, Studies in Religion and Society, Vol. 37 (Lewiston, Queenston, Lampeter: The Edwin Mellon Press, 1997).

Hagen, Kenneth, *Luther's Approach to Scripture as seen in his 'Commentaries' on Galatians 1519–1538* (Tübingen: J. C. B. Mohr [Paul Siebeck] 1993).

Heschel, Susannah, *The Aryan Jesus: Christian Theologians and the Bible in Nazi Germany* (Princeton, NJ: Princeton University Press, 2008).

Hinlicky, Paul R., 'Luther's Anti-Docetism in the Disputatio de divinitate et humanitate Christi (1540)' in *Creator est creatura: Luthers Christologie als Lehre von der Idiomenkommunikation* eds O. Bayer and Benjamin Gleede (Berlin and New York: Walter De Gruyter, 2007), 139–85.

Hinlicky, Paul R., *Paths Not Taken: Fates of Theology from Luther through Leibniz* (Grand Rapids, MI: Eerdmans, 2009).

Hinlicky, Paul R., 'A Leibnizian Transformation? Reclaiming the Theodicy of Faith' in *Transformations in Luther's Reformation Theology: Historical and Contemporary Reflections,* Vol. 32, Arbeiten zur Kirchen- und Theologiegeschichte. eds C. Helmer and B. K. Holm (Leibzig: Evangelische Verlagsanstalt, 2011), 85–103.

Hinlicky, Paul R., *Divine Complexity: The Rise of Creedal Christianity* (Minneapolis: Fortress, 2011).

Hinlicky, Paul R., Review of Peter Ochs, *Another Reformation: Postliberal Christianity and the Jews* (Grand Rapids, MI: Baker Academic, 2011 in the *Journal of Scriptural Reasoning*, Vol. 13, no. 2 (November 2014), http://jsr.shanti.virginia.edu/back-issues/volume-13-number-2-november-2014-navigating-john-howard-yoders-the-jewish-christian-schism-revisited/.

Hinlicky, Paul R., *Before Auschwitz: What Christian Theology Must Learn from the Rise of Nazism* (Eugene, OR: Cascade, 2014).

Hinlicky, Paul R., *Beloved Community: Critical Dogmatics after Christendom* (Grand Rapids, MI: Eerdmans, 2015).

Horňanová, Sidonia and Igor Kišš eds, *Ordinácia Žien za farárky v cirkvi* [The

Ordination of Women as Pastors in the Church] Zborník (Bratislava: Evanjelická bohoslovecká fakulta, Univerzity Komenského, 2007).

Juráš, Ján et al, eds, *Sláva Šlachetnýn II: Evanjelická cirkev a.v. a politika v 20. storočí* [Glory to the Noble Ones II: The Lutheran Church and Politics in the 20th Century] (Mikuláš: Spolok Martina Rázusa, 2012)

Kapitoly Odboja na Slovensku [Chapters in the Resistance Movement in Slovakia] (Bratislava: Ustav dejín KSS, 1968).

Kmeť, Norbert, *Postavenie cirkví na Slovensku 1948–1951* [The Stances of the Churches in Slovakia 1948–1951] (Bratislava, VEDA, 2000).

Kocka, Ján, 'Odkaz Osuského 'Prvých Slovenských Dejín Filozofie,' *Filozophia* 49/9 (1994).

Kolb, Robert and Wengert,T. J. eds, *The Book of Concord: The Confessions of the Evangelical Lutheran Church* (Minneapolis: Fortress, 2000).

Korec, Jan Chryzostom Cardinal S.J., *The Night of the Barbarians: Memoirs of the Communist Persecution of the Slovak Cardinal* trans. Peter-Paul Siska et al. (Bolchazy-Carducci, 2002).

Kováčová, Viera et al. eds, *Riešenie Židovskej otázky v spojeneckých krajinách nacistického Nemecka* [The Solution to the Jewish Question in the nations allied to Nazi Germany] (Banská Bystrica: Múseum Slovenskéhoe národného povstania, 2012)

Kusukawa, Sachicko, ed., *Philip Melanchthon: Orations on Philosophy and Education* trans. C. F. Salazar (Cambridge: Cambridge University Press, 1999).

Letz, Ján, *Slovenská kresťanská filozofia 20. storočia a jej perspektívy* [Slovak Christian Philosophy of the 20th Century and its Perspectives] (Spolok Slovákov v Polsku & Filosofická fakulta Trnavkej university v Trnave, 2010).

Lilje, Hanns, *The Last Book of the Bible*, English translation of German original (1940) (Philadelphia: Muhlenberg, 1957).

Lilla, Mark, *The Stillborn God: Religion, Politics and the Modern West* (New York: Vintage Books, 2008).

Lindbeck, George A., *The Nature of Doctrine: Religion and Theology in a Postliberal Age* (Philadelphia: Westminster, 1984).

Luther, Martin, *The Bondage of the Will* trans. J. I. Packer and O. R. Johnston (Grand Rapids, MI: Baker Academic, 2012).

Martyn, J. Louis, *History and Theology in the Fourth Gospel* (New York, 1968).

Masuzawa, Tomoko, *The Invention of World Religions* (Chicago and London: The University of Chicago Press, 2005).

Mauer, Wilhelm, *Historical Commentary on the Augsburg Confession,* trans. H. George Anderson (Philadelphia: Fortress, 1986).

Mildenberger, Friedrich, *Theology of the Lutheran Confessions* trans. E. Lueker (Philadelphia: Fortress, 1986).

Münz, Teodor, 'Náboženská filozofia na Slovensku v prvej polovici 20. Storočia,' *Filozofia* 49/7 (1994) 469.

Oberman, Heiko, *Luther: Man between God and the Devil* trans. E. Walliser-Schwarzbart (Yale University Press, 1989).

Ochs, Peter, *Another Reformation: Postliberal Christianity and the Jews* (Grand Rapids, MI: Baker Academic, 2011).

Ondrejovič, Dušan, 'PhDr. ThDr. h.c. Samuel Štefan Osuský 7.6.1888–14.11.1975', photocopy from the archives of the library of the Protestant Theological Faculty, Comenius University, Bratislava, accessed in 2014 with the aid of librarian Vlastislav Svoboda and Prof Dr Peter Gažik.

Palka, John, *My Slovakia, My Family: One Family's Role in the Birth of a Nation* (Minneapolis: Kirk House, 2012).

Pešek, Jan and Michal Barnovský, *Štátna moc a cirkvi na Slovensku 1948–1953* [State Power and the Churches in Slovakia 1948–1953] (Bratislava: VEDA, 1997).

Pešek, Jan, *Odvrátena tvár totality: Politické perzekúcie na Slovensku v rokoch 1948–1953* [Totalitarian Shunning: Political Persecution in Slovakia 1948–53] (Bratislava: Nádádci Milana Šimečku, 1998).

Reinhuber, Thomas, *Kämpfender Glaube: Studien zu Luthers Bekenntnis am Ende von* De servo arbitrio (Berlin & NY: Walter de Gruyter, 2000).

Royce, Josiah, *The Problem of Christianity* (Washington, DC: The Catholic University of America Press, 2001).

Steigmann-Gall, Richard, *The Holy Reich: Nazi Conceptions of Christianity, 1919–1945* (Cambridge: Cambridge University Press, 2003).

The Tragedy of Slovak Jews: Proceedings of the International Symposium at Banská Bystrica, 25th to 27th March 1992 (Banská Bystrica, Datei, 1992).

Teich, Mikuláš, Dušan Kováč, and Martin D. Brown, eds, *Slovakia in History*, (Cambridge: Cambridge University Press, 2013).

Trevor-Roper, H. R., ed., *Hitler's Table Talk 1941–1944: His Private Conversations*, New Updated Version trans. N. Cameron and R. H. Stevens (New York: Enigma Books, 2008).

Uhorskai, Pavel. *Uncompromising Faith: One Man's Notes from Prison*, trans. Jaroslav Vajda (St. Louis: Concordia, 1992).

Valčo, Michal and Andrej-Braxatoris-Sládkovič, eds, *Slovenské Národné Zhromaždenie v Turčianskom Sv. Martine 1861: Teologické aspekty memorandových udalostí a ich odkaz pre dnešok* [The Slovak National Assembly in St. Martin 1861: Theological Aspects of the Events surrounding the Memorandum on Slovak Nationality and their Message for Today] (Žilina: University Press, 2011).

Valčo, Michal and Daniel Slivka (eds), *Christian Churches in Post-Communist Slovakia: Current Challenges and Opportunities* (Salem,VA: Center for Religion and Society, Roanoke College, 2012).

Valčo, Michal and Katarína Valčová, *Teologické posolstvo Lutherovej reformácie a výzvy sučasnej doby* [The Theological Message of the Lutheran Reformation and the Challenges of the Contemporary Period] (Žilina: EDIS, 2012).

Valčo, Michal and Daniel Škoviera, *Katechizmus Leonarda Stőckela a jeho theologicko-filozofický odkaz* (Martin: Slovenská národná knižnica, 2014).
Weikart, Richard, *From Darwin to Hitler: Evolutionary Ethics, Eugenics, and Racism in Germany* (New York: Palgrave Macmillan, 2004).
Wink, Walter, *Naming the Powers: The Language of Power in the New Testament* (Philadelphia: Fortress, 1984)
Wink, Walter, *Engaging the Powers: Discernment and Resistance in a World of Domination* (Minneapolis: Fortress, 1992).
Witte, John Jr., *Law and Protestantism: The Legal Teachings of the Lutheran Reformation*, with a Foreword by Martin E. Marty (Cambridge UK: Cambridge University Press, 2002).
Wright, N. T., *The Climax of the Covenant: Christ and the Law in Pauline Theology* (Minneapolis: Fortress, 1992).
Žitňan, Andrej, *Evanjelická Cirkev Augsburgského Vyznania na Slovensku v Rokoch 1938–45* [The Lutheran Church in Slovakia 1938–45] Phd. Dissertation (2008: Evanjelická Bohoslovecká fakulta, Univerzity Komenského v Bratislava).

Index